NEWCASTLE UPON TYNE CITY LIBRARIES

D1556596

A–Z OF CARS

1945–1970

A–Z OF CARS
1945–1970

MICHAEL SEDGWICK

MARK GILLIES

First published 1986 by
Temple Press
an imprint of Newnes Books
Bridge House, London Road
Twickenham, Middlesex TW1 3SB
a division of
The Hamlyn Publishing Group Limited
and distributed for them by
Hamlyn Distribution Services
Rushden, Northants, England

Second impression 1987

Editor Charles Herridge

Designer Gerrard Lindley

Typeset by P&M Typesetting Ltd, Exeter

ISBN 0 600 333914

Printed in Spain

FOREWORD

Michael Sedgwick had the rare gift of being able to combine erudition with humour when he wrote motoring history. This quality marked all of his prodigious output, but perhaps it shone through most strongly in his A–Z encyclopaedia.

Commissioned by *Classic and Sportscar* to begin in its first issue in April 1982, the A–Z ran over 13 parts. The most remarkable thing about it – and only a man of Michael's energy could have tackled the task – was model by model analysis, the first time this had ever been attempted. A detailed guide to models of car is altogether more ambitious than the conventional encyclopaedia of marques of car. Naturally, there had to be restrictions so that the A–Z didn't fill the magazine for years to come, so Michael limited himself to European cars sold in Britain between 1945 and 1970. Any more would have tried even Michael's enthusiasm!

The A–Z was so full of controversial judgements that it sparked letters – some angry, some glowing – every time a new issue of *Classic and Sportscar* appeared. A good number of those letters asked when the A–Z would be published in book form. Well, here it is at last: see for yourself how it stands as one of Michael Sedgwick's finest achievements.

Mark Hughes
Editor
Classic and Sportscar

KEY

MODEL NAME. Years of manufacture (production figures). Body styles available. Engine position and driven wheels, cubic capacity (engine configuration, number of cylinders, valve gear).

F – front
R – rear
S – in-line engine
V – vee engine
HO – horizontally opposed engine
OHV – overhead valves
OC – overhead cam
DOC – double overhead cam
SV – sidevalve
SSlv – single sleeve valve
dSlv – double sleeve valve
IO – inlet over exhaust valves
TS – two stroke

ABARTH (I)

Carlo Abarth initially launched his firm as a tuning concern in 1950, specialising in the Fiat marque. His first car proper was the Tipo 207/A Spider of 1955, using Fiat parts, and this was followed rapidly by the first of his 600 based machines. Through the 1960s, Abarth continued to build cars based on the Fiat 500 and 600, as well as branching out into production of stunning little coupés with Fiat-based units. Racing activities pushed the company into liquidation in 1971, but Fiat took over the Abarth shop for its competition activities. 'Hot' Fiats today are marketed as 'Abarths'.

ZAGATO 750. 1957-61 (prod: n/a). 2-seater coupé. R/R, 747cc (S4 OHV). Essentially a Fiat 600, but what a difference. It's only 47ins high, with little bobbles on the roof for the occupants' heads. Does 95mph and over 40mpg, but the Fiat brakes can't always cope. Twin-cam 1-litre versions (*Bialbero*) were credited with 120mph. Imports started 1958. ➤

AC (GB)

AC stands for Autocarriers, the first car being a three-wheeler called the Sociable. Before World War II the firm's reputation was founded on a range of high quality sporting cars built in the 1930s under the management of the Hurlock brothers, who had taken over AC in 1930. Production of cars was resumed with a saloon in 1947, but the firm was really brought into prominence by the Ace of 1954; this was to be the inspiration for the V8-engined and very fast Cobra sports car. Since then, the only notable product has been the 427/428 range. AC struggled on until 1984 trying to produce the mid-engined ME3000: it still exists, but does not produce cars.

◄ **2-LITRE SALOON/DROPHEAD COUPÉ. 1947-56 (prod: 1300 approx). 2-door saloon, 4-door saloon, drophead coupé. F/R, 1991cc (S6 OC).** Pre-war design (rigid axles all round) with post-war styling. Ride hard, but triple carburettor, 76bhp engine gives 80mph top speed. Four-door saloons from late 1952, dropheads very rare. Not much fancied by collectors.

2-LITRE BUCKLAND TOURER. 1949-54 (see 2-litre Saloon for production figures). Sports-tourer. F/R, 1991cc (S6 OC). The nearest thing to a traditional family tourer in the period, and the most sought after of the beam-axle ACs. Mechanically identical to the saloons, although cars from November 1951 have fully hydraulic brakes instead of the earlier, less satisfactory hydromech type. ➤

ACE & ACE-BRISTOL. 1954-63 (prod: 226 Ace, 466 Ace-Bristol). Sports 2-seater. F/R, 1991cc (S6 OC), 1971cc (S6 OHV). The looks of a Ferrari *barchetta* with John Tojeiro's all-independently sprung chassis. The basically-1919 AC engine isn't really up to it, but with the Bristol's 120bhp (available from '56 on), there's 115mph on tap plus 0-60mph in 9secs. Much sought after. ➤

◄ **ACECA & ACECA-BRISTOL. 1955-63 (prod: 320). 2-seater coupé. F/R, 1991cc (S6 OC), 1971cc (S6 OHV).** The Ace looks as good in its hardtop form; it was also a hatchback before its time. As on the Ace, overdrive is a desirable option, and from 1958 you get disc front brakes on both cars. Watch out, though: unlike the Aces, the Aceca body is wood-framed, and could rot.

GREYHOUND. 1959-63 (prod: 80). 4-seater saloon. F/R, 1971cc (S6 OHV). Four-seater member of the Ace family, almost always Bristol-powered, although a handful had the old AC unit and 2 or 3 the Ford 2.6. Styling isn't as attractive as the two-seaters, and the car doesn't handle as well. Almost a 'sleeper'. ➤

◄ **ACE/ACECA 2.6. 1961-63 (prod: 47). 2-seater sports, 2-seater coupé. F/R, 2553cc (S6 OHV).** Originally a Ken Rudd conversion, but factory-available during the model's last years. How fast depends on how you tune your Ford Zephyr engine. Maybe not for the purist, but the best AC buy if you want to keep parts and maintenance costs down.

COBRA 289. 1962-69 (prod: 560). 2-seater sports. F/R, 4727cc (V8 OHV). Not for the sybarite is Carroll Shelby's cross-pollinated Ace with American Ford engine. It'll take you to 100mph in 14secs, and there are disc brakes, but even with some extra reinforcement the old 1954 chassis is working hard. Not many sold over here, so expect to pay for a good one. ➤

COBRA 427. 1965-69 (prod: 510). 2-seater sports. F/R, 6997cc (V8 OHV). Just about the ultimate in four-wheeled motorbikes, with a new coil suspension at the rear, and 400bhp: there have been street-legal versions with as much as 490bhp. They're making near-replicas in at least four countries, which could prove something. ➤

◄ **427/428. 1966-72 (prod: 51 convertible, 29 fastbacks). 2-seater convertible, 2-seater fastback coupé. F/R, 6997cc (V8 OHV), 7016cc (V8 OHV).** A marriage of Cobra mechanics and the later rear suspension in a luxury tourer. Manual and automatic both available, although latter (sadly) commoner. From 1967, the tamer (345bhp) 428 engine was fitted. Italian looks plus American performance.

ALFA ROMEO (I)

One of the great marques in motoring history, its main reputation has been for sporting cars, with a fantastic racing pedigree to back that up. First ALFA (Anonima Lombardo Fabbrica Automobili) came in 1910, with industrialist Nicolo Romeo taking over in 1915. Classic pre-World War II Alfa Romeos included Jano-penned 6C and 8C cars of the 1930s. After the war, the firm changed direction from production of bespoke and exclusive cars with the 1900. The classic Giulietta range of the 1950s and the 1750/2000 series of the late 1960s and early 1970s further enhanced Alfa prestige, but since then an attempt to move further down-market has seen disappointment for all concerned.

6C 2500SS. 1939-51 (prod: 474). 2-seater cabriolet, coupé, various specials. F/R, 2443cc (S6 DOC). Brought out just before World War II, this one came on a 104ins wheelbase frame and was good enough for over the ton. Majority of coachwork by Touring. Huge, 17ins perforated disc wheels are out of character, though some with wire wheels. All are good lookers, the last of the true bespoke Alfas. ➤

◄ **1900 TI. 1953-55 (prod: 17,243, all saloon types from 1951). 4-door saloon. F/R, 1975cc (S4 DOC).** The first mass-produced Alfa and, like all its kind, very rustprone. Very few imported, and all LHD with unpleasing column shift to four-speed 'box. Looks like a Vauxhall Velox from the back, but good for 100mph with the usual Alfa handling. Unlikely to be expensive–if you can find one.

1900 SUPER SPRINT. 1954-58 (prod: 1796). coupé (Touring), cabriolet (Pininfarina). F/R, 1975cc (S4 DOC). Very rare in England, and always LHD. They're prettier, however, than the saloons, have centre-lock wheels, and will do 110mph. Both four- and five-speed versions were made, but all have column change, and 'five on the tree' isn't much fun. ➤

◄ **GIULIETTA SPRINT/SPRINT VELOCE. 1955-62 (prod: 24,083 Sprint, 3058 Veloce). 2-seater coupé. F/R, 1290cc (S4 DOC).** Veloces have 90bhp instead of 80 and speed goes up from just over the ton to 110mph. Beautiful lines, a lovely engine, and lovely handling, but they're rust traps; anything made before late 1958 will have column shift, and there was no RHD before 1961.

2000 SPYDER. 1958-61 (prod: 3443). 2+2 seater sports. F/R, 1975cc (S4 DOC). Classical Alfa design with five-bearing twin-cam engine giving 115bhp to the saloon's 105, and handsome bodywork by Touring – unitary, of course, as on all Alfas after 1952. Five-on-the-floor is now the rule for the sporting types, but brakes are still drum-type. ➤

◄ **GIULIETTA BERLINA/BERLINA TI. 1955-62 (prod: 30,057 Standard, 144,213 TI). 4-door saloon. F/R, 1290cc (S4 DOC).** Despite a big production not many came here, although it was listed from 1957. RHD rare. It's an Alfa, every inch of it, and the TI's handling plus 98mph top speed makes it the fifties equivalent of the pre-war Lancia Aprilia and *Millecento* Fiat. Alas, column shift again on almost all of them.

2000. 1958-61. 4-door saloon. F/R, 1975cc (S4 DOC). Very seldom seen in this country, this one is an updated 1900 with the ugly angular styling and a five-speed all-synchromesh 'box. The lever's still on the column. Unlikely to be expensive, although parts will be. ➤

GIULIETTA SS/SZ. 1957-62 (prod: 1366 SS, 200 SZ). 2-seater coupé. F/R, 1290cc (S4 DOC). The full-house model with 100bhp twin-carburettor engine, five-on-the-floor, and special bodies: the SS is a long-tail by Bertone, and the SZ a Zagato square-tail. Listed in Britain in 1962, good for 120mph, and the last 30 had disc brakes. ➤

◄ **GIULIETTA SPYDER/SPYDER VELOCE. 1955-62 (prod: 14,300 Spyder, 2796 Veloce). 2-seater sports. F/R, 1290cc (S4 DOC).** Open version of the Giulietta with the same mechanics, although rust has decimated its ranks. One bonus – all the Spyders had floor change, whenever built. Again, RHD came with the 1962 models. Rust-phobia has kept prices down.

2600 BERLINA. 1962-68 (prod: RHD models, 425). 4-door saloon. F/R, 2584cc (S6 DOC). First 'six' listed in Britain since 1939, and you got floor change for your five-speed 'box with the RHD package. Servo assisted four-wheel disc brakes standard. Styling ugly and angular, and poor sales spell poor parts availability. Go for the sporting versions. ➤

◄ **2600 SPRINT. 1962-66 (prod: RHD models, 597). 4-seater coupé. F/R, 2584cc (S6 DOC).** The classical Bertone idiom, now with quad headlights, and good for around 120mph, thanks to its three-carburettor, 145bhp engine. Five forward speeds and all-disc brakes, as on the saloon. A true 'sleeper', still available in fair to good order for reasonable money.

2600 SPYDER. 1962-65 (prod: RHD models, 103). 2+2 seater sports. F/R, 2584cc (S6 DOC). A 98ins wheelbase gives you occasional back seats you don't get on the open Giulietta, and Touring's body is the one already fitted to 2000s. Specifications and performance as for the Sprint Coupé, but this one will probably set you back some if in good shape. ➤

GIULIA TI/SUPER. 1962-72 (prod. all types, 836,323). 4-door saloon. F/R, 1570cc (S4 DOC). Into the mass-production league at last with this ugly little saloon featuring a five-speed 'box, a rigid axle and coils at the rear, and servo disc-drum brakes. Output is anything from 92 to 102bhp according to type and year. Some early ones have all-drum brakes, but any sound one will do the ton. ➤

◄ **GIULIA SPRINT. 1962-68 (prod: 42,889). 2+2 seater coupé. F/R, 1570cc (S4 DOC).** Again the delightful coupé, with later twin-carburettor, 109bhp engine giving you 110mph, plus the usual handling. Brakes are disc/drum on early ones, all-disc on the 1966 GT Veloce. RHD generally available by now, but rust, as always, is a problem. For fun transportation, maybe choose a later model.

GIULIA SPYDER/SPYDER VELOCE. 1962-65 (prod: 9250 Spyder, 1091 Spyder Veloce). 2-seater convertible. F/R, 1570cc (S4 DOC). Pininfarina did this one, with 92bhp single-carburettor or 112bhp twin-carb engine. A five-speed 'box, of course, but you'll have to opt for the later Duetto if you must have all-disc brakes. All the usual plus and minus factors, of course, apply, but if you're lucky you might find one cheap. ➤

◄ **GT 1300 JUNIOR. 1966-72 (prod: 80,623). 4-seater coupé. F/R, 1290cc (S4 DOC).** Updated Giulietta coupé with the same economy, but four seats, five speeds, and all-disc brakes. More brake horses than the TI, ergo more speed. 447 cars were built to GTA specification with eight-plug heads, and on 96bhp they really will move. Both types available in Britain.

GIULIA 1300 TI. 1966-72 (prod: 144,213). 4-door saloon. F/R, 1290cc (S4 DOC). A combination of the 1.3-litre Giulietta mechanics and the Giulia shape, although it doesn't have the quad headlamps of later Giulia saloons. On 82bhp it'll give you the ton, and by now even basic Alfas offer five forward speeds and all-disc brakes. Listed in the UK from 1968. ➤

1750 BERLINA. 1967-72 (prod: 101,880). 4-door saloon. F/R, 1779cc (S4 DOC). Essentially an enlarged and tidied-up Giulia with more capacity and power, twin carburettors, hydraulically-actuated clutch, and dual circuit power disc brakes. The rust factor and large-scale production could hold the price down. In Britain from late 1968.

DUETTO. 1966-67 (prod: 6325). 2-seater convertible. F/R, 1570cc (S4 DOC). For our money, the prettiest of the Giulia family with new, low grille and inbuilt bumpers. The body's by Pininfarina, and the Duetto has the twin-carb, 109bhp version of the familiar engine. You get all-disc brakes, but no servo on this model.

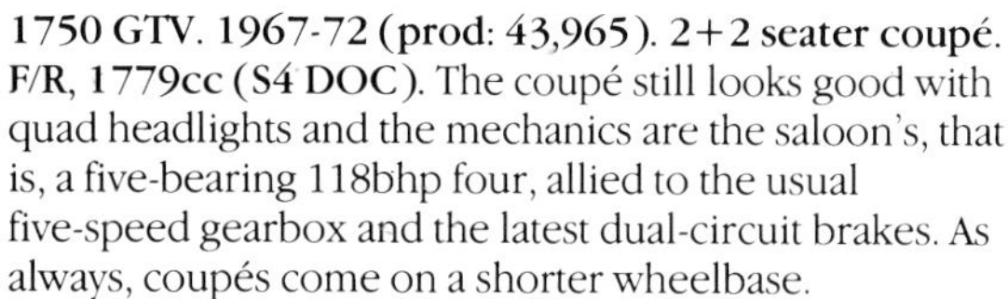

1750 GTV. 1967-72 (prod: 43,965). 2+2 seater coupé. F/R, 1779cc (S4 DOC). The coupé still looks good with quad headlights and the mechanics are the saloon's, that is, a five-bearing 118bhp four, allied to the usual five-speed gearbox and the latest dual-circuit brakes. As always, coupés come on a shorter wheelbase.

1750 SPYDER VELOCE. 1967-71 (prod: 8722). 2-seater convertible. F/R, 1779cc (S4 DOC). The Duetto's successor, but with the latest engine, transmission and chassis improvements and a sawn-off tail treatment. Worth watching in the collector market, if only because by this time there aren't many touring convertibles being made outside the supercar sector.

MONTREAL. 1970-77 (prod: 3925). 2-seater coupé. F/R, 2593cc (V8 DOC). For advanced students only, with its four-cam, fuel-injected dry-sump engine derived from the T33 sports-racer, although the rest is classic Alfa engineering. Bertone did the body (not one of his most elegant), and the Montreal does about 135mph. Few came to England, but they aren't in the big money yet.

2000 BERLINA. **1970-77 (prod: 89,840). 4-door saloon. F/R, 1962cc (S4 DOC).** Better looking than any Alfa saloon since the fifties, this one offered over 115mph from its 132bhp twin-carburettor engine. As usual there are all-disc servo brakes and a five-speed 'box. Later ones should still be rust-free, but as yet this one rates as a good secondhand buy rather than a collector's piece.

2000 GTV. **1970-77 (prod: 37,459). 2+2-seater coupé. F/R, 1962cc (S4 DOC).** The last of the traditional coupés, stylistically preferable to the current Alfetta-based wedge. Engine is to the same tune as the Berlinas, but it's an Alfa to its fingertips. Early ones are good bets – but watch that rust!

2000 SPYDER VELOCE. **1970 to date (prod: 22,000 to end 1977). 2-seater convertible. F/R, 1962cc (S4 DOC).** The good old formula – 132bhp, five forward speeds, and servo disc brakes, plus Pininfarina's ageless 1966 shape, and the usual rigid axle and coils at the rear. Not currently listed in UK, alas, although a dealer imported cars for RHD conversions.

ALLARD (GB)

Big, hairy-chested sporting cars were the staple of the Allard marque. The concept stemmed from Sydney Allard's pre-World War II trials special, which had divided axle ifs on a Ford V8 frame with an ex-GP Bugatti body. Its mud-plugging record saw demand for replicas, and pre-war cars came mainly with Ford engines. Post-war, the cars from Clapham became more civilised but were still extremely fast, with the Cadillac/Chrysler V8-engined J2 probably the most accelerative road car of its day. After 1953, sales of the smaller Palm Beach cars as well as the V8 cars fell due to competition from Jaguar. After 1958, the company's business was modifying Ford's 105E type Anglia.

K1. **1946-48 (prod: 151). 2-seater sports. F/R. 3622cc (V8 SV).** A sensation in 1946 with its waterfall grille and (then) staggering standing-start acceleration, thanks to a weight of under 22cwt. Engine, gearbox, and most other mechanics are Ford; if you wanted more power, you fitted the 3.9-litre Mercury. Brakes are hydraulic, and open cars always had floor change.

L. 1946-48 (prod: 191). 4-seater sports. F/R, 3622cc (V8 SV). A K1 with an extra 6ins of wheelbase and two extra seats. Front suspension (again) is of independent, divided-axle type with a Ford transverse set-up at the rear. A nice way to recapture the spirit of the thirties Anglo-American Sports Bastards before they started to put on weight. ►

◄ **M1. 1947-50 (prod: 500). 4-seater drophead coupé. F/R, 3622cc (V8 SV).** Historically the first truly civilised Allard, although style-wise perhaps the least successful of the initial postwar series. Late ones have the Ford Pilot's 'bent-wire' column shift. The Ford mechanics should keep servicing costs down.

P1. 1949-52 (prod: 559). 2-door saloon. F/R, 3622cc (V8 SV). Allard's best-seller and the model with which Sydney himself won the 1952 Monte Carlo Rally. Most powerful engine used was the 4.4-litre Mercury (say 115bhp) and column shift is standard. Lots of individuality but remember, the old Ford V8 is something of a gas guzzler. ►

◄ **J2/J2X. 1950-52 (prod: 173). 2-seater sports. F/R, 5420cc (V8 OHV).** Stark motorbike on four wheels with De Dion back end that can out-accelerate an XK120 when it's fitted with one of the big, short-stroke ohv American V8s, such as Cadillac, Oldsmobile or Chrysler. The dollar crisis, however, meant that British customers had to make do usually with the 4.4-litre ohv Mercury conversion.

K2. 1950-52 (prod: 119). 2-seater sports. F/R, 3917cc (V8 SV). More civilised K1 with full front styling, small luggage boot, and the usual choice of Ford or Mercury V8s for the home market, with Cadillac etc in the USA. Floor change is standard, thank goodness, and there is now coil spring front suspension. Rare in Britain. ►

M2X. 1951-53 (prod: 25). 4-seater drophead coupé. F/R, 3622cc (V8 SV). Drophead version of the P1 with A-shaped grille which makes appearance even more individual. Coil front springing, floor change, and the usual choice of engines, although anything native to Britain will have the faithful old Ford or Mercury. ➤

◀ **K3. 1952-55 (prod: 62). Roadster. F/R, 3622cc (V8 SV).** New-look Allard with the J2's De Dion rear axle, a tubular frame, fuel tanks in the rear wings, and a one-piece swing-forward bonnet. Seat is 56ins wide, and takes four abreast. Right-hand shift, but most of them went to the USA where you got a Cadillac engine and Hydramatic.

P2 MONTE CARLO. 1952-55 (prod: 11). 2-door saloon. F/R, 3622cc (V8 SV). Saloon version of the K3 on the 112ins wheelbase, with aluminium panels over a wood frame, and the M2X's A-grille. Power-operated bonnet gives access to the spare wheel as well. Heavy as well as rare, so try to find one with an American power train. ➤

◀ **SAFARI. 1952-55 (prod: 11). Station wagon. F/R, 3622cc (V8 SV).** Rare two-door woody based on the P2 – back to the windscreen, it's identical with the saloon. With a dry weight of some 1½ tons, it's not going to give you drag-strip performance using the regular 85bhp Ford flathead, but it's a real collector's piece. Ever seen one outside Earls Court?

PALM BEACH 21C/21Z. 1952-55 (prod: 8 21C, 65 21Z). 3-seater roadster. F/R, 1508cc (S4 OHV), 2262cc (S6 OHV). Allard's bid for the 'economy' market, using a K3-type chassis, but without De Dion axle. Even with the Ford Zephyr engine, it's no road burner, and if you find a Consul-powered version, swap units. A handful of later cars (1956-58) had twin-cam Jaguar engines. ➤

ALVIS (GB)

The glory days for Alvis ran from the 1920s to just before the outbreak of World War II – these were the years when the firm produced high quality sporting machinery. Alvis was founded in 1919, and as well as making cars it had an aero-engine division by 1937. After the war, it made the somewhat mundane – at least by pre-war Alvis standards – TA and TB series, with the best post-war product the Graber-bodied TD21 and its successor, the TE21. However, in 1966, Rover acquired a controlling interest and production of passenger cars ceased. The company now makes armoured vehicles.

◄ **TA14. 1946-50 (prod: 3311). Sports saloon, Carbodies drophead coupé, Tickford drophead coupé. F/R, 1892cc (S4 OHV).** Strictly a pre-war design, but with disc wheels instead of the old 12/70's wires. Mechanical brakes and rigid axles at both ends. Heavy on the controls, but very flexible and tough.

TB14. 1949-50 (prod: 100). 2-seater sports. F/R, 1892cc (S4 OHV). Rather horrible whale shape, although the door-mounted cocktail cabinet of the 1948 Show car was deleted from the production versions. Mechanics as TA14, but with twin carburettors and more power. As with all Alvises, Red Triangle Auto Services of Kenilworth offer an excellent parts service. ►

◄ **TA/TC21. 1950-55 (prod: 2074, inc TC21/100). Sports saloon, drophead coupé. F/R, 2993cc (S6 OHV).** Looks are pure traditional, but there's a new seven-bearing short-stroke engine, plus a return to IFS (coils, not the pre-war transverse leaf), and Alvis's first hydraulic brakes. Only about 85mph with the early single-carburettor engine, but 90 plus with the later twin carbs.

TB21. 1951 (prod: 31). 2-seater sports. F/R, 2993cc (S6 OHV). Body is the TB14's and so are the ponderous front wings, but the good old Alvis radiator is back once more. Unlike later closed 3-litres, still a single carburettor, but the advertised 95bhp should give nearly the ton, and the power unit is safe to 5000rpm. ►

TC21/100 GREY LADY. 1954-55 (prod: see TA/TC21). Sports saloon, drophead coupé. F/R, 2993cc (S6 OHV). Saloons have the thin pillars and plated window frames of later 'cooking' 3 litres, but the model is recognisable by its centre-lock wire wheels and bonnet airscoops. About 100bhp from the twin-carb engine gives 100mph, but only just. A nice gentleman's carriage. ➤

◄ **TC108G/TD21. 1956-63 (prod: 1098). 2-door saloon, drophead coupé. F/R, 2993cc (S6 OHV).** Styled most elegantly by Graber of Switzerland, although Park Ward bodied most of them. Better aerodynamics spell 110mph. Automatic available from 1959 with five-speed ZF 'boxes on 1963's manual cars. Disc front brakes in 1959, all-disc from 1962. Rust a problem, especially around the wheel arches.

TE/TF21. 1963-67 (prod: 458). 2-door saloon, drophead coupé. F/R, 2993cc (S6 OHV). Four-headlamp version of the Graber theme, with a choice of automatic or five-speed manual 'boxes. Power steering available (and desirable) from 1965. Sadly the last Alvis. Manual dropheads are the rarest and most desirable. ➤

AMPHICAR (D)

Originally the Eurocar, this strange amphibian, the brainchild of German Hans Trippel, was built in Karlsruhe from 1962. In late 1963, production transferred to Berlin's *Deutsch Waggon und Maschinenfabrik* where it survived in uncertain fashion until 1968. Rusting bodyshells and cash flow problems saw the demise of this machine.

◄ **AMPHICAR. 1961-67 (prod: approx 2500). 4-seater convertible. R/R, 1147cc (S4 OHV).** Just about the only amphibious private car to achieve commercial sales. Does 65mph on the road, and 7½ knots in the water, thus at best a compromise in either element. Corrosion and water sealing are problems, although mechanics are Triumph Herald and easily replaceable. Sold in Britain from 1964.

ARMSTRONG SIDDELEY (GB)

The firm came into being through the fusion of Armstrong-Whitworth's car-making activities with Siddeley-Deasy of Coventry in 1919. The products throughout the company's 41 years were always solidly built, easy to drive and comfortable rather than sporting. The last products from the firm were distinctly luxurious but were always too expensive compared to the main competition from Jaguar: the Sapphire 346 could have rivalled the Mk VII, but cost £205 more in 1954.

◄ **LANCASTER 16/18HP. 1946-52 (prod: 12,570, all 16/18 HP types to 1953). 6-light saloon. F/R, 1991cc or 2309cc (S6 OHV).** A stylistic sensation of 1945: 18hp engine standardised from mid-1949. Available with a Rootes-built four-speed synchromesh 'box, although the traditional Wilson preselector suits the car better (but watch repair costs!). Torsion-bar front suspension and hydro-mechanical brakes. Not much performance, but gentlemanly road manners.

HURRICANE 16/18 HP. 1946-53 (prod: see Lancaster). dropHead coupé, Typhoon 4-seater fixed-head coupé. F/R, 1991cc or 2309cc (S6 OHV). Mechanically the same as the Lancaster, but watch for wood rot and corrosion, especially in sills and screen pillars. Driving vision poor with the hood up. The fabric-roof Typhoon (dropped early 1950) was a hardtop coupé three years before Detroit dreamed up this label. Good ones available quite cheaply. ►

◄ **WHITLEY 18 HP. 1950-53 (prod: see Lancaster). 4-light saloon, 6-light saloon, limousine, sports station coupé. F/R, 2309cc (S6 OHV).** A more sporting style than the Lancaster which it replaced in 1952. 18 HP engine standard. Limousines on the 122ins wheelbase are very rare: even rarer in Britain is the Station Coupé, a coupé-utility in the Australian idiom. Synchromesh and preselector both available.

SAPPHIRE 3.4-LITRE/346. 1953-59 (prod: 7207). 4-light saloon, 6-light saloon. F/R, 3435cc (S6 OHV). Big, traditionally-appointed saloon with square-dimensioned hemi-head engine, good for 100mph with the optional twin carburettors. Sold with all-synchromesh, electrically selected preselector (caution!) or Rolls-Royce Hydramatic boxes. Good ones are splendid carriages, but the front wings are rust-traps, and you won't get more than 17mpg. ►

◄ **SAPPHIRE LIMOUSINE. 1955-59 (prod: see Sapphire 3.4 litre). Limousine. F/R, 3435cc (S6 OHV).** Rare long chassis variant for mayors: preselector standard. A lot of car on a 133ins wheelbase. The Armstrong Siddeley Owners' Club maintains an excellent spares service, a bonus in the case of a make that has now been extinct for over 20 years.

SAPPHIRE 234/236. 1956-58 (prod: 803, 234; 603, 236). Sports saloon. F/R, 2290cc (S4 OHV), 2309cc (S6 OHV). A triumph of non-styling, and a rust-trap. The 236 has the old ex-Whitley long-stroke six-cylinder engine and Lockheed Manumatic two-pedal transmission, but the 234's power unit is a big Sapphire minus two cylinders, a bit rough but giving 2.4 Jaguar performance. The car handles better than a Mk1 Jag, too. ➤

◄ **STAR SAPPHIRE. 1959-60 (prod: 980). 6-light saloon, limousine. F/R, 3990cc (S6 OHV).** Last and best of the Sapphires, with twin-carburettor 165bhp engine, servo disc/drum brakes, Borg-Warner automatic gearbox, and the power steering also available on the early 346 from 1956. Limousines (made only in 1960) had a single carburettor.

ASTON MARTIN (GB)

Somehow Aston Martin is still with us, producing magnificent V8-engined sports cars, the last true automotive dinosaurs. Although the firm was founded by Lionel Martin and Robert Bamford in 1914, initial production had to wait until 1922. Since then it has undergone periodic financial crises, yet has produced some stunning sports cars: Before the war, the cars were mainly 1½-litres and the company was on its third owner. After the war the David Brown Group took control (1947), and the DB series began, along with a racing programme that was to see Aston as World Sports Car Champions in 1959. Currently the company is owned by a consortium and is desperately looking to revitalise its current and somewhat dated range.

DB1. 1948-50 (prod: 15). Tourer, drophead coupé. F/R, 1970cc (S4 OHV). Interim model with 90bhp pushrod engine in a tubular chassis, with coil spring IFS and a live axle and coils at the rear. Dropheads are handsome beasts with their vee screens and wing-mounted spare wheels, but this one hasn't a lot more than scarcity value. ➤

◄ **DB2. 1950-53 (prod: 410). 2-seater coupé, drophead coupé. F/R, 2580cc (S6 DOC).** Marriage of W.O. Bentley's twin-cam Lagonda engine to Aston's tubular chassis from the DB1. The 116bhp Vantage engine is a desirable option, giving 115-120mph, although watch it, because some very early cars were made with column shift. Noisy, and spares expensive – when you can get them.

DB2/4 MK I. 1953-55 (prod: 564). 4-seater sports saloon, drophead coupé. F/R, 2580cc, 2922cc (S6 DOC). Saloons are now very occasional four-seater hatchbacks, and early 2.6 engines came in Vantage tune as standard. The 3-litre engine, for the 1954 and '55 seasons, restores the performance lost with the extra seats. Dropheads rare (only 70 made of all types to the end of 1955). Saloons can be found, but watch restoration costs ➤

◄ **DB2/4 MK II. 1955-57 (prod: 199). 4-seater saloon, hardtop coupé, drophead coupé. F/R, 2922cc (S6 DOC).** More angular rear wings distinguish this one, and the rear axle is more robust. Notchback 'hardtops' (34 made) and dropheads (only 24) are the more desirable variants, so think big money on either of these. Later Mk IIs could be had with 'hotter' camshafts giving 165bhp.

DB2/4 MK III. 1957-59 (prod: 551). 4-seater sports saloon, hardtop coupé, drophead coupé. You may or may not like the new droop snoot, but the final DB2 package gives you 162bhp, and there are Girling disc brakes at the front, plus a hydraulically actuated clutch and an overdrive option. Later cars can have automatic, too. ➤

◄ **DB4. 1958-63 (prod: 1110 all types). 4-seater sports saloon. F/R, 3670cc (S6 DOC).** Touring's body is more elegant than the old DB2 shape, and on 240bhp speed goes up to 140mph with a 0-60 time of around 7secs. Brakes are four-wheel power disc, overdrive was available from 1961, a 260bhp Vantage engine in 1962, and automatic in 1963. Short-chassis, lightweight GT is identifiable by cowled headlights; twin-plug engine gave 300bhp, a mere 81 were built.

DB4 GT ZAGATO. 1961-63 (prod: 19). 2-seater coupé. F/R, 3670cc (S6 DOC). Seen at the 1960 London Show, it's got the GT's 91ins wheelbase chassis and weighs less than 2800lbs in road trim. Output of 314bhp spells a fearsome performance, and on this one you don't get a brake servo. Even more expensive than the factory-bodied GT if you can find one. ➤

DB4 DROPHEAD COUFE. 1961-63 (prod: 70). Drophead coupé. F/R, 3670cc (S6 DOC). Specification of this one is stock 1961, a 240bhp engine with an overdrive option: automatic and Vantage options came in during the model's brief life. Another Aston in the high price-class today, although if you're content with a saloon it's surprising what you can get for a small outlay.

DB5. 1964-5 (prod: 1023). 4-seater sports saloon, drophead coupé, hardtop coupé. F/R, 3995cc (S6 DOC). More litres and more power: 282bhp in standard form and 314 with October 1964's Vantage option. Selectaride shockers and automatic became available during the model's run. All but the earliest manuals are five-speeders, courtesy ZF, and of course gearboxes are all-synchromesh. Weight is going up, too.

DB6. 1965-71 (prod: 1753). 4-seater sports saloon. F/R, 3995cc (S6 DOC). Better aerodynamics in this new shape with cut-off tail and a few extra inches of wheelbase. The option list includes the Vantage engine, limited slip differential, automatic and (with 1967 models) power steering. The Vantage's 325bhp is needed to offset ever growing weight. Thirsty, and therefore relatively cheap to buy.

VOLANTE. 1967-71 (prod: see DB6). Drophead coupé. F/R, 3995cc (S6 DOC). These make a lot of money, although collectors prefer manual to automatic. Attractive styling harking back to the DB5, and the usual option list, now including air conditioning as well. Weight is up to 3200lbs dry, though, and there's no comparing these luxury carriages with the old DB2.

DBS. 1967-72 (prod: 829). 4-seater sports saloon. F/R, 3995cc (S6 DOC). Plus, attractive wedge-shaped bodywork styled by Bill Towns, with quad headlamps and additional luggage space. De Dion rear end replacing the old live axle and coils. Handles nicely, and will top 140mph with the Vantage engine, but really needs more power. At present, rather a 'sleeper'.

DBS V8. 1969-72 (prod: 405). 4-seater sports saloon. F/R, 5340cc (V8 4OC). Adequate, if undisclosed, power at last for the DBS, plus standard power steering (except on a very few early cars) and Selectaride dampers. Only fuel injection engines offered up to 1972, and no convertibles. As yet fringe-collectable only: with a notoriously heavy clutch, maybe you should choose Chrysler's Torqueflite automatic on V8s.

ASTRA (GB)

One of those obscure small car firms that grew up in Britain in the Macmillan 'You've never had it so good' era, Astra produced its utility car at Hampton Hill in Middlesex from 1956-59. The firm was actually a subsidiary of the British Anzani Company, and the car was originally called the Jarc.

UTILITY. 1956-60 (prod: n/a). Station wagon. R/R, 322cc (S2 TS). Unusual mini station wagon with underfloor-mounted Anzani engine and three-speed motorcycle-type Burman gearbox. All independent springing and hydraulic brakes. Handling rather hoppity, although it did 55mph. Originally marketed as the Jarc Little Horse with 250cc Excelsior engine. Latterly sold only in kit form – did anyone buy one of these?

AUDI (D)

One of those companies which smacks of incest – there have been so many ties with other German firms. It was founded in 1909 by August Horch, who was not allowed to use his own name but chose instead its Latin form, 'Audi'. Early products were conventional and successful in competition. The last true Audi was the type R eight-cylinder of 1928, as the firm that year became part of the DKW group – subsequent models were always to some extent assembled cars. The Audi factory came under Soviet control after 1945, but the name was kept alive in the West as part of the revived Auto Union in 1949. Mercedes-Benz became a major shareholder in 1956, followed by Volkswagen in 1965. In 1966, the Audi marque name was revived, and since then the company has produced ever better cars.

60/70/80/SUPER 90. 1965-72 (prod: 416,852 all types). 2-door saloon, 4-door saloon, station wagon. F/F, 1496cc (60); 1696cc (70, 80); 1770cc (Super 90) (S4 OHV). Revival of a respected pre-war name by Auto Union, featuring a longitudinal four-stroke engine driving the front wheels. Four-speed all synchro, front disc brakes with servo option, live axle and torsion bars rear. British market dates: 70 1966, 80/Super 90 1967, 60 1968. Later versions much better.

AUSTIN (GB)

Now the dominant British car manufacturer, it was founded in 1905 by Herbert Austin (later Sir) whose earliest designs were conventional, reliable and somewhat boring. The Seven of 1922 was a revolution, and on this design the firm's fortunes were made. Most products through the pre-war period were dull but worthy, and the trend was continued after 1945. The British Motor Corporation was formed in 1952 between Austin and Morris, with the former firm emerging dominant. The most significant post-war car was, of course, the Mini, but fortunes are on the way up today thanks to a competent line-up which goes some way towards erasing the memory of some dreadful cars built in the late 1960s and early 1970s.

◄ **8HP. 1939-47 (postwar prod: 33,000 plus). 4-door saloon. F/R, 900cc (S4 SV).** Introduced 1939, but no tourers or 2-door saloons postwar. Four-doors almost invariably black with brown leather. Rigid axles, mechanical brakes, and a narrow track that doesn't help handling. Stolid little 40-45mpg workhorse.

10HP. 1939-47 (postwar prod: 49,000 plus). 4-door saloon. F/R, 1125cc (S4 SV). Around in this form with alligator bonnet from May '39, and from a best-selling line dating back to 1932. Spares no problem, thanks to a lively club. Like 8HP, has a welded-in integral floorpan that can rust. If you don't mind zero performance and 1937 American styling, a good family buy. ►

◄ **12/16HP. 1940-47/1945-49 (postwar prod: 6000 plus 12HP; 36,000 16HP). Saloon, station wagon (16HP only). F/R, 1525cc (S4 SV)/2199cc (S4 OHV).** Styling is enlarged 10, but no welded floorpan on the X-braced frame to rust. Usual beam axles and rod-operated brakes, plus the bonuses of sliding roof, opening screen and leather upholstery. 16 has Austin's first OHV private car engine (heresy!) and will give you 75mph and 25mpg, but acceleration is not its strong point.

A40 DORSET/DEVON. 1947-52 (prod: 354,000 plus). 2-door saloon, 4-door saloon, station wagon. F/R, 1200cc (S4 OHV). Austin's new look with OHV and coil spring IFS and pastel colours to liven up Cripps-era austerity. Sliding roof option; column shift on the last ones. Plus point: it's got a chassis. Minus points: uncertain hydromech brakes, woolly handling, and that '41 Chevrolet styling. Dorset two-door dropped early 1949. ►

A125 SHEERLINE. 1948-54 (prod: approx 9000). **Sports saloon, limousine. F/R, 3995cc (S6 OHV).** Poor man's Bentley Mk VI with attractive razor edge bodywork and traditional grille flanked by P100s. IFS, hydraulic brakes, and lots of wood and leather, but four-on-the-column, horrid instrumentation, and very undergeared. Limousine (new for 1950) very rare. Becoming collectable. ►

◄ **A135 PRINCESS.** 1948-56 (prod: approx 3000). **Sports saloon, touring limousine, limousine. F/R, 3995cc (S6 OHV).** Vanden Plas's luxury Austin, more streamlined and less pleasing than Sheerline aesthetically, although aluminium panelling means no rust problems. Early ones have 130bhp three-carburettor engines to cope with the weight, but these less common on facelifted Mk II (1951). Limousines from 1953. Optional automatic, 1956.

A70 HAMPSHIRE. 1949-50 (prod: n/a). **Saloon, station wagon. F/R, 2199cc (S4 OHV).** Austin's answer to the Standard Vanguard with the OHV Sixteen engine in an A40-type chassis with coil IFS and hydromech brakes. Four-on-the-column, poor handling, and not much more room than in a Devon. Seldom seen today, but this isn't the engine's fault...it is pretty well unburstable. ►

◄ **A90 ATLANTIC CONVERTIBLE.** 1949-50 (prod: see Saloon). **4-seater convertible. F/R, 2660cc (S4 OHV).** Aimed at an unappreciative US market which didn't want an abbreviated stick-shift four-cylinder at Buick price, for all those Indianapolis long-distance records. Coil front springs, gold lettered instruments, column shift, a power-top option, and even plated streaks *à la* Pontiac down the beetling bonnet. Heavy brakes and awful handling.

A90 ATLANTIC SALOON. 1950-52 (prod: approx. 10,000 inc. convertible). **2-door sports saloon, F/R, 2660cc (S4 OHV).** Fabric roofed hardtop with wrap around rear window, better for British market than convertible. Low axle ratio and better low-speed acceleration. Full hydraulic brakes replace hydromech from 1951. Wonderful engine which redeemed itself in the original Austin-Healey. ►

A40 SPORTS. 1951-53 (prod: 3800). 4-seater convertible. F/R, 1200cc (S4 OHV). Semi-sports type, and a non-starter in the sales stakes, despite Jensen's pretty body based on their Interceptor Cabriolet. In twin-carburettor form the engine gives 50bhp: hence 80mph possible. Column shift on '52s and '53s. Usual non-handling, but no parts problems. Coming up in the collector stakes.

A70 HEREFORD. 1951-54 (prod: 50,000). Saloon, station wagon, convertible. F/R, 2199cc (S4 OHV). Four-light bulboid styling spells room for six in the Hampshire's replacement, now with fully hydraulic brakes. Good for 80mph, but rolls appallingly. Still a separate chassis. Woody wagons rare, and the power-top convertibles (1951) rarer still.

A30. 1952-56 (prod: 225,000). 2-door saloon, 4-door saloon, station wagon. F/R, 803cc (S4 OHV). First unitary Austin and their answer to the Morris Minor, soon to share its engine and gearbox. Lighter and more frugal than the Morris, *but* hydromech brakes and a narrow track that makes the A30 hazardous in crosswinds. Structure surprisingly durable. Two-door from late 1953, Countryman wagon 1955.

A40 SOMERSET. 1952-54 (prod: n/a). 4-door saloon, convertible. F/R, 1200cc (S4 OHV). Hereford styling in the A40's still separate chassis with hydraulic brakes: column shift standard. Convertibles from late '52, although A40 wagons (still made) are van-based and retain the older shape. Lasts very well; a sound one is well worth the £400 you'll pay. Handling? The less said the better.

A40/A50/A55 CAMBRIDGE. 1955-58 (prod: n/a). 4-door saloon. F/R, 1200cc/1489cc (S4 OHV). Unitary construction at last with hole-in-the-wall style grille, although sliding roof still an option. 1.2-litre A40 1955/6 only: A55 (bigger boot and back window) from 1957. Van derivatives still made into early 1970s. The last 1½-litre saloon with a shape peculiar to Austin.

A90/A95/A105 WESTMINSTER. 1955-59 (prod: n/a). Saloon, station wagon. F/R, 2639cc (S6 OHV). Scaled-up Cambridge with BMC's new C-type 'six' and column shift. A105 (from mid-'56) is the high-performance variant with two-tone finish, all the extras and that mid-50s fad, triple overdrive. Wagons only in the A95 line (from October '56), when automatic also became available throughout this range. ➤

◄ **A35 SALOON 1957-59 (prod: 375,000). 2-door saloon, 4-door saloon. F/R, 948cc (S4 OHV).** Facelifted A30 with the latest 948cc A-type engine and bigger rear window. Smaller (13in) wheels but higher overall gearing to compensate. A great little saloon-car racer in its day. Handling as lethal as the A30's, but also lasts just as well. Excellent shopping car for one's wife.

A35 COUNTRYMAN. 1957-62 (prod: n/a). Station wagon. F/R, 948cc (S4 OHV). Two-door all-metal wagon which out-lived the saloons, the van version going on to '68. Furnishings van-like and sound damping negligible. Also made (as were 1956 A30s) as a very rare Aussie-style Coupé Utility. ➤

◄ **PRINCESS IV. 1957-59 (prod: 200). Sports saloon. F/R, 3995cc (S6 OHV).** Last Princess to carry the Austin badge: for later models, see Vanden Plas. Slab sides and razor edge roofline suggest the latest Cadillac Sevilles. Hydramatic transmission, power steering, servo brakes and tubeless tyres all standard, and it did 100mph. Scarcity might just lend enchantment, but handling won't. Nor will a 12mpg thirst.

A40 FARINA MKS I-III. 1958-61/1961-67 (prod: 340,000). 2-door saloon, station wagon. F/R, 948cc/ 1098cc (S4 OHV). Better looking and roomier A35 replacement courtesy of Pininfarina, and a well-loved little hack in its day: still common, which suggests good tinworm-resistance. Wider track, but still not fun to drive, larger engine came in October 1962. Early ones had the A35's hydromech brakes. Countryman wagon is in fact an early hatchback saloon. ➤

A55/A60 CAMBRIDGE. 1959-61/1961-69 (prod: n/a). **Saloon, station wagon.** F/R, 1489cc/1622cc (S4 OHV). Immortal BMC—Farina family saloon beloved of country cabbies, also badged as MG, Morris, Riley or Wolseley. Dull, worthy and indestructible. 1.6-litre engine, tail fins (!) and automatic option 1961, diesel engine available '66, but never even front disc brakes. Some time every British motor museum will have to have one.

A99/A110 WESTMINSTER. 1959-61/1961-68 (prod: n/a). **Saloon.** F/R, 2912cc (S6 OHV). The 1½-litre Farina's big sister, also with Wolseley or Vanden Plas badging. Always servo front disc brakes, plus overdrive/automatic options. A110 with longer wheelbase, and preferable as it has four-speed as standard instead of three. Power steering available from July, 1962. Undistinguished.

1100/1300. 1963-73/1967-73 (prod: n/a). **2-door saloon, 4-door saloon, station wagon.** F/F, 1098cc/1275cc (S4 OHV). Mini development with east-west engine plus Hydrolastic suspension and front disc brakes: Austin came a year after Morris version. Automatic option late 1965, station wagons March 1966. Early two-doors for export only. Still quite enjoyable, but rust is a killer, especially in the rear subframe. Caution enjoined.

1800. 1964-75 (prod: n/a). **Saloon.** F/F, 1798cc (S4 OHV). Mechanically a blown-up 1100 using a detuned five-bearing MGB engine set across the front. Automatic available from '68: rather necessary power steering had been an option from previous autumn. Always felt too wide, but a dependable if uninteresting family saloon. Also sold as a Morris or Wolseley.

3-LITRE. 1967-71 (prod: 10,100). **Saloon.** F/R, 2912cc (S6 OHV). 1800 hull with improved Hydrolastic suspension incorporating a self-levelling device, a longitudinal engine (the MGC's seven-bearing version, not the old C-type), rear drive, and front disc brakes. Option list includes overdrive, automatic, and power steering. Never caught on. Scarcity value only.

MAXI 1500. 1969-80 (prod: 450,000 all variants, to 1981). 5-door saloon. F/F, 1485cc (S4 OC). Only just in our period, and early ones with that dreadful cable linkage for the five-speed 'box are best left alone. Fifth impossibly high. Suspension as on 3-litre but front drive and a new OHC engine on east-west mounting. The Maxi redeemed itself in later life, and is much mourned. ➤

AUSTIN-HEALEY (GB)

In October 1952, the Donald Healey Motor Co showed a stunning open sports car at the Earls Court Motor Show. It became Austin's answer to Sir John Black's Triumph TR2, and proved immensely popular in the USA. The four- and six-cylinder Healey 100s, along with the later 3000 model, were masculine sports cars in the best tradition, and they were backed up by the humble Sprite which was later badged as an MG Midget. Final A-H models were assembled at Abingdon, not Longbridge, and the marque name disappeared.

◄ **100/4. 1953-56 (prod: 14,012). Sports 2-seater. F/R, 2660cc (S4 OHV).** A worthy home, at last, for the Altantic's engine. BN2s (1955-6) have four speed 'boxes with overdrive, instead of three speed with dual overdrive. Contemporary 100M variant featured high compression head and 110bhp output. Most cars went for export: beware corrosion on vehicles now over a quarter of a century old.

100S. 1954-56 (prod: 50). Sports 2-seater. F/R, 2660cc (S4 OHV). Rare competition variant with 132bhp alloy-head engine, alloy body panels, straight four-speed 'box with overdrive, and all-disc brakes. Hard to find, especially in Britain. Could be expensive, whereas reasonable 'cooking' 100/4s can still be found for fair money. ➤

◄ **100/6. 1956-59 (prod: 14,436). Sports 2-seater, sports 2+2. F/R, 2639cc (S6 OHV).** Wire wheels and overdrive are desirable extras. Avoid early (1956-7) BN4 cars with 120bhp engines, slower and less accelerative than the Fours. From late '57 there's a six-port head and more power, but a BN6 designation means two seats and not the improved power unit.

3000 Mk I. 1959-61 (prod: 13,650). Sports 2-seater, sports 2+2 seater. F/R, 2912cc (S6 OHV). More power still – 132bhp on the BT7 series – plus front disc brakes, though overdrive, once again, is an option. All big Healeys are desirable, but body rot is a horrible problem. Two-seater rare, ergo more money. Anything offered too cheaply may be a restoration tragedy. ➤

3000 Mk II. 1961-63 (prod: 11,563). Sports 2-seater, sports 2+2 seater. F/R, 2912cc (S6 OHV). Again more urge, with triple SUs: difficulty in setting them up saw twin carbs back from 1962. Recognisable from older cars by its convex grille. Late ones (BJ7) have a brake servo option, though this refinement only became standard on the Mk IIIs. Two-seater very rare, 34 only sold on the home market. Again watch for body corrosion, especially around the back. ➤

◄ **3000 Mk III. 1963-68 (prod: 16,321). Sports 2+2 seater. F/R, 2912cc (S6 OHV).** Last and best of the big bangers, with brake servo, nearly 150bhp, a new wooden facia and better appointments. There are also more of them around and they've had less time to rot. Again, occasional seats are compulsory.

SPRITE I. 1958-61 (prod: 38,999). Sports 2-seater. F/R, 948cc (S4 OHV) The original Frogeye with one-piece, lift-up bonnet/wing assembly ... long a cult car on both sides of the Channel. There's no MG sub-variant, either. You'll be lucky to find one without body or bonnet problems. Still, we've seen restore-while-you-drive specimens quite recently at reasonable prices, although they're on the up. ➤

◄ **SPRITE II. 1961-62/1962-64 (prod: 20,450/11,215). Sports 2-seater. F/R, 948cc/1098cc (S4 OHV).** This one's been tidied up with a certain loss of individuality, though the conventional bonnet lasts better and the opening boot is a bonus. Go for the later (Oct 1962) series with bigger, 56bhp engine and wire-wheel option. Front disc brakes standard on all Mk IIs.

SPRITE III. 1964-66 (prod: 25,905). Sports 2-seater. F/R, 1098cc (S4 OHV). As for Mk II but with windows that wind, doors that lock and proper semi-elliptics at the back instead of those hoppity quarter-elliptics on earlier marks. An extra 3hp compensates for some of the extra weight, but you've still got usual body rot problems. With no 'Octagonal cachet', Sprites come cheaper than Midgets. ➤

SPRITE IV. 1966-69 (prod: 14,350). Sports 2-seater. F/R, 1275cc (S4 OHV). Engine is basically Mini-Cooper S detuned to 65bhp and at last you get a permanently attached hood, a very desirable refinement. Just a fraction faster than a Mk III but acceleration figures about the same. Sprites have a good rust record, so this one shouldn't have deteriorated too far.

SPRITE V/AUSTIN SPRITE. 1969-71 (prod: 8443). Sports 2-seater. F/R, 1275cc (S4 OHV). The last 1029 were badged as plain Austins and are real rarities, but the oval MG-style grille means loss of identity, and do you really want black sills and Rostyle wheels? Collapsible steering columns on later cars. Main merit on this one is that it's had less time to rust.

AUTO UNION (D)

Auto Union was formed in 1932. The name actually covered a combine of Audi, DKW, Horch and Wanderer. After the war, the four factories were nationalised, but two former executives reformed the combine in West Germany in 1949, basically to produce the West German versions of DKWs. The DKW Type 1000 was marketed only as an Auto Union until 1962.

1000SP. 1958-65 (prod: 6640). Sports 2-seater coupé. F/F, 980cc (S3 TS). Only touring car to carry this name, but really just the good old three cylinder DKW tuned to give 55bhp and dressed up by Baur to look like a mini-Thunderbird. Front disc brakes from March 1963. Rare and little known here, so you might find a clean one for a song.

BENTLEY (GB)

The most widely revered Bentleys come from the 1921-30 period, when W.O. Bentley's firm produced the archetypal vintage sports car. Shaky finances and the attempt to launch a luxury model as the depression started saw the firm fail, Rolls-Royce taking over and producing its own radically different Bentley car in 1933. After the war, the Bentley was more sporting and cheaper than Rolls-Royce products, but with the exception of the 1952 Continental the firm's Rolls-Royce and Bentley products were virtually identical from there on. Current models, led by the Turbo R, are moving away from that.

◄ **MK VI. 1946-51/51-52 (prod: 5201). 4-door saloon, drophead coupé, numerous customs. F/R, 4257cc/ 4566cc (S6 IOE).** Choice of special bodies limitless, though 80 per cent of production carried the rust-prone Standard Steel coachwork. Customs tend to be aluminium-panelled, but there are no off-the-shelf replacement bits. On Standard Steels, first tell-tale sign of trouble is bubbling round the sidelamps. 18mpg on two-star fuel a bonus, 4.6-litre engine from mid-1951.

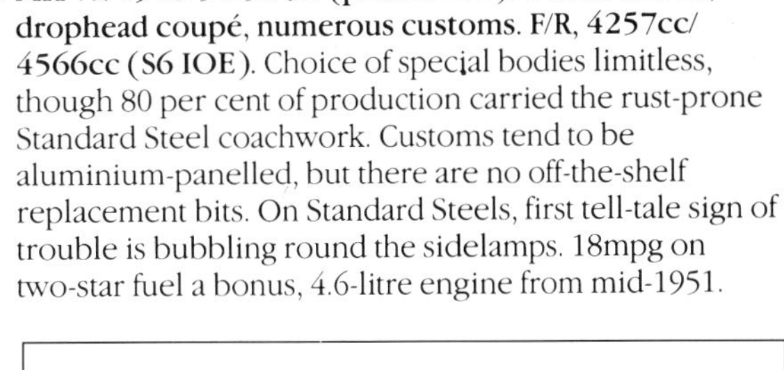

R-TYPE. 1952-55 (prod: 2320). 4-door saloon, drophead coupé, numerous customs. F/R, 4566cc (S6 IOE). Bigger boot and 4.6-litre engine, plus an automatic option standardised on late cars. Specials even rarer than on Mk VI, which is why you must pay handsomely for a good drophead. Straight Standard Steels come cheaper, though Mk VI corrosion problems apply. ►

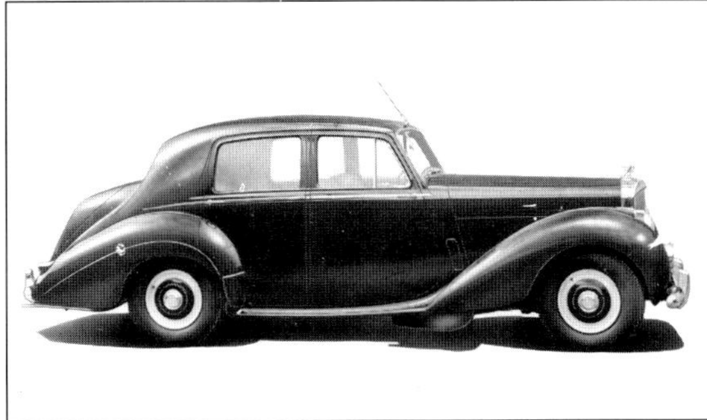

◄ **CONTINENTAL R. 1952-55 (prod: 207). 2-door saloon. F/R, 4566cc/4887cc (S6 IOE).** H.J. Mulliner's superb shape on almost all of these, the ultimate in post-war Bentleys. Three figure cruising with minimal wind noise, plus 20mpg. 4.9-litre engine on late cars, manual more fancied than automatic, but LHD means column shift, alas. Pay an arm and a leg for a good one, but expect awful body repair bills on the less good.

S1. 1955-59 (prod: 3107). 4-door saloon and a few specials. F/R, 4887cc (S6 IOE). Preferred to early V8 S-types and in any case simpler and more frugal. Long chassis (35 built) merely rare. Desirable power steering from 1957. Corrosion problems at back of chassis as well as on body. Commoner than Rolls-Royce, ergo a lot cheaper. ►

◄ **CONTINENTAL S1. 1955-59 (prod: 431). 2-door saloon (H.J. Mulliner), 2-door saloon (Park Ward), drophead coupé. F/R, 4887cc (S6 IOE).** Not quite as popular as the R Continental with Park Ward's closed cars usually coming the least expensive. Manual very rare, and not after early 1957. Again, as on regular S1s, go for one with power steering. Dropheads rare and very expensive.

S2, 1959-62 (prod: 1932). 4-door saloon. F/R, 6230cc (V8 OHV). First and least fancied of the V8s, though Rolls-Royce versions now outnumber Bentleys. Power steering and automatic standard from now on, plus an air conditioning superfluous in Britain. Better to go for an S3. Long wheelbase still rare (57 cars). ➤

◄ **CONTINENTAL S2. 1959-62 (prod: 388). 2-door saloon (H.J. Mulliner), 2-door saloon (Young), 4-door Flying Spur saloon (H.J. Mulliner), 4-door saloon (Young), drophead coupé. F/R, 6230cc (V8 OHV).** Four shoe front brakes and a higher axle ratio than on standard cars, plus a wide choice of bodies you won't find on regular S2s. Less valuable than the sixes, and closed cars still (relatively) cheap ... especially the rather controversially styled Flying Spurs.

S3. 1962-65 (prod: 1318). 4-door saloon. F/R, 6230cc (V8 OHV). Another good last-of-the-line buy with higher-compression engine, though the obvious recognition feature is the quad headlights. The 32 long-chassis cars have only the merit of rarity and probably sheltered lives. Even if the S3 is rarer than the parallel Silver Cloud, it's still about 25 per cent cheaper. No special bodies on this one. ➤

◄ **CONTINENTAL S3. 1962-65 (prod: 312). 2-door saloon, 4-door Flying Spur saloon, drophead coupé. F/R, 6230cc (V8 OHV).** The last Bentley without an exact RR counterpart, though watch it, there are a few Royces made to the same specification. Improvements on regular S3s include greater power assistance to the steering as well as those quad headlights. Young's 20 saloon bodies on this chassis just about represented their swansong.

T1. 1965-70/1970-77 (prod: 1867 to end 1976). 2-door saloon, 4-door saloon, drophead coupé. F/R, 6230cc/ 6750cc (V8 OHV). Bentley up-to-date with monocoque hull, all-independent, self-levelling suspension, dual-circuit servo disc brakes and all the other goodies. There are 10 Silver Shadows to every Bentley so scarcity counts ... 2-doors (98) and dropheads (41) are very rare indeed and already collectable. ➤

BERKELEY (GB)

Laurie Bond was one of that strange breed of designers who flaunted convention. The Berkeley was one of his designs, built by Charles Panter's firm of caravan manufacturers from 1956-61 in Biggleswade. Technically clever, the cars never really caught on, possibly because of the revolution in passenger car design presaged by the Mini.

◄ **B60/B65. 1956-57/1957-58 & 1961 (prod: approx 2000, all 4-wheeled models). Sports 2-seater.** F/F, 322cc/328cc (S2 TS). Laurie Bond's engaging miniature with three-piece, rustproof plastic unitary construction, chain-driven front wheels, and three-speed (four-speed on later cars) motorcycle-type gearbox. Excelsior-powered B65 preferred to earlier Anzani-engined B60. Looks like a baby Austin-Healey, but flat out at 65.

B90. 1958/59 (prod: see B60/65). Sports 2-seater, sports 4-seater. F/F, 492cc (S3 TS). Austin-Healey looks now matched to Sprite performance, thanks to Excelsior's aircooled triple-carburettor three, rated at 30bhp. Weighs less than 800lb, and the floor change (on late B65s as well) an improvement on the original column shift. For reliability, though, the B65 has a happier record. ►

◄ **B95/B105. 1959-61 (prod: see B60/65). Sports 2-seater, hardtop 2-seater.** F/F, 692cc (S2 OHV). The ultimate in Berkeleys with Royal Enfield's parallel-twin Constellation motor. In high-compression 50bhp tune the B105 should do just that speed, thanks to its modest 784lbs dry weight. Easily identifiable from lesser models by its big rectangular grille.

T60. 1959-61 (prod: 2500 approx). Sports 2-seater. F/F, 328cc (S2 TS). A B65 with trailing arm suspension to the single rear wheel instead of the four-wheeler's swing axles and coils. Excelsior Twin engine and four-speed box. Possibly the best fun-trike between the last of the old Morgans and the Triking. Berkeleys as a whole haven't got into the money yet. ►

BMW (D)

BMW has undergone so many near catastrophes that it is amazing it has survived. Initially a firm making aero-engines, it then produced motorcycles before making the Dixi, an Austin Seven manufactured under licence. In 1933, BMW revealed its own design, which was succeeded by some fine pre-war touring cars. After the war, the firm nearly died for want of capital to build a new plant, and then embarked on a disastrous spell building Isetta bubble cars from 1955, which nearly resulted in bankruptcy in 1959. The 'New Class' of the early 1960s saw order restored, and paved the way to the highly respected range of executive, luxury and sporting cars of the 1980s.

◄ **501. 1951-56 (prod: 8951). 4-door saloon. F/R, 2077cc (S6 OHV).** The good old pre-war 326 plus four-on-the-column and horrible bulboid styling, but minus the free wheel. The few cars sold in Britain have the overbored engine: early ones, however, run to 1971cc and a rather inadequate 65bhp. Either way, the V8 model is a better buy.

501 V8/502. 1955-63 (prod: all types 13,500). 4-door saloon. F/R, 2580cc/3168cc (V8 OHV). The prestige alternative to a Mercedes in its homeland – faster, more 'U' and a better seller. Servo brakes on de luxe models, and front discs on some of the last ones. Even with the 2.6 engine it's good for 100mph, but it's as ugly as the six and comes quite cheap. Floor change with rare RHD option. ►

◄ **503. 1956-59 (prod: 413). Fixed-head coupé, cabriolet. F/R, 3168cc (V8 OHV).** Meant to rival the 300S Mercedes, but didn't quite. A 140bhp twin-carburettor edition of the big V8 spells 115mph, but the Goertz-styled bodies are a trifle ponderous, and there's still column shift, compulsory because no official RHD option. Could be cheap, if only because so few people have heard of it.

507. 1956-59 (prod: 250). Roadster, hardtop coupé. F/R, 3168cc (V8 OHV). Goertz pulled all the stylistic stops out on this beauty, with a high-compression 150bhp engine and a 135mph potential using a 3.42 axle option. Servo brakes: front discs on some later cars. A five-star classic, and not as complex as the 300SL. Mint specimens are not cheap. ►

ISETTA. 1955-65 (prod: approx 160,000). 2-seater rolltop cabriolet. R/R, 245cc/298cc (S1 OHV). Archetypal bubble and sometime correct wear for the Kings Road. Rolltop convertible with swing-up front door and jointed steering column attached thereto. British production (at Brighton) consisted of three-wheeler versions, though the original article was a narrow-track four-wheeler with differential-less back end. Cheap fun, though connoisseurs prefer the Heinkel.

600. 1958-59 (prod: 35,000). 2-door saloon. R/R, 585cc (HO2 OHV). Enlarged Isetta with swing up front door and a single side one for the back-seat passengers. 6ins shorter than a Mini and drives rather like a VW Transporter, though less choppily thanks to a lower C of G. LHD only.

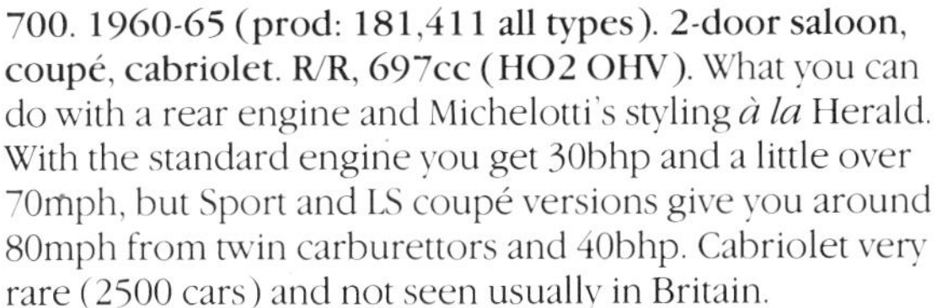

700. 1960-65 (prod: 181,411 all types). 2-door saloon, coupé, cabriolet. R/R, 697cc (HO2 OHV). What you can do with a rear engine and Michelotti's styling *à la* Herald. With the standard engine you get 30bhp and a little over 70mph, but Sport and LS coupé versions give you around 80mph from twin carburettors and 40bhp. Cabriolet very rare (2500 cars) and not seen usually in Britain.

1500/1800. 1962-64/1964-72 (prod: 23,544/147,160). F/R, 4-door saloon. 1499cc/1773cc/1766cc (S4 OC). Complicated range, all with unitary construction, four-cylinder OHC engines, disc/drum brakes, MacPherson struts at the front and IRS. The hottest one available in Britain was the 1800TI with twin Solexes and 110bhp: the hairier five-speed TI/SA wasn't listed here.

2000. 1966-72 (prod: 143,464). 4-door saloon. F/R, 1990cc (S4 OC). Bigger-engined 1800 with round-the-corner headlamp styling; sold here in single-carb 100bhp and twin-carburettor 120bhp (TI, Tilux) guises, also with short-lived Frazer Nash-BMW badging. Servo brakes on all 2000s, with a dual-circuit system from late 1968.

2000CS. 1966-69 (prod: 8883). 4-seater coupé. F/R, 1990cc (S4 OC). First of BMW's modern coupés (by Karmann) with quad headlights. CS with twin carbs and 120bhp is the desirable one, though the 'cooking' CA was also offered here. Most of the latter had automatic, available on the 1800s and 2000s, though not the 1500s. Less thirsty, if less fun, than the six-cylinder coupés. ►

◄ **1502/1600-2/1602. 1975-77/1966-75 (prod: 750,000 all 02 series). 2-door saloon, 3-door Touring (hatchback). F/R, 1499cc, 1573cc (S4 OC).** The basic BMW of the period with the usual hemi-head OHC slant four engine, four-speed 'box, all-independent springing and dual-circuit servo brakes. Five-speed high-performance variants not usually seen in Britain. End-of-the-run 1502s were stripped economy two doors using 75bhp engines in place of the earlier 85bhp type.

1600 CABRIOLET. 1967-71 (prod: see 1502/1602). 4-seater cabriolet. F/R, 1573cc (S4 OC). Full cabriolet by Baur, who made about 4000 bodies for BMW between 1967 and 1975. In British buyers' guides 1969 only. 85bhp engine and mechanical specifications as per 1600-2 or 1602, which (remember) are the same car despite the semantics. ►

◄ **2002/2002 Tii/2002 TURBO. 1968-75 (prod: see 1502/1602). 2-door saloon, 3-door Touring (hatchback), cabriolet. F/R, 1990cc (S4 OC).** UK availability from 1970, Tii from 1972. Automatic and five-speed variants listed, latter standard with LHD-only 170bhp Turbo (1973-4). Cabriolets are of Targa-type with fixed rollbar. Other engines are 100bhp single carburettor, and the 130bhp Tii with Kugelfischer fuel injection.

2500/2800. 1969-77 (prod: 132,303 to 1974). 4-door saloon. F/R, 2494cc/2788cc (S6 OC). First of a distinguished line of sixes based on the fours, with speeds of 110-120mph according to cylinder capacity. All-disc servo brakes, automatic and power steering options. 2500 was available in Britain throughout its life, so good low-mileage specimens a possibility. ►

2800CS. 1968-71 (prod: 9400). 4-seater coupé. F/R, 2788cc (S6 OC). A delightful car, turbine smooth in the high 5000s (rpm), though manual versions have only four speeds where one might expect five. Automatic available. Quad headlights and all-disc brakes as on the six-cylinder saloons. The standard power steering isn't the car's best point, but these big BMWs have an excellent service record.

BOND (GB)

Bond produced Laurie Bond's eccentric three-wheeler Minicar at Preston from 1949 to as late as 1965. From 1965 it diversified with four-wheeler GT coupés, but in 1969 Reliant bought out the firm, closed the Preston works and transferred production to its Tamworth factory, where the only Bond car produced was the 'Bug', an odd sporting three-wheeler.

MINICAR. 1948-65 (prod: n/a). 2+2. F/F, 122cc (S1 TS). Laurie Bond's Minicar adopted various guises in its life span, early models featuring a front mounted Villiers two-stroke motorcycle engine driving single front wheel by chain. Rear suspension and front brakes later additions. Unusual.

EQUIPE GT4/GT4S. 1963-70 (prod: n/a). 4-seater coupé. F/R, 1147cc/1296cc (S4 OHV). Triumph Herald chassis with Spitfire-tune twin-carb engine (1300cc from February 1967) and the Spitfire's front disc brakes. Glass-fibre body shells but the GT4 uses Vitesse doors and the GT4S with quad headlights, opening boot and greater headroom (1965 on) isn't much better looking. Main attractions are rarity and ease of parts supply.

875. 1966-70 (prod: n/a). 4-seater saloon. R/R, 875cc (S4 OC). Bond's first challenge to Reliant in the three-wheeler sector, which explains its demise when eventually taken over by Reliant. Leading-arm front suspension with a Hillman Imp power pack (fortunately de-tuned) in the tail. Rustproof glassfibre bodywork, but no beauty, even in final Mk II form with rectangular headlamps.

EQUIPE 2-LITRE (prod: n/a). 4-seater coupé, convertible. F/R, 1998cc (S6 OHV). Vitesse with Bond treatment and quad headlights. Convertible from October 1968, when Mk II specification introduced with the later (and better-handling) type of Vitesse rear suspension. Coupés prettier than the GT4S, though we've seen more handsome dropheads. Rear seats less occasional than on competing models.

BUG. 1970-74 (prod: 1620). 2-seater coupé. F/R, 700cc (S4 OHV). Way-out Reliant-type three-wheeler with Reliant mechanics and styling by Tom Karen. With its 10ins wheels, sawn-off tail, wedge-nose, streamlined-in rectangular headlights, swing up cockpit canopy and bright tangerine paintwork, it can't be mistaken for anything else. Hair raising with 75mph top speed and 0-60mph in 23-odd secs. ➤

BORGWARD (D)

Carl Borgward owned the Hansa, Hansa-Lloyd and Goliath works, which produced a vast range of cars before 1939. The Hansa name was applied to Borgward cars from 1939, but nothing particularly outstanding was produced until 1949, when the Hansa 1500 made its debut at the Geneva Salon. The last Borgward was an odd looking 2.3-litre limousine, which lasted only 10 months before the collapse of the group in 1961.

◄ **1800/1800D. 1952-54 (prod: 8111/3226). 2-door saloon, 4-door saloon, station wagon, cabriolet. F/R, 1758cc (S4 OHV/OHV diesel).** Available UK from late 1953: diesel model had more sporting performance than contemporary rivals. One of the first all-new post-war designs from Germany, with backbone frame, all-independent springing and all-synchromesh box. Ugly slab-sided bodywork in the Phase II Vanguard idiom.

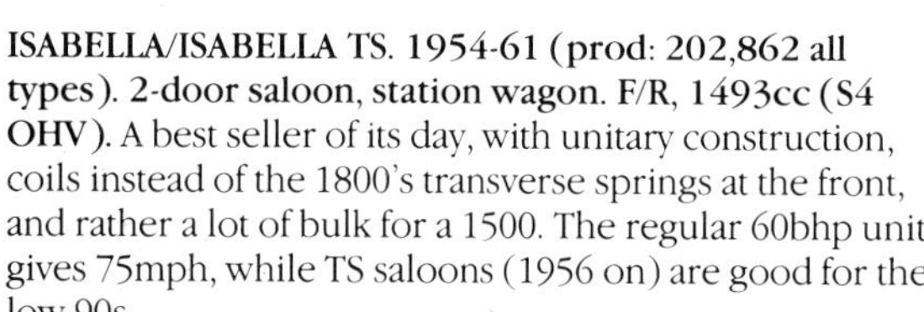

ISABELLA/ISABELLA TS. 1954-61 (prod: 202,862 all types). 2-door saloon, station wagon. F/R, 1493cc (S4 OHV). A best seller of its day, with unitary construction, coils instead of the 1800's transverse springs at the front, and rather a lot of bulk for a 1500. The regular 60bhp unit gives 75mph, while TS saloons (1956 on) are good for the low 90s. ➤

◄ **ISABELLA COUPE/CABRIOLET. 1955-61 (prod: see Isabella). 2+2 seater coupé, 2+2 seater cabriolet. F/R, 1493cc (S4 OHV).** Classy coupé – and a very rare drophead – was an excellent performer, with 95mph top speed and fine road manners, although column change was standard for the four-speed 'box. The story goes that the car was built to prevent Mrs Borgward buying a VW Karmann Ghia . . .

2.3 SALOON. 1959-61 (prod: n/a). Saloon. F/R, 2240cc (S6 OHV). An interesting swansong with pneumatic suspension all round, unitary construction, servo brakes and a choice of Isabella's four-speed all-synchromesh 'box or a Hobbs automatic. A little underpowered, and the money ran out before it could be properly developed. Very rarely seen in Britain. ➤

BRISTOL (GB)

The Bristol Aeroplane Co branched out into car manufacture in 1947 with an anglicised version of the pre-war BMW 327, and Bristol Cars, which came into being in 1960, is still going strong with a range of luxurious, fast and somewhat battleship-like cars. Most significant in some ways were their six-cylinder engines, which powered Cooper, Frazer Nash and AC cars. These units were derived from the famous pre-war BMW engine, but by 1962 more power was needed. Hence the adoption of American V8 engines.

◄ **400. 1947-50 (prod: 700). 2-door saloon. F/R, 1971cc (S6 OHV).** Looks what it is, a hand-made BMW-based saloon with wind tunnel derived aerodynamics, wood instead of plastic inside, one-shot lubrication and a built-in radio. Most had 85bhp three carburettor engines, though some earlier examples made with less powerful single-carb units.

401. 1949-53 (prod: 650). 2-door saloon. F/R, 1971cc (S6 OHV). Styling and construction (light alloy panels over a steel-tube frame) of the body by Touring of Italy, though their own rare pre-production version has a dreadfully fussy front end. Good factory service and 25-30mpg, but these don't make a lot of money. ➤

◄ **402. 1949-50 (prod: 20). 4-seater cabriolet. F/R, 1971cc (S6 OHV).** Pininfarina-inspired. Has the 401's shorter radiator grille with additional side slats. Chassis extended rearwards to take bigger fuel tank aft of the axle. For all its concealed hood, not one of the better looking milestone convertibles, and it didn't sell.

403. 1953-55 (prod: 300). 2-door saloon. F/R, 1971cc (S6 OHV). Improved 401 with 'hotter' camshaft giving 100bhp output, a front anti-roll bar and Alfin brake drums. Perhaps the best of the early Bristols, but not in the big money league, yet. ➤

◄ **404. 1954-55 (prod: 44). 2-seater coupé. F/R, 1971cc (S6 OHV).** Known in its day as the 'Businessman's Express', and the first Bristol to feature the 'hole in the wall' grille, one-piece forward-tilting bonnet, and front wing mounted spare wheel. Alloy body panels again, but watch the wood framing. Engine options of up to 140bhp, giving 110mph.

405 SALOON. 1954-58 (prod: 297). 4-door saloon. F/R, 1971cc (S6 OHV). Styling and front-end treatment as 404, but a much heavier car on a 114ins wheelbase. Overdrive, electrically operated fuel reserve, radial-ply tyres and screenwash standard: will cruise at around 90mph. Drainage channel problems in the roof can provoke rot. ➤

◄ **405 DROPHEAD COUPÉ. 1954-56 (prod: 43). 4-seater drophead coupé. F/R, 1971cc (S6 OHV).** Classical ragtop by Abbott with 'hole in the wall' grille and spare wheel housed in the nearside front wing. Standard 405 mechanics. Rarity should lend enchantment, but the last really good one to come under the hammer sold for a pittance.

406. 1958-61 (prod: 292). 2-door saloon. F/R, 2216cc (S6 OHV). Angular 2-door body better looking than the four-door 405. Same spare wheel location, but steel-framed body. Enlarged engine gives the same 105bhp, but overdrive and disc brakes standard and appointments most luxurious. Rather overweight, and the earlier sixes may be preferable. ➤

406 ZAGATO. 1960-61 (prod: 7). 4-seater coupé. F/R, 2216cc (S6 OHV). Smaller than the stock 406, and with 450lbs of *avoirdupois* pruned off, too. Triple Solexes and Abarth manifolding boost power to 130bhp, and with a top speed of 120mph, this is probably Bristol's fastest touring six. The styling doesn't quite come off. Rare enough to be expensive.

407. 1962-63 (prod: 300). 2-door saloon. F/R, 5130cc (V8 OHV). First of the Anglo-American Bristols with 250bhp Chrysler engine married to a three-speed Torqueflite automatic transmission. Coils at the front instead of the traditional BMW transverse set-up, all-disc brakes and 125mph on tap, plus a rather stodgy dignity. A thirsty engine spells modest prices.

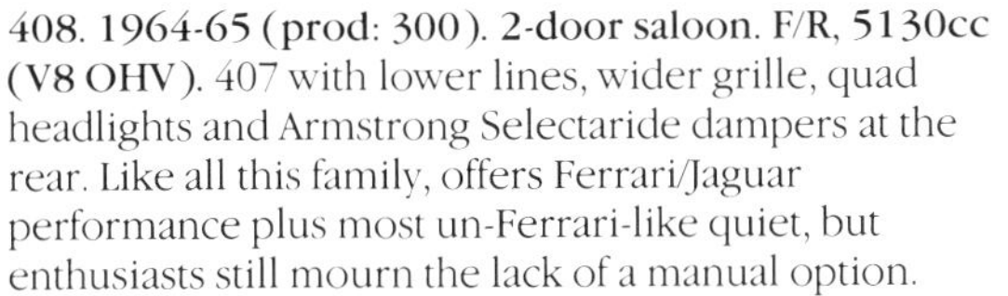

408. 1964-65 (prod: 300). 2-door saloon. F/R, 5130cc (V8 OHV). 407 with lower lines, wider grille, quad headlights and Armstrong Selectaride dampers at the rear. Like all this family, offers Ferrari/Jaguar performance plus most un-Ferrari-like quiet, but enthusiasts still mourn the lack of a manual option.

409. 1966-67 (prod: 300). 2-door saloon. F/R, 5211cc (V8 OHV). Softly, softly, especially in the ride department. Disc brakes by Girling instead of Dunlop, and a few more cubic inches, though output still around 250bhp. Other improvements – a sealed cooling system, a stainless steel exhaust, a pre-engaged starter and (for 1967) power steering. No longer a sports car.

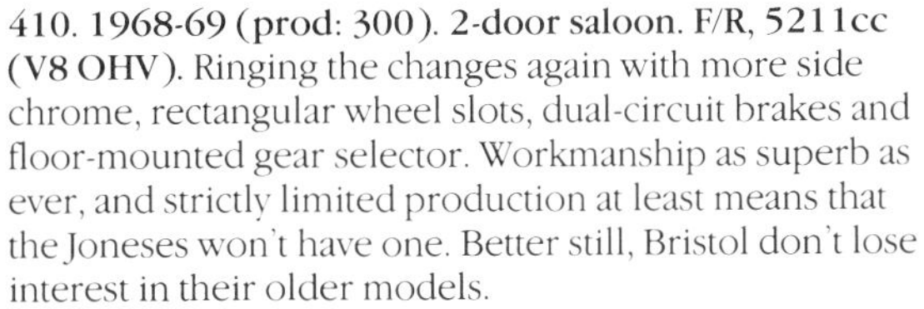

410. 1968-69 (prod: 300). 2-door saloon. F/R, 5211cc (V8 OHV). Ringing the changes again with more side chrome, rectangular wheel slots, dual-circuit brakes and floor-mounted gear selector. Workmanship as superb as ever, and strictly limited production at least means that the Joneses won't have one. Better still, Bristol don't lose interest in their older models.

411. 1970-76 (prod: 600). 2-door saloon. F/R, 6277cc/ 6556cc (V8 OHV). Progressively improved through five series: Notable changes are through-flow ventilation (1973) and the 6.6 litre engine (1974). Genuine wood and leather, of course, plus power windows, and an air-conditioning option. A future collectable, though look to the older V8s if you want a bargain. ➤

BRITANNIA (GB)

Acland Geddes initiated the Britannia project in 1957, but a lack of urgency and cohesion meant that the GT car, with Ford Zephyr power, was never a serious proposition. The company also made a number of relatively unsuccessful Formula Junior cars designed by John Tojeiro, but by the end of 1960 Britannia was in the hands of the receiver.

◄ **GT. 1958-1960 (prod: 6). 2-seater coupé. F/R, 2553cc (S6 OHV).** Short-lived attempt to marry Raymond Mays-headed Zephyr engine to John Tojeiro-designed all-independent chassis and neat glass-fibre body. Lack of development and a list price of £2400 – more than an XK150S – meant that the project never got off the ground, although five of the six are known still to exist.

BUCKLER (GB)

One of the neatest and most successful products of the 1950s kit car boom was the Buckler. Derek Buckler's Berkshire-based firm, in business from 1947 to 1962, made extremely high quality chassis and bodies to take, mainly, Ford mechanicals. The company's decline was due both to Buckler's failing health – he was to die in 1964 – and the fact that Buckler finances were always shaky.

VARIOUS. 1949-1962 (prod: 500). Although most of the 500 Bucklers built were supplied in kit form or even as a bare chassis, Derek Buckler's firm justified inclusion in our A to Z because in the early days some Mk Vs and 90s (both 1172cc Ford-based space frame two-seaters) were factory-built. The DD1 and DD2 had de Dion rear suspension and often Climax FWA engines, but the later kit cars did not have a fixed specification. ➤

CISITALIA (I)

A tiny firm with a reputation far beyond its achievements, founded by Pierre Dusio in 1946. Sports versions of the cars came always with beautiful bodywork, some, by Pininfarina, among the best of early postwar styling. In 1950, production of the 1100cc cars resumed under new sponsorship, but the company lost its pre-eminent position, and ended its life disappointingly by making Fiat 600 based machines.

◄ **GS. 1946-48 (prod: n/a). 2-seater coupé. F/R, 1089cc (S4 OHV).** Their outstanding car and a styling landmark for Pininfarina. Light, multi-tubular welded-up frame with Millecento Fiat mechanics even down to the transmission handbrake. Good aerodynamics spell 105mph with the regular 50bhp engine, and over 120mph with the full-house competition unit. Never officially imported.

CITROEN (F)

One of the giants of the automotive industry, and one of the most idiosyncratic and technically daring. André Citroën started the firm to make gears in 1913, but by 1919 had branched out into car manufacture. His first really successful design was the 5CV of 1922, which was cheap, dull and indestructible, while his first major technical tour de force, the *Traction Avant* front-drive car of 1934, virtually ruined the company and forced a sell-out to Michelin. After the war, the firm first produced the Boulanger-designed 2CV in 1949, a classic of utility motoring which is still in demand today, and the DS of 1955. Citroën still makes idiosyncratic cars, but in 1976 became part of the Peugeot-Talbot group.

LIGHT 15 (11 LEGERE). 1935-57 (prod UK post-war: approx 13,500). 4-door saloon. F/F, 1911cc (S4 OHV). Not sold in Britain after '55. The immortal *traction* with its heavy steering, superb roadholding and three-speed 'box with awkward dashboard shift. Projecting rear boot from 1953. Slough specification gave you wood and leather trim, 12-volt electrics, chromium plated radiator and a choice of colours. Rust a crucial problem. ►

◄ **BIG 15 (11 NORMALE). 1935-57 (prod UK post-war: approx 1100). 4-door saloon. F/F, 1911cc (S4 OHV).** A short post-war British run (1953-55) makes this model much rarer than the Light 15 over here. All Slough-built cars have projecting boots. An extra 7ins of wheelbase spells more legroom but more weight and parking problems, ergo men only.

6/6H. 1939-55/1954-55 (prod UK post-war: approx 1700). 4-door saloon. F/F, 2866cc (S6 OHV). The big 15CV beloved of Inspector Maigret and his adversaries. Slough-built from 1949, hydropneumatic rear springing option (6H) from 1954. A real vintage model with the usual three speed 'box and dashboard change, 16ft long and with a 46ft turning circle. Fun for the strong armed, but a maintenance nightmare. ►

2CV. 1948 to date (prod all saloons to end of 1981: 3,462,237). 4-door convertible saloon. F/F, 375cc/ 425cc (HO2 OHV). The immortal garden shed on wheels with interconnected self-levelling suspension: almost everything is quick-detachable, and just as easily replaced. Only made by Slough 1954-59, and imports not resumed till the seventies. Avoid the early 375cc species: the 425cc unit came in during 1954.

DS19. 1956-65 (prod all D-types 1956-75: 1,415,719) 4-door saloon. F/F, 1911cc (S4 OHV). Revolutionary when it came out – self-levelling hydropneumatic suspension, power gearshift, clutch and brakes (with inboard front discs), but tiny brake pedal can be disconcerting. Impossible to restore and a rust trap, so leave old ones alone. In any case this brilliant car deserved something better than the 1935 long-stroke engine.

ID19/DW. 1957-66/1964-66 (prod: see DS19). 4-door saloon. F/F, 1911cc (S4 OHV). Simplified DS with detuned engine and no power assists, though the hydropneumatics are still there. DW (1964) is a British special with DS power unit and appointments plus ID mechanics, possibly the best combination since the engine has fewer ancillaries to feed. But again, why choose an old one?

DS DECAPOTABLE. 1963-71 (prod: see DS19). Drophead coupé. F/F, 1911cc/2175cc (S4 OHV). Full-house DS converted by Chapron, quoted in UK 1963-68 only. From 1966 with 2.2-litre short-stroke engine; swivelling headlamps, 1968. Later ones could have power steering, fuel injection and five speed gearbox. All the complexity plus the structural headaches of a unitary top-chop. You'll be lucky to find a saveable one.

SAFARI. 1957-75 (prod: see DS19). Station wagon. F/F, 1911cc/1985cc/2175cc (S4 OHV). Called a *'break'* or a *'commerciale'* in France, according to the standards of interior appointments. Basically a big, roomy wagon to ID specifications, but short-stroke engine fitted later, and standardised for UK market from 1966-67. More metal to rust.

DS19/20/21/23/PALLAS. 1966-75 (prod: see DS19). 4-door saloon. F/F, **1985cc/2175cc/2347cc** (S4 OHV). Nomenclature infuriating, but Pallas is a luxury model, and all have the later short-stroke engines. Power steering and swivelling headlamps by '68, fuel injection available 1970. 2.3-litre engine, five-speed manual and three-speed automatic boxes join the list from 1973. You may find a late one that doesn't need derusting.

BIJOU. 1960-62 **(prod: 211). 2/4 seater coupé.** F/F, **425cc** (HO2 OHV). British attempt to inject some *chic* into the 2CV, but the down-by-the-bows attitude is off-putting. Weighs more than the standard saloon, and isn't a carry-all. Leave it to French fanatics in quest of 'different' Citroëns, though the glassfibre body won't rust.

AMI 6. 1961-69 **(prod: 1,840,159). 4-door saloon, station wagon.** F/F, **602cc** (HO2 OHV). Really an up-market 2CV with the same interlinked coil and leading arm suspension and all-indirect four-speed gearbox controlled from the dash. Plus, the enlarged flat-twin gives 22bhp and pushed the Ami along at 65mph. Minus, the hideous saloon body with concave rear window. Station wagon introduced 1966.

AMI 8. 1969-78 (prod: see Ami 6). 4-door saloon, station wagon. F/F, **602cc** (HO2 OHV). The extra couple of French CV spell a few more bhp, front disc brakes, and (thank goodness) goodbye to that ghastly breezeway rear window. A good little hack, but most people will prefer the honest-to-God non-styling of the 2CV and Dyane.

DYANE. 1968-1982 (prod to end 1981: 1,401,145). 4-door convertible saloon. F/F, **425cc/602cc** (HO2 OHV). Cleaned up and streamlined 2CV with all the traditional qualities. Smaller engine listed in Britain 1968 only, and you won't get front disc brakes on anything older than a 1978. Splendid little hack with more actual performance than you'd suspect.

SM. 1970-75 (prod: 12,920). 4-seater coupé. F/F, 2670cc/2974cc (V6 4OC). The Citroën-Maserati marriage didn't last long, but it was worth it for this combination of handling and complexity. Citroën suspension plus a four cam V6 and five-speed 'box. Top speed 135mph, fuel injection from mid-72, automatic (with 3-litre unit) available mid-73, but Peugeot bought Citroën and killed the SM before RHD could become an option. ➤

CONNAUGHT (GB)

The 1950s were a fertile time for British racing and sports car fans. Kenneth McAlpine and Rodney Clarke's Connaught concern originally built sports racing cars and then branched out into Formula 2 and Grand Prix racing car manufacture. In this activity, until the money started running out after 1955, it was quite successful.

◄ **L2. 1949-51 (prod: 27 incl L3SR). Sports 2-seater. F/R, 1767cc (S4 OHV).** Their only street machine, with a Lea-Francis 14 engine boosted to give 98bhp. Streamlined, forward tilting one-piece bonnet, but retains the Leaf's beam front axle and mechanical brakes. Later L3SR was stark, cycle-winged affair with torsion-bar front suspension. Both good for the ton.

COSTIN (GB)

To build his own car was a bold move by Frank Costin when he was left without a job by the bankruptcy of Marcos in 1971. The Amigo, with its wooden chassis, was doomed to failure, however, costing far too much money when it finally came on sale in 1972. The eight cars were built at Little Staughton, Bedfordshire, with backing from Paul Pycroft.

AMIGO. 1970-71 (prod: 8). 2-seater coupé. F/R, 1975cc (S4 OC). Frank Costin's gamble that didn't pay off. Using Vauxhall mechanics (from the Victor) the 'standard' VS model had a quoted top speed of 134mph, the Hart-tuned CS faster still. Costin (the cos in Marcos) employed Marcos-style monocoque wooden box type construction in the 13cwt Amigo. ➤

DAF (NL)

Dafs first appeared in 1958, the product of a firm which had been making commercial trailers since 1928. Unique transmission was their main distinguishing feature, giving the cars their 'easy driving' tag. In 1965, this belt drive transmission was adapted to both military and racing (Formula 3) uses. In 1975, the firm was acquired by Volvo, but since then Volvo Car BV has ousted Daf models from its inventory.

◄ **750/DAFFODIL/33. 1962-75 (prod incl 600: 312,367). 2-door saloon. F/R, 746cc (HO2 OHV).** The basic DAF (early 600cc versions barely made the British market) with air-cooled flat-twin engine and infinitely variable, stepless V-belt drive – you just select forward or reverse and go. The answer to the clueless aunt's prayer, though there weren't really enough brakes even for 60mph. Early ones are getting rare.

44. 1966-75 (prod: 167,905). 2-door saloon, station wagon. F/R, 844cc (HO2 OHV). The bigger version of the SAT twin engine pushes this one along at 70-75mph, and Michelotti's restyle is less ugly, if the droop-snoot individuality of the little car has been lost. Still drum brakes only, so let's choose the Renault-engine 55 for serious driving.

55. 1968-72 (prod all types: 164,231). 2-door saloon, station wagon. F/R, 1108cc (S4 OHV). With the Renault 8 engine this one can move, to the tune of 80mph plus. Front disc brakes are standard, and DAF remained faithful to those belts right up to the end. The 63bhp Marathon was available by 1972, for those in quest of more urge.

55 COUPE. 1968-72 (prod: see 55). 4-seater coupé. F/R, 1108cc (S4 OHV). In basic form hardly a sports car, with no gears to change and not even the sensation of shifting. 90mph possible with later Marathon engine. Like all DAFs, of course, it's got all-independent springing. Might eventually become collectable.

DAIHATSU (J)

One of the oldest Japanese firms involved with the motor car, although back in 1907 it produced only internal combustion engines. The firm's first vehicles of 1930 were three-wheeled vans, with the Bee three-wheeler of 1950 its initial entry into the passenger car market: the first four-wheeler was 1963's Compagno. Products from the 1960s and 1970s were pretty boring in the main, and the company continues to make solid but unexciting cars.

COMPAGNO. 1964-70 (prod all types: approx 120,000). 2-door saloon, station wagon, spyder. F/R, 797cc/958cc (S4 OHV). Nicely made but ordinary little car with separate chassis, drum brakes, torsion-bar front suspension and semi-elliptics at the rear. Just about good for 70mph with the smaller engine. The first Japanese car ever marketed in Britain: British buyers got a built-in radio for their £798 ... but did any ever make it off the show stands to the roads?

DAIMLER (GB)

The oldest British manufacturer, founded in 1893, although now a part of Jaguar Cars. Early Daimlers were imported from Germany, and during the Edwardian era the cars became luxury carriages. In 1910 the firm was acquired by BSA, and after the Great War the Daimler was adopted as the car for the Royal Family. After 1945 the firm lost direction, with production of vast straight-eight luxury carriages alongside the more down-market Conquest series. Last real Daimlers were the Majestic series and the SP250 sports car, but these were phased out after the Jaguar takeover in 1960. Daimler now makes a limousine and up-market Jaguars.

◄ **DB18. 1939-50 (prod: 3365 post war). Saloon, drophead coupé. F/R, 2522cc (S6 OHV).** Re-styled pre-war design with prettier body and more luggage space. Mechanics unchanged – four-speed fluid flywheel, worm drive, and mechanical brakes. Bonuses include sliding roof, automatic chassis lubrication, and a fuel reserve. Dropheads (by Tickford) are expensive.

DB18 SPORTS SPECIAL. 1949-53 (prod: 608). 2/3 seater drophead coupé, Hooper Empress saloon. F/R, 2522cc (S6 OHV). Not really sports for all those 85bhp and twin carbs: it weighs 3600lbs. But it'll waffle along in overdrive top with 400rpm showing and has pleasant road manners. Barker's all-panelled coupé preferred, though its ash frame can rot. A pleasant gentleman's carriage. ►

◄ **DB18 CONSORT. 1950-53 (prod: 4250). Saloon. F/R, 2522cc (S6 OHV).** Updated DB18 with the curved radiator grille and hydromech brakes of the Sports, plus a hypoid bevel back end. Lacks some of the older model's elegance, though can be found cheaper.

DE27/DH27. 1946-51 (prod: 205/50). Saloons, various limousines. F/R, 4095cc (S6 OHV). Poor man's edition of the straight-eight and nearly as big, especially the 150in wheelbase DH27 made for Daimler Hire. Unlike pre-war heavies, these have coil spring ifs, hydromech brakes and (thank goodness) detachable cylinder heads. Too ponderous for the enthusiast, but the ambulance version may still be a parts source. ►

◄ **DE36. 1946-53 (prod: 205). Saloon, limousine, drophead coupé, numerous specials. F/R, 5460cc (S8 OHV).** Britain's last production straight-eight and the basis for the earlier Docker Spectaculars that used to enliven Earls Court (remember the Green Goddess drophead?). Mechanics similar to the DE27's with detachable head. Seven Royal families (including ours) bought them, but it's over 220ins long and weighs close on three tons.

REGENCY. 1952-54 (prod: 51). Saloon, Hooper Empress sports saloon. F/R, 2952cc/3468cc (S6 OHV). A perpetual student of a car that never really got into production. It's a blown up Consort with hydromech brakes, hypoid back end, and of course, the Daimler Fluid Flywheel. One-piece curved screen. Later ones (including a solitary sports drophead) with 3.5-litre engine. Regency II is a better bet.

REGENCY II. 1955-56 (prod: 153/66). Saloon, Sportsman saloon, Hooper Empress sports saloon. F/R, 3468cc/4617cc (S6 OHV). 'Production' Regency with more litres though not much more performance. Automatic chassis lubrication. The attractive four light Sportsman with wrap round rear window (and all 4.5-litre cars as well) had full hydraulic instead of hydromech brakes and an overdrive top gear. Empress razor-edge saloon is a panelbasher's nightmare.

CONQUEST. 1953-56 (prod: 4568). Saloon. F/R, 2433cc (S6 OHV). Yes, it cost £1066 without purchase tax when new! Shorter, lighter Consort replacement with short-stroke 75bhp engine, torsion-bar front suspension. Automatic chassis lubrication and wood and leather trim still there: so are hydromech brakes. The pressed steel body is a rust trap, though driveable examples are cheap and plentiful.

CONQUEST CENTURY. 1954-58 (prod: 4818). Saloon. F/R, 2433cc (S6 OHV). Alloy head and twin carbs boost output to 100bhp, and give you 90mph the stock Conquest cannot dream of. Once, briefly, a force in saloon car racing. Automatic option from 1957, standard from that September. Rust problems as on the regular model, so it won't cost you much more.

CONQUEST CENTURY DROPHEAD COUPÉ. 1954-55 (prod: 234). Coupé. F/R, 2433cc (S6 OHV). Introduced a little before the Century saloon: same mechanics plus a Carbodies four-seater body as fitted to the Lanchester Leda, with half-power top – you have to pull it forward from the 'de ville' position. Some saloon panels spell saloon type rust, but good survivors have been breaking reasonable money for some time now.

CENTURY ROADSTER/SPORTS DROPHEAD COUPÉ. 1954-55/1956-57 (prod: 65/54). 2-seater Sports, 2/3-seater drophead coupé. F/R, 2433cc (S6 OHV). A real sports Daimler for the first time since 1908. Roadster is an ugly beast with one piece wrap round screen, bonnet air intakes, and tail fins, making the traditional Daimler radiator look out of place. Coupé prettier but heavier. Alloy bodies and a genuine 100mph are bonuses.

DK400 REGINA. 1955-60 (prod: 132). Limousine. F/R, 4617cc (S6 OHV). Almost the last traditional Daimler with both separate chassis and four-speed fluid flywheel 'box: there are even the odd customs, though these are very rare. Huge 63ins rear track allows for three-abreast occasional seats. No overdrive on this one. A 95mph trip to the cemetery?

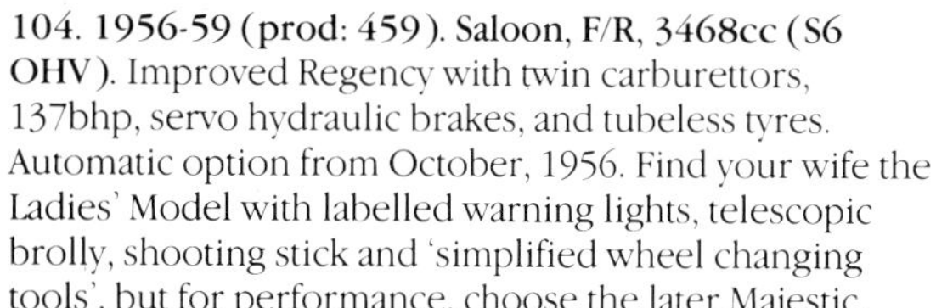

104. 1956-59 (prod: 459). Saloon, F/R, 3468cc (S6 OHV). Improved Regency with twin carburettors, 137bhp, servo hydraulic brakes, and tubeless tyres. Automatic option from October, 1956. Find your wife the Ladies' Model with labelled warning lights, telescopic brolly, shooting stick and 'simplified wheel changing tools', but for performance, choose the later Majestic.

MAJESTIC. 1958-62 (prod: 940). Saloon. F/R, 3794cc (S6 OHV). The 104 theme again with more cc and bhp, plus all-disc brakes (not yet listed on Jaguar's saloons), and compulsory automatic. 100mph and 10secs to 50mph, but more bulboid lines present a repair problem, and, like other Daimler saloons of these days, it rusts. Mk IX Jaguar performance with dignity.

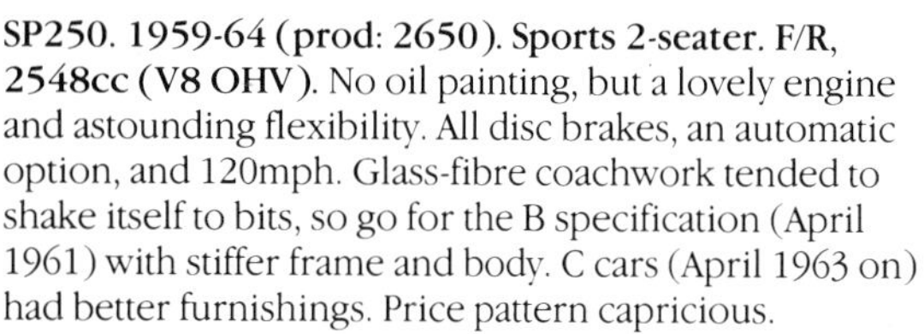

SP250. 1959-64 (prod: 2650). Sports 2-seater. F/R, 2548cc (V8 OHV). No oil painting, but a lovely engine and astounding flexibility. All disc brakes, an automatic option, and 120mph. Glass-fibre coachwork tended to shake itself to bits, so go for the B specification (April 1961) with stiffer frame and body. C cars (April 1963 on) had better furnishings. Price pattern capricious.

MAJESTIC MAJOR. 1960-68 (prod: 1180). Saloon. F/R, 4561cc (V8 OHV). Once unkindly described as a '120mph funeral taxi', but look again – you've got 220bhp, automatic, power steering (on all but a few very early ones) and the usual sure-footed handling. Once more they rust, but for anyone handy with sheet metal work, surely a bargain best buy.

DR450. 1961-68 (prod: 864). Limousine. F/R, 4561cc (V8 OHV). Elongated two-tonner Majestic Major, though mercifully the eight light show prototype was a one-off. Like the saloons, it's got both a chassis and rust problems. Both, too, have a real honey of an engine, but limited production spells parts headaches in that department.

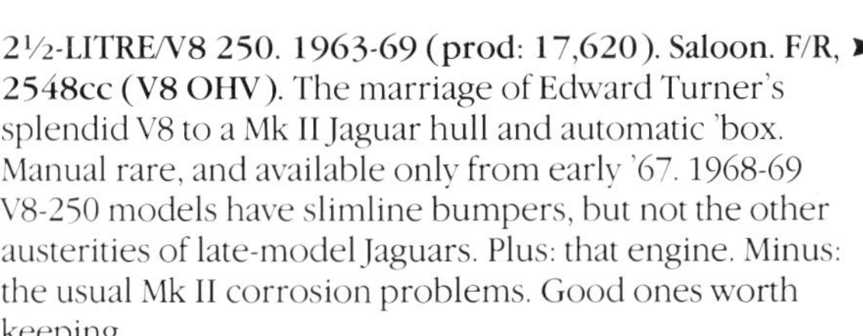

2½-LITRE/V8 250. 1963-69 (prod: 17,620). Saloon. F/R, 2548cc (V8 OHV). The marriage of Edward Turner's splendid V8 to a Mk II Jaguar hull and automatic 'box. Manual rare, and available only from early '67. 1968-69 V8-250 models have slimline bumpers, but not the other austerities of late-model Jaguars. Plus: that engine. Minus: the usual Mk II corrosion problems. Good ones worth keeping.

DS420. 1968 to date (prod to end 1978: 2380). Limousine. F/R, 4235cc (S6 DOC). Princess replacement built up on a 420G Jaguar floorpan with the famous twin-cam six, automatic power steering and all-independent springing. Looks a bit too like the old Burney Streamline to please the eye. Rare enough to be a future collectable.

DATSUN (J)

A giant of the Japanese motor industry, Datsun's history dates back to 1912, when it started as the Kwaishinsha Motor Car works with an experimental machine, followed in 1914 by the first DAT car. These were produced until 1926, and car manufacture was not resumed until 1931. The firm continued through the 1930s with a range based on the British Austin Seven. Early post-World War II products were based on the Austin A50, and most of the firm's cars built from 1960 to date have been, by and large, fairly mundane. They have, however, sold in huge numbers, and Nissan established a manufacturing base in Britain in 1984.

◄ **SUNNY B10. 1966-70 (prod: 435,877). 4-door saloon, station wagon. F/R, 988cc (S4 OHV).** Semi-elliptics at the rear and drum brakes on this one, available in UK from 1969. The pretty little coupé wasn't sold here at all. As a secondhand buy, better to go for the 1200 (1971), which had discs at the front and is good for 85mph.

BLUEBIRD 1300/1600. 1968-71 (prod: 1,696,974). 4-door saloon, station wagon. F/R, 1295cc/1595cc (S4 OHV). First Datsun to be marketed seriously over here, though less than 3500 of all models found buyers in 1969/70. Four-speed all-synchro 'box and all four wheels independently sprung, but disc front brakes and station wagon bodies only with the bigger engine. ►

◄ **1800. 1968-73 (prod: n/a). Saloon, station wagon. F/R, 1815cc (S4 OHV).** Datsuns of this period are confusing, but this is the Cedric, popular as a taxi in Australia. Five bearing engine gives an advertised 105bhp and nigh on 100mph. Otherwise closely related to the Bluebird. A three-speed heater fan, two-speed wipers and an electric screenwash were part of the UK-market package.

2000. 1968-74 (prod: n/a). Saloon, station wagon. F/R, 1998cc (S6 OC). First of the six-cylinder imports with the now familiar seven bearing overhead cam unit and power disc/drum brakes. Watch it, though – there were some examples of an older pushrod design brought in, usually as station wagons. Beam rear axle on all these types in our period. ►

◄ **240Z. 1969-74 (prod: all Z-series to end 1980: 722,852). Sports coupé. F/R, 2393cc (S6 OC).** Became the world's best-selling sports car. 240 specification embraces 24-valve engine churning out 161bhp, twin Hitachi carburettors (fuel injection came later), all-independent springs, power disc/drum brakes and (unusually for a Japanese car) rack and pinion steering. UK imports from late 1970.

DELAGE (F)

Louis Delage was a real motor industry maverick, a perfectionist who would build only the finest vehicles. He started modestly enough in 1905 with a conventional shaft drive single-cylinder 6½hp car, and this was followed by equally conventional touring machines, early examples having De Dion engines. It was in racing that the firm made its mark, and after World War I it made superb touring cars and several vastly expensive forays into Grand Prix racing and record breaking. It was acquired by Delahaye in 1935 and thereafter the cars evolved into slightly more florid versions of that make. Along with Delahaye, it died in the Hotchkiss merger.

◄ **D-6-3L. 1946-52 (prod: approx 250). Sports saloon, drophead coupé. F/R, 2988cc (S6 OHV).** Last of the line: like the Delahaye, has the Cotal electric 'box, but bonuses of hydraulic brakes and higher-revving short-stroke engine. Bodywork usually slab-sided, over-blown and heavy: pre-war D-6-70 is essentially the same car and more attractive.

DELAHAYE (F)

One of the Grandes Marques, best known for its stunning sports cars built in the 1930s. The history of the firm dates back to the dawn of motoring, when Emile Delahaye branched out into car production in 1894. Before the Great War, the range was diverse, although this was to change in the 1920s when the firm only offered horrifically dull, 'cooking' vehicles. After 1935, when the marque acquired Delage, it made sporting cars as well as venturing into Grand Prix racing. This was its heyday, as after the war the French government's penal taxation nearly killed off luxury car manufacture. The firm merged with Hotchkiss in 1953, but only trucks and Jeeps were made.

135MS. 1936-53 (prod: approx 2000, inc pre-war). Various, but usually drophead coupés in England. F/R, 3557cc (S6 OHV). Splendid classic available in various tunes up to 135bhp with triple carburettors. Cotal gearbox gives four speeds forward or reverse, but some cars had crash-type manual transmission. Always rhd, but watch those Bendix brakes on a 110mph tourer. Post-war chassis serials in the 80,000s. Prices are high. ►

DELLOW (GB)

Basically, the Dellow was evolved for that peculiarly English form of motor sport, trialling, and was built by K. C. Delingpole and R. C. Lowe, who used a Ford 10 engine in an A-shaped tubular chassis with a very simple two-seater body. In 1956, the firm produced the Mark VI with all enveloping body, and in doing so sacrificed the originality which had made the earlier vehicles so popular; few were sold.

◄ **MKS I/II/III. 1949-57 (prod: approx 500, all types). Sports 2-seater, sports 4-seater. F/R, 1172cc (S4 SV).** A trials iron with Ford 10 mechanics in an A-shaped tubular frame with quarter-elliptic rear springs. Bodywork very basic: fiddle brakes available for driving tests. Later ones had coils at the back. Mk III (1952) with doors and occasional rear seats. Unusual but hairy, especially in supercharged form.

DE TOMASO (I)

One of those wonderful Italian sports car manufacturers who have tried to challenge the might of Ferrari, but have always failed because of the inherently kit-car nature of their machinery. Initially, Argentine Alejandro de Tomaso made racing cars, and followed them up with a range of supercars, including the Mangusta. His 1970s products included the Pantera, still made in 1985, but the firm's finances have always been precarious.

◄ **PANTERA. 1970 to date (prod: approx 700 to 1973). 2-seater coupé. R/R, 5763cc (V8 OHV).** First De Tomaso to be made in commercial quantities and derived from the Mangusta. Up to 350bhp with hotter versions of Ford's mid-mounted 351 engine, a five-speed transaxle, 11in ventilated disc brakes and 175mph advertised for the GTS version (from early 1973). Early ones overheated. Good secondhanders sell handsomely in the US, so watch this one.

DKW (D)

Like BMW, DKW initially made motorcycles, branching out into car manufacture in 1928. In 1932 the firm became part of the Auto Union combine – Auto Union was re-established in the Federal Republic in 1949, and DKW resumed building cars in 1950. The firm came under Daimler-Benz control in 1958, and was bought by Volkswagen in 1965.

SONDERKLASSE 3-6/GROSSER 3-6. 1953-59 (prod: 230,598). 2-door saloon, 4-door saloon, station wagon, 4-seater coupé, 2 and 4-seater cabriolets. F/F, 896cc (S3 TS). The old two-stroke theme updated with longitudinal engine, hydraulic brakes, and four-speed synchromesh 'box, though if you buy an early left-hooker you may find it's only got three speeds. There's a free wheel and it's a better cold starter than some of its rivals. Wide choice of bodies – four-door introduced in 1955. ►

◄ **1000/1000S. 1958-63 (prod: 171,008). 4-door saloon, 4-seater coupé. F/F, 980cc (S3 TS).** Identifiable by the wrap around screen and tidier, cross-hatched oval grille. Output up to 44bhp (50bhp with S engine) giving 80mph. For: it's got a separate chassis and bodies are well made. Against: petroil lubrication and a nasty column change. Rare in England.

JUNIOR/F11/F12. 1959-63/1963-65/1963-65 (prod: 237,587/30,738/82,506). 2-door saloon. F/F, 741cc/796cc/889cc (S3 TS). Small three-cylinder saloons with all-synchro 'boxes for later 1000s. 796cc engine in De Luxe Junior (1961-63) and F11, 889cc in all F12s. Saxomat automatic clutch option, but rare F12 Cabriolet not seen here. Front disc brakes on C12. Not very interesting. ►

F102. 1964-66 (prod: 52,753). 2-door saloon, 4-door saloon. F/F, 1175cc (S3 TS). Last of a line going back to 1931. Four-door 1966 only. If you like early Audis and two-stroke engines, this is the car for you. Looks like a simplified Audi and the chassis/body structure is almost identical. ➤

ELVA (GB)

The car's name is derived from the French for 'she goes' ('Elle va'), and the original 1955 Frank Nichols design was a low cost sports racing car with power unit to suit the customer's pocket. The most successful car was the Courier road-going sports machine. The firm was taken over by Trojan Ltd in 1964, with manufacture ceasing after 1969.

◄ **COURIER. 1958-61 (prod: approx 400). Sports 2-seater, coupé. F/R, 1489cc/1588cc (S4 OHV).** First street Elva with tubular ladder frame, 1.5-litre Riley (later MGA) engine and gearbox and a rigid axle and coils at the back. Glassfibre bodies. Export only 'till 1960, when sold in kit form over here. Rough and tough, but good for 95-100mph.

MK III/T-TYPE MK IV. 1962-69 (prod: approx 100). Sports 2-seater, coupé. F/R, 1622cc/1498cc/1798cc (S4 OHV). Later, Trojan-built cars with Triumph rack and pinion steering and irs on the Mk IV. Coupés have ugly 105E Anglia-type rear windows, or prettier fastback coupé (rare). Specification varies, but front disc brakes standard and inboard rear discs optional. Engines MG (initially A 1600, then B) or Ford Cortina GT. Very few made after 1965. ➤

ENFIELD (GB)

This firm was owned by Greek Shipping magnate John Goulandris, and its only automotive efforts were the 8000 electric car – which flopped miserably – and the Safari saloon, which appeared on the Jeep stand at the 1972 Turin Show. Aluminium speed boats and guns were other company products.

◄ **8000. 1969-71 (prod: 103). R/R, electric motor.** Only 42 of these little electric runabouts reached the public (no wonder with a price tag of £2808 in 1975), the Electricity Council took the rest. Aluminium panels over a space frame, coil spring ifs, hydraulic brakes and even Dunlop Denovo tyres and full factory rustproofing. First of the few or first of the many?

FACEL VEGA (F)

Jean Daninos' *Forges et Ateliers de Construction d'Eure et Loire* manufactured a wide variety of high quality metal products, but was best known for supplying complete car bodies to Panhard, Simca and Ford France – these were specialist bodies, not run-of-the-mill saloons. However, he had a dream of producing a Grand Routier in the best Delage/Delahaye tradition, and the result, in 1954, was the Facel Vega. One of the first European cars to use American V8 power allied to continental styling and chassis behaviour, the cars sold well but never in enough quantity. A move down-market with the Facellia, powered by the firm's own engine, proved disastrous, and the Facel concern folded in 1964.

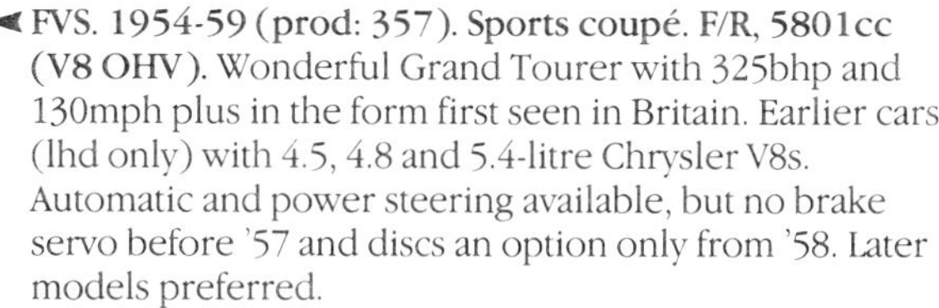

◄ FVS. 1954-59 (prod: 357). Sports coupé. F/R, 5801cc (V8 OHV). Wonderful Grand Tourer with 325bhp and 130mph plus in the form first seen in Britain. Earlier cars (lhd only) with 4.5, 4.8 and 5.4-litre Chrysler V8s. Automatic and power steering available, but no brake servo before '57 and discs an option only from '58. Later models preferred.

EXCELLENCE. 1958-64 (prod: 230). 4-door saloon. F/R, 5801cc/6268cc (V8 OHV). Four-door extended wheelbase Facel: specifications otherwise as coupé's, though 6.3-litre engine from 1959. Usually automatic, but a few manuals. Only 13 sold new in Britain. Pillarless doors a headache, and nobody loves this one. Thus there's a chance of something different for not much outlay ... if you don't mind a 17 footer doing 12mpg. ►

◄ HK500. 1959-61 (prod: 500). Sports coupé. F/R, 6286cc (V8 OHV). Uprated FVS, still with vertical headlamp clusters, aircraft-type facia and console, and those roly-poly seats. With the twin quadrajet-carburettor option there are 360 brake horses. Power steering standard with automatic, but anything made before April 1960 may still have drum brakes so be careful.

FACEL II. 1962-64 (prod: 184). Sports coupé. F/R, 6286cc (V8 OHV). Lower, more angular roofline means better vision, poorer driving position. Options up to 390bhp plus power disc brakes, Borrani wheels, stick instead of pushbuttons on automatic models, and Armstrong Selectaride dampers on British-market cars. Usual awful thirst, but a good club has the parts situation properly organised. ►

◄ **FACEL III. 1963-64 (prod: 1500). Coupé, cabriolet. F/R, 1780cc (S4 OHV).** If you want a ragtop Facel, you'll have to choose the small car. This one's reliable, thanks to its twin-carb pushrod engine straight out of Volvo's P1800. On 108bhp it's not much slower than a Facellia, but it's heavier and the handling suffers. Seldom seen in Britain. Its development, the Facel 6 with Austin-Healey 3000 unit (26 made) was not imported at all.

FACELLIA. 1960-63 (prod: 1258). Coupé, cabriolet. F/R, 1647cc (S4 DOC). Small Facel with their own twin-cam unit giving 114bhp and 114mph ... but, alas, a well-founded reputation as a piston burner and travelling oil leak. Early ones were convertibles with or without hardtop; coupés from 1961. Some with drum brakes in 1960, but power discs on most. They did eventually sort the engine out, so try for a later car. ►

FAIRTHORPE (GB)

From 1954 to 1978 the Fairthorpe concern, founded by Air Vice Marshal D. C. T. Bennett, produced bizarre cars. Its first products were glass fibred-bodied minicars, followed by the strange looking but good handling Electron sports cars. In 1965, Torix Bennett developed the TX, later the TX GT. Quite fast and stylish, they were never refined enough to be a threat to cars like the Ford Capri.

◄ **ATOM. 1954-57 (prod: 44). 2-seater coupé. R/R, 646cc (S2 OHV).** Plastic-bodied sporty bubble with central backbone frame, and all-independent springing. Brakes are hydraulic, but some motorcycle features – positive-stop gearbox and chain drive. Big-twin BSA gives 75mph. Other engines available were 250cc and 350cc BSA singles and Anzani's 322cc two-stroke twin.

ATOMOTA. 1958-60 (prod: n/a). 2-seater coupé. R/R, 646cc (S2 OHV). More sophisticated Atom derivative with live (hypoid) rear axle, coil rear springs and car-type syncromesh four-speed 'box. Better looking than the Atom and sold only with the big BSA twin. Like later Fairthorpes, marketed in kit-form as well as complete. Very rare. ►

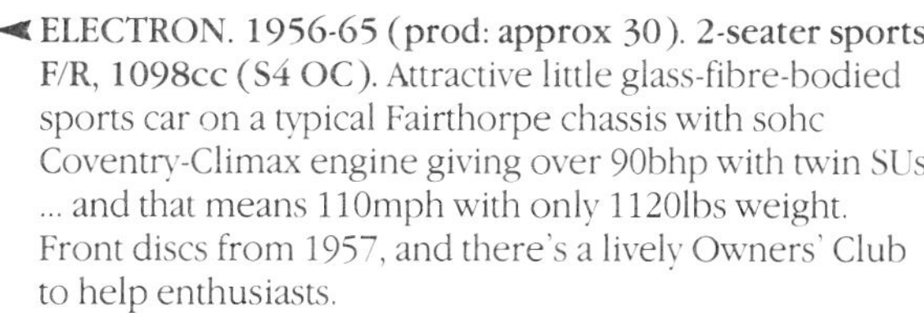

◄ **ELECTRON. 1956-65 (prod: approx 30). 2-seater sports. F/R, 1098cc (S4 OC).** Attractive little glass-fibre-bodied sports car on a typical Fairthorpe chassis with sohc Coventry-Climax engine giving over 90bhp with twin SUs ... and that means 110mph with only 1120lbs weight. Front discs from 1957, and there's a lively Owners' Club to help enthusiasts.

ELECTRON MINOR/EM3/EM4/EM5/EM6. 1957-73 (prod: approx 500). 2-seater sports. F/R, 948cc/1147cc/1296cc (S4 OHV). Poor man's Electron with twin-carburettor Triumph engine: Herald in the early ones, Spitfire from EM3 (1963) onwards. 1.3-litre unit (from 1969) gives 75bhp – quite exciting in a two seater weighing just over 1000lbs. Very spartan though later cars have better looks. Options included hardtops and superchargers. Front discs from 1966.

ELECTRINA. 1961-63 (prod: approx 20). 4-seater sports saloon. F/R, 948cc (S4 OHV). An Electron Minor for a small family and its luggage. Usual chassis and glass-fibre body, drum brakes and 50bhp twin-carb Herald engine, ergo no mechanical problems. Ugly little car – especially from the front – and it didn't last long.

ZETA. 1960-65 (prod: approx 20). Sports 2-seater. F/R, 2553cc (S6 OHV). Strictly a bomb: the Electron chassis/body set up with a 2.5-litre Ford Zephyr engine shoehorned in. Front disc brakes, rack and pinion steering. You could have the power unit to almost any tune, but with six Amals fed by twin SU pumps, what price 137bhp and 120mph? Drive-to-meeting rather than drive-to-work.

ROCKETTE. 1963-67 (prod: approx 25). Sports 2-seater. F/R, 1596cc (S6 OHV). Zeta for apprentices – same chassis but 70bhp Triumph Vitesse straight six engine and four-speed gearbox with or without overdrive. First cars had a horrible goitrous central third headlamp sprouting out of the bonnet, to make it look different. Later ones lost this and had better appointments.

TX-GT. 1967-73 (prod: all TX types to date, approx 50). 2-seater coupé. F/R, 1998cc (S6 OHV). First car with Torix Bennett's ingenious transverse-rod braking-type irs. Otherwise the mixture as before, with glass-fibre body (a coupé this time) over a typical Fairthorpe frame, front disc brakes and coils at the front. Standard power pack is Triumph's GT6 with overdrive 'box, giving over 110mph.

TX-S/TX-SS. 1969-76 (prod: see TX-GT). 2-seater coupé. ➤ F/R, 1296cc (S4 OHV); 1998cc/2499cc (S6 OHV). Prettier four-light coupé with the TX-GT's chassis and springs. S models use the twin carb Triumph GT6 engine up to 1973, four-cylinder Spitfire units thereafter; the six is good for 120mph. For still more urge, try the SS with fuel injected TR6 motor which should really pull those 1750lbs along. TX1500 (four-cylinder) and TX2000 (six-cylinder).

FALCON (GB)

Another of those cars which started life from its maker's production of glass-fibre shells between 1958 and 1964. Car kit-production using space frame chassis began in 1961: bodies were made by Falcon Shells of Waltham Abbey/Epping, kits by Falcon Cars of Hatfield. The firm died when founder Peter Pellandine had a bad road accident.

◄ 515. 1963-64 (prod: 25). 2-seater sports. F/R, 1498cc (S4 OHV). The closest Falcon Shells Ltd got to producing a complete car, though the few that were made were more often than not sold as kits. Typical of the special breed, the 515 was Ford-based, had a pretty glass-fibre body on a tubular chassis, an independent front end and a live rear axle. Falcons, generally, are a rare species.

FERRARI (I)

One of the great names, all the more remarkable considering it has been around only since 1940. Enzo Ferrari, ex-racing driver and team manager for Alfa Romeo through the 1930s, went his own way when Alfa resumed control of its racing activities in 1938. His first product, the Tipo 815, was Fiat based, but in 1946 the firm started making its first V12 engine. Through the 1950s road cars were essentially hand-built, very fast and sensational looking. As well as making some of the finest sports cars ever, the firm has won innumerable sports car and Grand Prix races. Fiat has been the majority shareholder in the firm since 1969, but that has not meant any sacrifice in the quality of the cars.

166. 1948-53 (prod: 97), 2-seater sports, fastback coupé. F/R, 1995cc (V12 DOC). ➤ The first true production Ferrari, and a car which inspired one of the truly great automotive shapes – Touring's Barchetta. The V12 engine was a Colombo masterpiece, and Luigi Chinetti won the marque's first Le Mans in one in 1949. A jewel, and prices reflect that fact.

◄ 212. 1951-53 (prod: approx 80). Various. F/R, 2563cc (V12 DOC). First Ferrari to be seen on British roads. Specifications vary, but this is the classical Colombo type, with one ohc per bank, massive seven bearing crankshaft, box-section frame, transverse-leaf ifs and beam rear axle. Tricky and delicate five-speed 'box. 130-150bhp according to tune, and 120mph. Expensive to buy and even more so to restore.

342/375 AMERICA. 1951-52/1953-54 (prod: approx 18). **Various. F/R, 4102cc/4522cc (V12 DOC).** Immensely complicated, and early ones liable to brake fade. Only four speeds, but synchromesh on all of them. Early engines gave 200bhp, but the competition 4.5-litre unit disposed of 350bhp and even in street tune should top 130mph. Unless it's cheap, think high.

410 SUPERAMERICA. 1955-60 (prod: approx 13). **Various. F/R, 4962cc (V12 DOC).** This time 340bhp from 5-litres, with twin master cylinders for the brakes and the 250's coil spring ifs. Usually with coupé and cabriolet bodies by Pininfarina. Later ones have inboard rear brakes, and some have discs, too. Again, for the very rich.

400 SUPERAMERICA. 1960-62 (prod: approx 75). **Coupé, spyder, cabriolet. F/R, 3967cc (V12 DOC).** Last of the Americas and it'll almost certainly be lhd, which early Ferraris weren't? Triple-carburettor engine gives 340/400bhp. Two-seater bodies only, though all have servo disc brakes, and some have overdrive to the four-speed 'box. 160mph plus, but once again very expensive.

250GT. 1956-64 (prod: n/a). **Coupé, 2+2 coupé, cabriolet. F/R, 2953cc (V12 DOC).** The first 'volume' production Ferrari: most of them have Pininfarina's 2+2 coupé body. Coil-spring front suspension and four-speeds with overdrive standard on 2+2s. Power around 220/240bhp and up to 140mph. Disc brakes from 1960 when UK imports started in earnest. Aluminium bodywork rather fragile.

250GTB BERLINETTA. 1959-63 (prod: 102). **2-seater coupé. F/R, 2953cc (V12 DOC).** The short (94.5in) wheelbase with Scaglietti body: no overdrive on these, though Dunlop disc brakes standardised in 1960. Conventionally-located gearbox (as on all 250s) and beam rear axle. Outputs of up to 290bhp quoted for the three carburettor engine, so they'll be quite a lot faster than the 2+2 – and more expensive.

250 CALIFORNIA. 1959-63 (prod: 159). 2-seater spyder. F/R, 2953cc (V12 DOC). Mechanical specification as for the GTB with the short wheelbase, straight four-speed 'box and full-house engine. Easier to find in the USA and rhd very rare. Very definitely a sports two-seater and not a cabriolet. Again one of the expensive ones, so if money is an object, stay with the 2+2.

275GTB. 1965-66 (prod: 465). 2-seater coupé. F/R, 3286cc (V12 DOC). Specification embraces five-speed transaxle, dual-circuit servo disc brakes and all-independent springing. This one's on the short (94.5in) wheelbase. Pininfarina did the bodies and top speed is around the 150mph mark. A few made with six carburettors and 320bhp. Not as expensive as a GTS.

275GTS. 1965-66 (prod: 200). 2-seater spyder. F/R, 3286cc (V12 DOC). Again Pininfarina, and mechanics as GTB, except for Borrani wire wheels where coupés usually wear cast-alloy. Ragtops add weight, so you lose about 5mph top speed. Scarcity spells high prices, and most of them are firmly on the other side of the Pond.

275GTB4/NART SPYDER. 1966-68 (prod: 280/9). 2-seater coupé, 2-seater spyder. F/R, 3286cc (V12 DOC) The ultimate in 275s with dry-sump lubrication, six Webers and 300bhp, plus the usual all-independent suspension and five-speed transaxle of this family. Short chassis, of course, and a 165mph potential. Very expensive, and the few open cars all went to America.

330GT. 1964-67 (prod: 2,086, all 330 variants). 2+2 seater coupé. F/R, 3967cc (V12 DOC). The conventionally located gearbox has four speeds and overdrive, and there's a beam axle. 150mph luxury on the long chassis, with electric fans in the cooling system, and such options as power steering and air conditioning. Not very rare, and so reasonably priced.

330GTC/GTS. 1966-68 (prod: 600/100). 2-seater coupé, 2-seater spyder. F/R, 3967cc (V12 DOC). Double-cam 4-litre 300bhp engine married to the short chassis with irs, and a predictable 150mph. Limited slip differential standard: air conditioning optional on coupés. Usual lovely Pininfarina bodies, but once again ragtops come very expensive indeed. ➤

◄ **500 SUPERFAST. 1964-66 (prod: 37). 2-seater coupé. F/R, 4962cc (V12 DOC).** Ultimate development of the America line, all with the same style Pininfarina body. Long chassis, beam rear axle, and 400bhp, or 170-plus mph. Seldom-seen (12 only) Series II cars have five-speeds instead of four-plus-overdrive, but this one can set you back more even than a good Daytona.

365 CALIFORNIA. 1966-67 (prod: 14). 2-seater spyder. F/R, 4390cc (V12 DOC). First of the 4.4-litre cars with Pininfarina body, five-speed 'box, and power steering as standard, plus wire wheels. Only two made with right hook. Foglamps retract, though headlamps are fixed and hooded. Unusual also as an open car on the longer wheelbase. ➤

◄ **365 GT 2+2. 1967-71 (prod: 801). 2+2-seater coupé. F/R, 4390cc (V12 DOC).** 330 replacement with the California's 320bhp engine, and a combination of constant level irs and a conventionally located gearbox. Package includes power steering, limited slip diff., and air conditioning. Alloy or wire wheels, and a little 'soft' for the fanatic. It's a Ferrari, nevertheless.

365GTC/GTS. 1967-70/1968-69 (prod: 150-200/approx 20). 2-seater coupé, 2-seater spyder. F/R, 4390cc (V12 DOC). Updated short chassis 330 with the latest 4.4-litre engine: three double-choke Webers fed by electric and mechanical pumps. Usual mechanical specification, i.e. five-speeds, limited slip differential, and irs. Very desirable, as the last of this line. ➤

365GTB4 DAYTONA. 1968-74 (prod: 1005). 2-seater coupé, 2-seater spyder. F/R, 4930cc (V12 4OC). Collectable almost before production ceased. The all-alloy, dry sump engine with its six Webers pushes out 352bhp, and you've the usual five-speed transaxle. Retractable headlamps from 1971. Only 50 Spyders made, 1969/70. ➤

◄**DINO 206. 1968-69 (prod: 150). 2-seater coupé. R/R, 1987cc (V6 4OC).** A new generation, with transverse mid engine, five-speed, all-synchro, transaxle, and all-coil independent suspension, good for 145mph and round 20mpg. Mostly badged as Dinos, not Ferraris. Handling superb, but bugs not all ironed out in 1968, so choose the later 246.

DINO 246GT/GTS. 1969-74/1972-74 (prod: 2732/680). 2-seater coupé, 2-seater spyder. R/R, 2418cc (V6 4OC). More powerful engine with cast iron block in place of the 206's aluminium one, spelling 150mph and up to the ton in less than 18secs. Spyder, alas, is only another Targa, not a proper open car. Not fun to work on, but it's surprising what you can pick up for reasonable money. ➤

FIAT (I)

Not just a maker of cars, Fiat is an Italian industrial colossus, making ball bearings, aero-engines and railway rolling stock, among other things. The firm's standing can be gauged by current boss Gianni Agnelli being reckoned the most powerful man in Italy: the firm also controls Ferrari and Lancia. Fiat was founded in 1899 by Giovanni Agnelli and Count Carlo Biscaretti, who took over the small Ceirano factory. Throughout its history the company has marketed everything from vast touring cars down to the smallest utility vehicles. It is now a multi-national company, producing cars in Argentina as well as having its products made under licence in the USSR and Poland.

500C. 1949-54 (prod: 376,368). 2-seater cabriolet, station wagon. F/R, 569cc (S4 OHV). The good old *Topolino* in its final, best form with ohv and rear tank: a genuine 60mph plus the familiar 50-plus mpg. Delightful to drive, and horrible to work on. Watch the sills and avoid earlier, woody-type wagons: all-steel from 1952. UK availability, late 1954. ➤

8V. 1952-53 (prod: n/a). 2-seater coupé. F/R, 1996cc. (V8 OHV). Running against the Fiat utility grain, this one was a true beauty with a one-off V8 engine producing 105bhp, and giving a top speed of 110mph. All round independent suspension was used, but Fiat never really marketed it properly, and most of the Fiat V8-engined cars made came from the Siata works. ➤

◄ **1100-103. 1953-62 (prod: 1,019,378). Saloon, station wagon. F/R, 1089cc (S4 OHV).** First unitary *Millecento*. Available in UK 1954. For: splendid performance, economy and handling, especially TV (1954-56) with central cyclops headlamp and 53bhp engine. Against: rust, squashed Mk I Consul looks, and that horrible transmission handbrake.

1100D. 1962-66 (prod: 408,997). Saloon, station wagon. F/R, 1221cc (S4 OHV). 'False' 1100 with the bigger engine, improved styling, wrapround rear window, and (thank goodness) a handbrake working on the rear wheels. Otherwise same remarks apply as to earlier models, but all 1100s are great fun to drive, if you can find one without terminal corrosion. ➤

◄ **1100R. 1966-70 (prod: 300,000 approx). Saloon, station wagon. F/R, 1089cc (S4 OHV).** Last of the line, and good fun to the end. A 48bhp engine spells nearly 80mph, and you've now got front disc brakes plus floor change instead of the unpleasant four-on-the-column of fifties Fiats. Later made in India. A possible spares source?

1200. 1957-60 (prod: 400,066). Saloon. F/R, 1221cc (S4 OHV). Fiat's answer to the Simca Aronde, and first use of the 1.2-litre engine and wrapround rear window. 82mph on 55bhp, though a little more ornate than the regular article. Plus: it corners a treat. Minus: rust, four on the column, and that abominable handbrake. ➤

1400. 1950-58 (prod: 120,356). Saloon, cabriolet. F/R, 1395cc (S4 OHV). Fiat's 'Standard Vanguard', incredibly oversquare and also incredibly overgeared, ergo acceleration negligible. Awful styling, but a full six-seater and very tough. Rare in Britain, where it didn't appear till '54: cabriolets and diesel versions not sold here. Later cars with wrapround rear windows. ➤

◄ **1900. 1952-58 (prod: 15,759). Saloon, hardtop coupé. F/R, 1901cc (S4 OHV).** Up-market 1400 with such gimmicks as an average speed calculator, plus 16 more brake horses and a fifth speed. They meant to fit the 8V sports engine, but didn't. Coil rear springs spell lots of roll, and if you think Italian stylists are infallible, take a look at the *Gran Luce* hardtop.

600/600D. 1955-60/1960-70 (prod: 891,107/ 1,561,000). Saloon, convertible saloon. R/R, 633cc/ 767cc (S4 OHV). How to cram four people into something smaller than a *Topolino*. Handles nicely, but very noisy and rustprone. Abarthised versions good for 80 plus, and later D cars are the best of the 'cookers' since they'll do over 60 and don't have that transmission brake. Still made in Argentina and Yugoslavia. ➤

◄ **600 MULTIPLA. 1955-66 (prod: see 600). Station wagon. R/R, 633cc/767cc (S4 OHV).** Full forward control minibus for six, 139in long and 62in wide. Mechanics as 600, with the bigger engine from 1960. Woolly gearchange and choppy ride when driven solo. Some late cars have the angular 850T van body and more headroom. A possible solution to the co-operative morning commute?

NUOVA 500/500D. 1957-60/1960-75 (prod: 181,036/ 2,900,000). 2-seater cabriolet. R/R, 479cc/499cc (S2 OHV). Minimal transportation, with a busy aircooled twin at the back of a 600-type, all-independently sprung hull. Early ones gutless and to be avoided, but the 499cc car has a vintage feel and cruises at 50-55mph. Gearbox very crash indeed: double-declutch both ways. Too noisy and cramped for long runs – and it rusts. ➤

◄ **500 GIARDINIERA. 1960-77 (prod: approx 327,000). Station wagon. R/R, 499cc (S2 OHV).** Baby wagon with a surprising load capacity, thanks to mounting the engine flat under the floor. Mechanics otherwise as for 500 cabriolet, including drum brakes, and no synchro to the end. Later ones by Autobianchi and badged accordingly, though UK imports ceased in 1971.

1800/2100/2300. 1959-68/1959-61/1961-68 (prod: approx 185,000, all types). Saloon, station wagon. F/R, 1795cc/2054cc/2280cc (S6 OHV). Four-bearing sixes: Lampredi did the engines and Pininfarina the styling, and they're good performers. Luxury 2100s and 2300s have quad headlamps. Disc brakes from 1961. Quiet and smooth, but avoid early cars with the 1400-type coil rear springing, while handling was never a strong point anyway. ➤

◄ **1500S/1600S. 1959-62/1963-66 (prod: approx 47,000, including 1500 cabriolet). 4-seater cabriolet. F/R, 1491cc/1568cc (S4 DOC).** Twin-cam Osca engine in an 1100-base platform which avoids that unhappy coil-sprung back end. 120bhp and 105mph, front disc brakes from '61 (all-disc from '63), and the last cars had five-speed 'boxes. Main debits are an oil-burning engine and the usual rust. Pushrod versions preferred.

1500 CABRIOLET. 1963-67 (prod: see 1500S/1600S). 4-seater cabriolet. F/R, 1481cc (S4 OHV). Apart from the absence of a bonnet bulge (and of quad headlights from late cars) hard to distinguish quickly from a Fiat-Osca, though not nearly as fast. Servo front disc brakes, however, plus a thoroughly reliable pushrod four. Another rust-trap, though, and few cabriolets of either type made with rhd. ➤

1300/1500. 1961-67/1961-68 (prod: approx 600,000, all types). Saloon, station wagon. F/R, 1295cc/1481cc (S4 OHV). Styling is angular-period Pininfarina, with four synchronised ratios on the column. Front disc brakes are standard, and the handbrake is on the rear wheels: the last long-chassis 1500s have discs at the back, too. Semi-elliptic rear springs improve the handling. The 1500 has a delightfully smooth engine and will see 90mph. Against: looks, rust. ➤

◄ **2300S. 1961-68 (prod: see 1800/2100/2300). 4-seater coupé. F/R, 2280cc (S6 OHV).** Poor man's Ferrari, with Ghia-styled coachwork on a 2300 floorpan. Power discs to all four wheels, and twin-carb. 135bhp engine, ergo 115-120mph. Heavy on the controls, and festooned with idiot lights, plus a couple of warning bells (!). Power windows standard. Great fun, but tinworms love it, too.

850. 1964-71 (prod: 1,780,000). 2-door saloon. R/R, 843cc (S4 OHV). Those who say rear-engined saloons don't handle should try this one. More room than on a 600, plus a genuine 70mph, though corrosion remains a menace. Some imported with Idroconvert 2-pedal drive (avoid). Best of the bunch is 1969's Special, with coupé-tune engine and front disc brakes. ➤

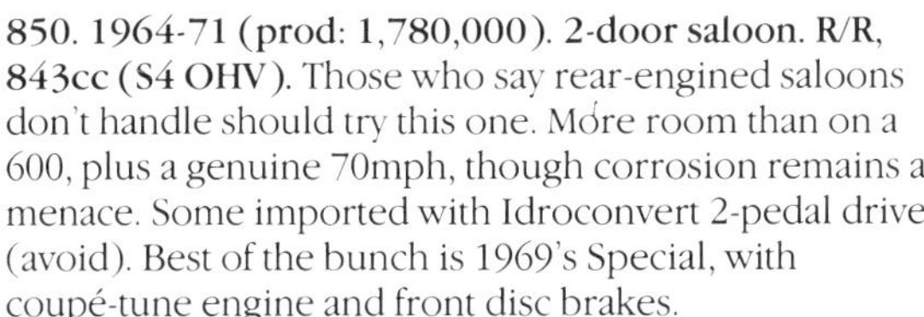

◄ **850 COUPÉ. 1965-73 (prod: 380,000). 4-seater coupé. R/R, 843cc/903cc (S4 OHV).** A little honey that'll average 45mph *and* 45mpg on long runs. Front disc brakes standard: 903cc engine from mid-1968, boosting top speed into the middle 90s. Handling superb, but luggage space limited, rear seats useless, and ventilation lousy. Late, rust-free ones covetable and cheap.

850 SPYDER. 1965-73 (prod: 140,000). 2-seater sports. R/R, 843cc/903cc (S4 OHV). Bertone's open 850, without the coupé's ventilation headaches. Mechanics the same, with the bigger 52bhp engine arriving during '68. More fun than a Spridget, but alas, most of them went to the USA and rhd was never listed. Allegedly a 903 will do the ton if you risk 7000rpm ... ➤

124/124 SPECIAL. 1966-73 (prod: 1,280,000 to 1972). Saloon, station wagon. F/R, 1197cc/1438cc (S4 OHV). Wonderful little workhorse with a surprising performance: even 1.2-litres will do 90. New and better type coil rear springing, plus all-disc brakes. Specials (saloons only) feel too fast for chassis. Today's Russian Ladas are look-alikes with the same structure, but a different engine. ➤

◄ **124 COUPÉ. 1966-72 (prod: 380,000 approx). 4-seater coupé. F/R, 1438cc/1608cc (S4 DOC).** Cogged-belt dohc engine and servo-assisted discs all round on this one. Rear seats usable if uncomfortable, handles a treat, but you're lucky if you get 25mpg. Quad headlights (1969) don't improve looks but that year's 1600cc option gives you more power, and always go for the lovely five-speed 'box introduced then. Wheel arch rust a nightmare.

124 SPYDER. 1966-72 (prod: n/a). 2-seater sports. F/R, 1438cc/1608cc (S4 DOC). Short-wheelbase relative of the 124 coupé: same remarks apply, only on this one you're spared the quad headlamps. Again, the good one is the five-speed 1600, fifth being a very usable gear. Still being made for the USA with 2-litre fuel-injected engine, but never seriously marketed here, and never any right-hand drive. ➤

◄ **125. 1967-72 (prod: 603,870). Saloon. F/R, 1608cc (S4 DOC).** Put the twin-cam 1600 sports engine into a reinforced 124 hull, and you get a 100mph saloon, distinguishable from lesser Fiats by its quad headlights. Automatic available, also a five-speed Special model (1968), though fifth is very much an overdrive. Much nicer than its successor, the 132.

DINO 2000/2400. 1967-69/1969-73 (prod: approx 7500). 2+2 coupé, 2-seater spyder. F/R, 1987cc/2418cc (V6 4OC). Always rather over-shadowed by the mid-engined Ferrari, with which it shares power units and five-speed all-synchromesh gearboxes. Bertone did the coupé and Pininfarina the spyder. Irs on 2400s, and transistorised ignition on all but the earliest cars. No rhd, so won't be too expensive if you can find one. ➤

128. 1969 to date (prod: 3,107,000 all types to 1978). ➤ 2-door saloon, 4-door saloon, station wagon. F/F, 1116cc (S4 OHC). The first Fiat with east/west engine driving the front wheels. Front disc brakes and all-independent McPherson suspension. Very sensitive handling and modest thirst – 38mpg in give and take conditions. Rust record pretty hairy, so go for a late one, maybe one of those pretty little coupés introduced in 1971.

◄ 130. 1969-75 (prod: 15,000). Saloon. F/R, 2866cc/3235cc (V6 DOC). Prestige family saloon with a Dino-type bottom end, but cogged-belt rather than chain drive for half the number of camshafts. Torsion bars at the rear and power steering: only automatics sold in Britain. A fast and quiet *autostrada* cruiser, but not particularly exciting. Most cars will have the 3.2 engine, introduced in 1972.

130 COUPÉ. 1972-75 (prod: 4600). 4-seater coupé. F/R, ➤ 3235cc (V6 DOC). Beautifully appointed classic-from-birth by Pininfarina, with all-independent suspension, all-disc brakes and power steering. Automatic, alas!, compulsory in Britain, though some left-hookers made with five-speed ZF 'boxes. 165bhp not really enough, but it's headed straight for the collector stakes.

FORD (Germany)

The parent company in America started building Model Ts in Berlin in 1925, with the Model A following in 1927. A new factory in Cologne was built, with production beginning in 1931 with the Rheinland model. All pre-1939 German Fords were basically to American or British design, but after the war Ford Germany went its separate way with Taunus designs. However, there was increasing rationalisation of Ford's European ranges after 1968, with, for example, the Capri offered in both Britain and Germany. Today the story is different, Ford in Cologne effectively operating as Ford of Europe's design centre; all up-market products are manufactured there.

◄ TAUNUS 17M. 1957-60 (prod: 239,978). 2-door saloon, 4-door saloon, station wagon. F/R, 1698cc (S4 OHV). Not unlike a contemporary Consul, with McPherson front suspension, oversquare four-cylinder engine, and hydraulic brakes. Four on the column and Saxomat automatic clutch were catalogued options, but here we got three-speeders with synchromesh on bottom. Smaller engined variants not imported.

TAUNUS 17M. 1961-64 (prod: 669,731). 2-door saloon, ➤ 4-door saloon, station wagon. F/R, 1698cc (S4 OHV). Roughly paralleling the Mk III Zephyr 4, but rather better looking, and available with 75bhp TS engine for extra urge. Four on the column standard, and still only drum brakes. Scarcity value – no more – in Britain, though the TS would do 90mph and 0-60mph in 15 secs.

TAUNUS 12M/12MTS. 1963-66 (prod: 672,695). 2-door saloon, 4-door saloon, station wagon. F/F, 1183cc/ 1498cc (V4 OHV). Historical interest, mainly, as the first production fwd Ford (16 years before the Fiesta), and the first use of the soon-common V4 engine. TS models were credited with 90mph on 65bhp, but though this one appeared at Earls Court, it never sold in any numbers over here. ►

◄ **TAUNUS 17M. 1964-67 (prod: 516,991). 2-door saloon, 4-door saloon, station wagon. F/R, 1699cc (V4 OHV).** Rear drive and a V4 engine this time, in something that resembled a tidied-up Corsair. As its Dagenham rival was V4-powered by '66 anyway, the later Taunus had no *raison d'être* in Britain. Four on the floor for export plus front disc brakes and an automatic option.

TAUNUS 20M/20MTS. 1964-67 (prod:193,068). 2-door saloon, 4-door saloon, coupé. F/R, 1998cc (V6 OHV). Cologne led Dagenham again: there were no British V6 Fords till 1966. The engine gave 85 or 90bhp according to tune: four on the floor was regular equipment, as were disc front brakes, with a servo on the TS. Coupés were much better looking than the contemporary Capri. ►

FORD (Great Britain)

Until 1932, Ford of Britain made only right-hand-drive versions of American products at Trafford Park, Manchester. However, following the opening of a new integrated plant at Dagenham in Essex, British designed products followed. All through the 1950s and 1960s, Ford produced its own designs in Britain, the most successful being the Cortina ranges, begun in 1963 as an answer to the BMC Mini. The Cortina shot Ford to the top of the best sellers' lists, and the Escort range further strengthened that hold. Today the firm is still the biggest seller in England, but competition from Austin Rover and Vauxhall has started to threaten.

◄ **ANGLIA EO4A. 1940-48 (prod: 58,864, inc pre-war). 2-door saloon. F/R, 933cc (S4 SV).** The original Anglia, little more than 1938's 7Y 8hp with built-out boot and rectangular bonnet. Mechanical brakes, transverse-leaf springs at both ends, and the ultimate in choppy riding. Almost invariably black, though a colour choice in '40 and again in '48. 1172cc engines in export models.

ANGLIA E93A. 1949-53 (prod: 108,000). 2-door saloon. F/R, 933cc (S4 SV). EO4A with sloping grille and central painted bar, reminiscent of the 1937-8 Ten. Basic, go-anywhere transportation: 60mph and 30/35mpg plus considerable discomfort. It's got a chassis and doesn't rust as badly as the opposition. Commoner than squared-bonnet types. ►

PREFECT. 1939-53 (prod: 379,339, inc pre-war). 4-door saloon. F/R, 1172cc (S4 SV). Announced in October 1938 as a restyled Ten, but only 4-door models available after the war. Colour choice again from '48, and new bonnet/grille with recessed headlamps from 1949. Later pre-war cars have centred instruments, so can be confused with 1945-48s. All the usual Ford virtues and vices. ➤

◄ **V8 PILOT. 1947-50 (prod: 22,189). 4-door saloon, estate car. F/R, 3622cc (V8 SV).** Marriage of the pre-war 22hp chassis/body to the classic '221' flathead engine. Rod-operated Girling brakes and bent-wire column shift. Very tough, hence a high survival rate: there's a good club as well. Pilots come cheaper than their pre-war counterparts. Wagons (1949-50) very rare: pickups (nominally export only) scarcer still.

CONSUL EOTA. 1951-56 (prod: 231,481). 4-door saloon. F/R, 1508cc (S4 OHV). Into the modern age with unitary construction, upstairs valves, McPherson-strut ifs, and hydraulic brakes. Three on the column bearable, but styling totally uninspired, and they've almost all rusted out by now. Good ground clearance and not fast enough to expose endemic handling weaknesses. ➤

◄ **ZEPHYR I EOTTA. 1951-56 (prod: 152,677). 4-door saloon. F/R, 2262cc (S6 OHV).** A Consul with a different grille and two extra cylinders, giving 80-plus mph. In its day a favourite with tuners, who could give it Jaguar performance, but never Jaguar handling. More fun, though, than a contemporary Austin or Vauxhall. Some estate-car (Farnham) conversions by E.D. Abbott.

CONSUL I/ZEPHYR I CONVERTIBLE. 1952-56 (prod: N/A). 5-seater convertible. F/R, 1508cc/2262cc (S4/S6 OHV). First seen at the '51 Show, but few sold before '53. Top chop by Carbodies: the hood is manually operated on Consuls, but the Zephyr's is power-actuated, if only as far as the *de ville* position. Never common: rust plus structural problems killed them off, so survivors probably expensive.

ZODIAC I EOTTA. 1954-56 (prod: 22,634). 4-door saloon. F/R, 2262cc (S6 OHV). Jazzed-up Zephyr: not much more performance, except on paper, but two-tone paint helps break up those slab sides, and you also get whitewall tyres and twin spot/fog lamps. No convertibles, though possibly a few estate-car conversions still around.

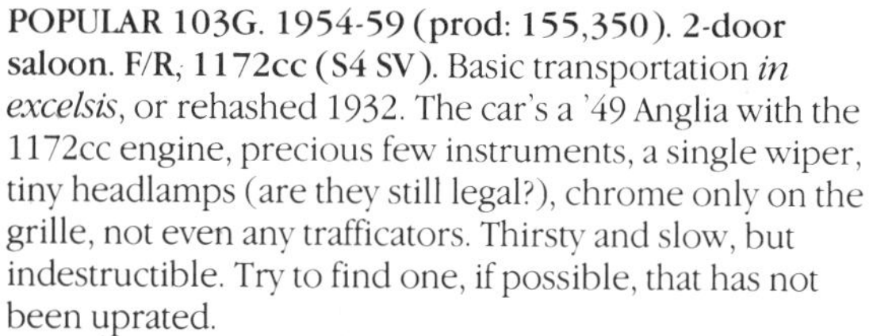

POPULAR 103G. 1954-59 (prod: 155,350). 2-door saloon. F/R, 1172cc (S4 SV). Basic transportation *in excelsis*, or rehashed 1932. The car's a '49 Anglia with the 1172cc engine, precious few instruments, a single wiper, tiny headlamps (are they still legal?), chrome only on the grille, not even any trafficators. Thirsty and slow, but indestructible. Try to find one, if possible, that has not been uprated.

ANGLIA 100E. 1954-59 (prod: 348,841). 2-door saloon. F/R, 1172cc (S4 SV). Structurally it's Consul/Zephyr with McPherson front suspension, semi-elliptics at the back, and unitary body, though the redesigned engine with its pump cooling is still a long-stroke flathead. Ride, handling and stopping powers incomparably better than the old Anglia's, but it won't usually better 30mpg, and all the character has gone.

PREFECT 100E. 1954-59 (prod: 100,554). 4-door saloon. F/R, 1172cc (S4 SV). Mechanically the Anglia's twin with unitary construction, hydraulic brakes etc, and using the same 87-in wheelbase, which makes for rather narrow doors. Convex, vertical-barred grille identifies it from the front. Some Anglias and Prefects (1956 on) had 2-pedal drive: such systems usually best left alone.

ESCORT/SQUIRE. 1956-60 (prod: 33,131/17,812). Estate car. F/R, 1172cc (S4 SV). There'd been proprietary Utilecon conversions of the old 5cwt van, but these were Ford's first factory-built small wagons. Escorts are 5cwt vans with Anglia grilles, seats and windows: Squires have the Prefect grille and wood strakes on the side. Mechanically, they're identical.

CONSUL II 204E. 1956-62 (prod: 350,244). 4-door saloon, estate car. F/R, 1703cc (S4 OHV). Restyled Consul with a longer wheelbase, better weight distribution, and a bigger engine to boost top speed to over 80mph. Lower roof lines and plated window frames from February 1959. Cars made from the summer of '61 were called Consul 375s, but only to avoid confusion with the Classic, also nominally one of the Consul range!

ZEPHYR/ZODIAC II 206E. 1956-62. (prod: 350,244). 4-door saloon, estate car. F/R, 2553cc (S6 OHV). The sixes updated on the same lines as the Consul, with improved low-line types appearing early 1959. 80plus bhp from the latest 2½-litre engine spells 90mph. Borg-Warner triple overdrive optional, also automatic from October '56. Only convertibles are worth money.

CONSUL/ZEPHYR/ZODIAC II CONVERTIBLE. 1956-62 (prod: n/a). 5-seater convertible. F/R, 1703cc/2553cc (S4/S6 OHV). Carbodies' second effort, and Ford's last in this direction, with the ragtop Zodiac in the range this time. Manual tops standard on Consul: others with the old semi-power type inherited from Mk I. The usual overdrive and automatic options are available. Rust has decimated the model's ranks, but it is possible to find a good one.

POPULAR 100E. 1960-62 (prod: 126,115). 2-door saloon. F/R, 1172cc (S4 SV). A stripped (if not too stripped) 100E Anglia replacing the old sit-up-and-beg Pop of the fifties. Mechanical specification the same as the Anglia's even down to three-speed gearbox. Of no particular interest except that if you fancy late flathead Fords, these'll have had less time to corrode.

ANGLIA 105E. 1960-67 (prod: 945,713). **2-door saloon, estate car. F/R, 997cc (S4 OHV).** A real performer, with its very-over-square, rev happy ohv engine, and four speeds at last. Suspension is the 100E's but the reverse-slope window is unmistakable. Estate car version (104,000 built) from October '61. Handling a little uncertain, and rust has taken its toll, too.

ANGLIA SUPER 123E. 1962-67 (prod: 72,955). **2-door saloon. F/R, 1197cc (S4 OHV).** Longer-stroke engine in de luxe Anglia saloon to push top speed from the mid-70s to the low 80s, and give better acceleration. Even at the end, in '67, there was, however, no disc-brake option. Some estate cars got the 1200 engine, too.

PREFECT 107E. 1960-61 (prod: 38,154). **4-door saloon. F/R, 997cc (S4 OHV).** If you want a rare Dagenham Ford with reasonable looks, this is it. Externally recognisable from the flathead 100E version by its plated side flashes, but with the new 39bhp engine and four-speed 'box, there's 75mph plus new standards of acceleration. Not much collector-interest yet.

CLASSIC 109E/116E. 1961-62/1962-63 (prod: 84,694/ 26,531). **2-door saloon, 4-door saloon. F/R, 1340cc/ 1498cc (S4 OHV).** An ugly beast with all the nastier Detroit styling fads – reverse-slope rear window, hooded quad headlights, and tail fins. Front disc brakes and four on the floor standard, though there was a column-shift option. Go for the later five-bearing 1500 engine and all-synchro 'box. May become collectable, but so far the auction crowd has given it the bird.

CAPRI 109E/116E. 1961-62/1962-64 (prod: 11,143/ 7,573). **2-seater coupé. F/R, 1340cc/1498cc (S4 OHV).** Nobody loved it when it was new: really only a sporty Classic without much performance, apart from the rare 1½-litre GT (2002 made) which offered a frightening 95mph. Development history and base specifications as per Classic saloon. A case of Sleepers Awake, though not as yet.

CORTINA 113E/CORTINA SUPER 118E. 1963-66 (prod: 887,801). 2-door saloon, 4-door saloon, estate car. F/R, 1198cc/1498cc (S4 OHV). The anatomy of a bestseller, or the safe way's the known way. Classical Ford layout, plus four-speed all-synchro 'boxes as standard, and a five-bearing-engine for Supers. Automatic available on Supers 1964: front disc brakes on all from 1965. Some day there'll be an early Cortina cult.

CORTINA GT 118E. 1963-66 (prod: 74,399). 2-door saloon, 4-door saloon. F/R, 1498cc (S4 OHV). This one had front disc brakes from the start, and with a Weber carburettor output is up to 83bhp. Interior trim is more luxurious, too. Surprisingly, an automatic option from 1964, with through-flow ventilation standard on this (and all Cortinas) from '65.

LOTUS CORTINA I. 1963-66 (prod: 4012). 2-door saloon. F/R, 1558cc (S4 DOC). Marriage of the twin-cam, twin-carburettor 105bhp Lotus engine to a Cortina bodyshell, lowered and with coil rear springing (semi-elliptics 1966) and servo disc/drum brakes. Wide rim wheels and cream paint with green side flashes identify this one. 108mph and 21mpg, and there can't be many left. A current collectable.

ZEPHYR 4 MK III 211E. 1962-66 (prod: 106,936). 4-door saloon, estate car. F/R, 1703cc (S4 OHV). Consul replacement with the latest all-synchro 'box and power disc/drum brakes. No convertibles, and station wagons rare. Overdrive available, also an automatic never listed on Mk II Consuls. Column shift standard on these.

ZEPHYR 6 Mk III 213E. 1962-66 (prod: 107,400). 4-door saloon, estate car. F/R, 2553cc (S6 OHV). A full width grille distinguishes this from four-cylinder cars: there's also a floor change option as well as the usual overdrive and automatic variants. Abbott's estate-car conversions once again very rare. Cloth trim on some later Zephyrs of both types.

ZODIAC Mk III. 1962-66 (prod: 77,781).4-door saloon, estate car. F/R, 2553cc (S6 OHV). Rarest of this family, with power boosted from 98 to 109bhp, giving a 100mph potential. Immediately recognisable by its six-light styling and quad headlights, but otherwise similar to Zephyr 6, with the usual options. Executive (1965-66) was a luxury edition with all the extras thrown in.

CORSAIR 120E. 1964-65 (prod: 137,734). 2-door saloon, 4-door saloon. F/R, 1498cc (S4 OHV). Wedge-nosed saloon, not unlike the contemporary German Taunus, to fill the gap between Cortinas and Zephyrs. Mechanics ordinary, i.e. 60bhp single-carburettor engine, four on the floor (with column-shift option), and front disc brakes. Good for about 85mph and easy on fuel, but otherwise undistinguished.

CORSAIR GT 120GT. 1964-65 (prod: 21,857). 2-door saloon, 4-door saloon, F/R, 1498cc (S4 OHV). Same treatment as the Cortina GT, i.e. more luxurious interiors plus a dual-choke Weber carburettor instead of the regulation Solex. Good for 90-95mph. Preferable to early V4 versions which had a somewhat tarnished reputation, but again without distinction.

CORSAIR V4. 1966-70 (prod: 135,000 inc GT). 2-door saloon, 4-door saloon, estate car. F/R, 1663cc (V4 OHV). Bigger front disc brakes, but no other significant changes beyond the engine switch. V4 unit gives 81bhp so there's some more performance at the price of some roughness. New options include an estate car and automatic.

CORSAIR V4 GT/2000. 1966-70 (prod: see V4). 2-door saloon, 4-door saloon, estate car. F/R, 1996cc (V4 OHV). More cc and 93bhp now. 2000 takes over 1967: sold only as 4-door saloon with servo brakes, radial tyres, and wooden facia (from mid-year). Executive models have fancy grilles, twin reversing lamps, vinyl roofs and other goodies.

GT40, 1966-68 (prod: 31 road cars). 2-seater coupé. R/R, 4727cc (V8 OHV). A mid-engined bolide with all-independent springing weighing 2000lbs. In the fifth gear of its ZF all-synchromesh 'box it'll turn 154mph and 0-100 takes 11.8secs, all this on a mere 335bhp. Racers have been converted into street machines and vice versa, but think high. Mark III (illustrated) was a better equipped and tamer road version.

ZEPHYR 4/6 Mk IV 3008/3010E. 1966-72 (prod: approx 140,000). 4-door saloon, estate car. F/R, 1996cc/2495cc (V4/V6 OHV). Last of the all-British big Fords, now with vee engines, irs, and all disc brakes (servos optional on fours, standard on sixes). The regular package has four on the column, but floor shift, overdrive and automatic are options. So, for the first time, is power steering.

ZODIAC/EXECUTIVE IV 312E. 1966-72 (prod: 42,000). 4-door saloon, estate car. F/R, 2994cc (V6 OHV). Zephyr 6 with quad headlights, horizontal-barred grille (the central star badge came in '68), and a more powerful 3-litre V6 engine. Floor shift and power steering standard, the latter from October '67. Executives have all the extras thrown in, and a choice of overdrive or automatic transmission. A few convertible conversions were made and sold privately by Crayford.

CORTINA II STANDARD/SUPER. 1967-70 (prod: approx 800,000). 2-door saloon, 4-door saloon, estate car. F/R, 1297cc/1599cc (S4 OHV). Fully restyled Cortinas, all with five-bearing engines and front disc brakes. Automatic available. From 1968 on, improved bowl-in piston type engines standardised, with more power for the 1300, and the 71bhp 1600 unit replacing the older 1.5-litre type.

CORTINA II GT. 1967-70 (prod: approx 89,000). 2-door saloon, 4-door saloon. F/R, 1498cc/1599cc (S4 OHV). Badges replace chrome strip on the outside of these latest, restyled GTs, and there's a new instrument panel, 83bhp bowl-in piston 1600cc engine on '68s and later cars. Radial ply tyres also standardised on late models.

CORTINA II LOTUS/CORTINA TWIN CAM. 1967-70 (prod: 4000). 2-door saloon. F/R, 1558cc (S4 DOC). Twin Cam name in 1970 only: the usual twin-carburettor Lotus engine plus servo brakes, wide rim wheels, and an options list embracing things like limited slip diffs. and oil radiators. Matt black grille is an identification feature. Good for 105mph, but neither as exciting nor as sought after as Mk I.

CORTINA 1600E. 1968-70 (prod: 55,833). 4-door saloon. F/R, 1599cc (S4 OHV). The 'E' stands for 'Executive' but it's a bit more than that. There's a late-type 88bhp GT engine, the lowered suspension is off the Lotus model, and the package includes quad lights, wood facia, wide rim wheels, leather-rimmed steering wheel, and reversing lamps, plus black tail panels on later cars. Already attracting collector-interest. A further total of 2749 2-door 1600Es were for export only.

ESCORT/ESCORT DE LUXE. 1968-74 (prod: 1,076,118 all types). 2-door saloon, 4-door saloon, estate car. F/R, 1098cc/1298cc (S4 OHV). Roomier and more bland in appearance than the superseded Anglia, but with rack and pinion steering albeit (in our period) still drum brakes: front discs and servos available, and so is automatic transmission. Even the cooking engine gives 53bhp, so performance is quite reasonable.

ESCORT GT. 1968-74 (prod: see Escort). 2-door saloon, 4-door saloon. F/R, 1298cc (S4 OHV). A bit more powerful than the standard article, thanks to a 75bhp engine with Weber carburettor. 4-door saloons from 1969. Standard equipment includes servo front disc brakes, wide rim wheels, a close ratio 'box, and remote control. Should do 90mph, but why buy an old one?

ESCORT TWIN CAM. 1968-71 (prod: n/a). 2-door saloon. F/R, 1558cc (S4 DOC). First of the hairy Escorts with reinforced bodyshell and the twin cam Lotus engine in 105bhp form. Remote control, servo front disc brakes, and 115mph performance. Flared wheel arches to take wider-rim wheels. Cars made up to June 1969 have the original Escort's rectangular headlamps.

ESCORT RS1600. 1970-74 (prod: n/a). 2-door saloon. F/R, 1599cc (S4 DOC). Reinforced body as on Twin Cam, but now with the 16-valve Cosworth BDA unit featuring cogged-belt camshaft drive. Invariably white with black interior trim. 120bhp spells 113mph, and it will run on low-octane fuel. Going to be collectable, if only because it asked to be driven into the ground.

ESCORT MEXICO. 1970-74 (prod: n/a). 2-door saloon. F/R, 1599cc (S4 OHV). Named to commemorate London to Mexico Rally winning Escort. It looks like an RS1600, apart from its colour-contrast stripes, and the reinforced structure, suspension, brakes and even instrumentation are pure RS. The engine isn't, being a straightforward Kent-type pushrod unit disposing of 86bhp. Still, it'll do the ton, plus 28mpg. A nice, uncomplicated fun-car.

CAPRI 1300/1600. 1969-72 (prod: all British and German models, 742,149). 4-seater coupé. F/R, 1298cc/1599cc. (S4 OHV). You personalised this one just like a Mustang, but everything's got a 101-in wheelbase, McPherson front suspension, rack and pinion steering, four-speed 'box and front disc brakes. The 1600GT will run close to the ton on 94bhp, and has a brake servo, whereas a base 1300 makes do on 61bhp. Automatic available on 1600s.

CAPRI 2000GT/3000GT. 1969-72 (prod: see Capri 1300/1600). 4-seater coupé. F/R, 1996cc/2994cc (V4/V6 OHV). Higher-performance Capris with servo brakes, vee engines, and speeds of over 100mph. Automatic is available, and optional packs include X (interior trim), L (external decor) and R (Rostyle wheels, sports steering wheel, matt black bonnet, and other psychological aids to more mph).

CAPRI RS2600. 1970-72 (prod: see Capri 1300/1600). 4-seater coupé. F/R, 2637cc (V6 OHV). The original hairy version, using 150bhp fuel-injected version of the German V6 engine, alloy wheels with 6in rims, and quad headlights. Ventilated discs on later cars, and in street form it was good for 125mph with 0-60 coming up in 8.2 secs. Ancestor of the British made RS3100 (3091cc) made in 1973-4.

FRAZER NASH (GB)

A company with a reputation far larger than it deserves on the basis of the number of cars built. Like so many British sports car firms of the 1920s, it suffered several financial crises. Cars built in the 1930s were mainly stark, unsophisticated and fast, but by 1936 the majority of cars coming through the Isleworth showrooms were BMWs with Frazer Nash badging. After 1945, Frazer Nash sports cars were modern and sophisticated, using a development of pre-war BMW running gear: by the time production ceased the cars, which had never been cheap, were just far too expensive to be competitive.

◄ **LE MANS REPLICA/LE MANS REPLICA II. 1948-52/1952-53 (prod: 34). Competition 2-seater. F/R, 1971cc (S6 OHV).** Originally the 'High Speed', but given a new name after its 1949 Le Mans third place. Stark Bristol-powered (three carburettors and 120bhp) bolide with cycle wings: engine differs from 'cooking' versions in having bigger valves and ports, magnesium sump. Later Mk II even starker, with 125bhp and de Dion back end. Very much a classic, *ergo* expensive.

FAST ROADSTER/MILLE MIGLIA. 1948-49/1950-52 (prod: 11). Sports 2-seater. F/R, 1971cc (S6 OHV). Four-bearing 18-pushrod Bristol unit derated to 90-100bhp on an 8 to 1 cr for this model, with aerodynamic body and front-wing mounted spare wheel, but still good for over the ton. Synchro 'box has the old BMW/Bristol feature of a free-wheel on bottom. Specifications vary from car to car: Mille Miglia family includes two one-off dropheads (1949 and 1950 show models). ►

◄ **TARGA FLORIO. 1952-56 (prod: approx 14). Sports 2-seater. F/R, 1971cc (S6 OHV).** Mille Miglia replacement with full-width light-alloy body in classical 'Nash tubular frame and, again, rack and pinion steering, torsion bar rear springing, and 2LS brakes. Sold with Gran Sport (125bhp) or 'Turismo' (100bhp) engines, but even the latter hauls 1800lbs at over 110mph.

FIXED HEAD COUPÉ. 1953-56 (prod: 3). 2-seater fixed head coupé. F/R, 1971cc (S6 OHV). Designed for LeMans and only production closed 'Nash ever. Usual 96-in wheelbase, de Dion back end optional. New wide grille with venetian blind, extra fins to brake drums, centre lock wire wheels and wrapround rear window. Available in any stage of tune from 100bhp to 150bhp. ►

◄ **SEBRING. 1954-56 (prod: 3). Sports 2-seater. F/R, 1971cc (S6 OHV).** Not as stark as a Le Mans Replica: suitable for roadwork or club-racing. Light (1750lbs), with 24-gallon tank. Front-end styling and centre-lock wheels as coupé: usually de Dion rear axle, too. Buyers' guide quoted 140bhp on an 8.8 to 1 cr, but every car individually tailored.

CONTINENTAL GRAN TURISMO COUPÉ. 1957-58 (prod: 2). Sports 2-seater, F/R, 3168cc (V8 OHV). Represents the company's last fling. Beautiful beast powered by BMW's V8 engine and clothed with bodywork utilising Porsche-style roof and doors. Debut was 1958 Motor Show but alas production never got under way. ➤

FRISKY (GB)

Captain Raymond Flower designed this vehicle for Meadows, well-known maker of proprietary engines. The cars were built in Wolverhampton early on, with the bodies made at the nearby Guy factory. In 1961 the firm moved to Sandwich in Kent and cars were listed until 1964, but as for so many manufacturers of micro-cars the 1950s were the Golden Age of economy.

◄ **SPORT. 1958-59 (prod: n/a). 2-seater coupé. R/R, 324cc (S2 TS).** Odd glassfibre bodied minicar with ladder frame, close-set rear wheels, no diff., chain drive, and Dubonnet front suspension. Reasonably civilised appointments. Lingered on into 1964, latterly as a three-wheeler. Specifications above cover the 16bhp Villiers twin, but some 'trikes have smaller singles (Villiers) or twins (Excelsior).

GILBERN (GB)

One of the firms successfully to make the transition from producing kit cars to genuine complete cars – even though some were sold in component form to beat purchase tax. Gilbern was started in 1959 by Giles Smith and Bernard Friese, and they marketed some fine sporting products until 1973. It was the death of Wales' last manufacturer.

GT. 1959-67 (prod: approx 280). 2+2-seater coupé. F/R, 948cc/1558cc/1622cc/1798cc (S4 OHV). Welsh-built kitcar: handsome little machine with glassfibre body on a tubular frame with Austin A35 front suspension, MG four-speed 'box, and BMC back end with live axle and coils. Some with 1098cc Coventry-Climax: other units A and B-type BMC. Overdrive available 1963. Good for 110mph with later MGB engine. ➤

◄ **GENIE. 1966-70 (prod: approx 200 approx). 4-seater saloon. F/R, 2495cc/2994cc (V6 OHV).** Upmarket Grand Tourer with Ford V6 engine and gearbox in usual frame with BMC rack and pinion steering and back end. All with front disc brakes: some with fuel injection. The 3-litres will top 120mph, but Genies are fairly rough-riding. Twin split fuel tanks, 6½ gallons each.

◄ **INVADER. 1969-74 (prod: approx 600). 4-seater saloon, estate car. F/R, 2994cc (V6 OHV)** Improved Genie with 144bhp carburettor Ford V6 engine: remainder of specification as before. Options include dual overdrive and automatic. GT estate cars 1971-72 only. Final Mk IIIs (1972 Show on) had overdrive, power windows as standard, and were the only Gilberns not sold in kit form. Last of the line is often the best bet.

GILL (GB)

Another dreadful English product of the 1950s, the Gill was built by the British Anzani Company in London W1. As well as the two-seater illustrated, the firm also built a four-seater seriously intended as a taxi – it was not taken too seriously, and the firm traded only for the one season, 1958.

GETABOUT. 1958 (prod: n/a). 2-seater coupé. R/R, 322cc (S2 TS). Minicoupé using the chassis and Anzani twin engine of the Astra Utility, with alloy-panelled body, all-independent springing, and hydraulic brakes. 60mpg claimed, but at £500 maybe the most expensive bubble. Almost certainly the rarest British one, too. Ever seen one? ►

GINETTA (GB)

The enthusiastic Walklett brothers, Bob, Ivor, Trevor and Douglas, made their first production vehicle, the G2, in 1958. Before 1968, the cars were remarkably successful in club racing, and thereafter the firm's most popular product was the G15 coupé, with Hillman Imp power unit, until the imposition of VAT in 1973 killed the fiscal attraction of component cars.

◄ **G4. 1961-68 (prod: approx 390). Sports 2-seater coupé. F/R, 997cc/1498cc (S4 OHV).** 1000lb (or less) sporting kit-car with Ford mechanics in a tubular space frame with front disc brakes and all-coil springing, independent at the front. With a tuned 1500, it gave 115mph and 0-50 in under 7 secs, plus handling to match. Revived in Mk IV guise, 1981.

G15. 1967-74 (prod: 796). 2-seater coupé. R/R, 875cc (S4 OC). Mechanics and suspension are Hillman Imp, which means that lovely 'box. Putting the engine ahead of the rear axle improves the handling, and you get front disc brakes, denied to Imp owners. 55bhp spells 100mph and 40mpg, though avoid very early ones without the frontal radiator, as they run hot. ►

GITANE (GB)

Produced for one season only, 1962, by G. F. Plant at West Bromwich, this was an ambitious attempt to produce a Mini based GT coupé. However, the price was too high for any market impact, and plans to develop the Italian Giannini engine fell through. The car was mooted as an Engish Abarth.

GT. 1962 (prod: 6). 2-seater coupé. R/R, 997cc (S4 OHV). Looks and sounds Italian, but made by a dumptruck builder from Wolverhampton. Mini mechanics at the back of a tubular spaceframe, Mini suspension, inboard disc brakes at both ends, centre-lock wire wheels, and fuel tanks up front. Said to do 135mph, and production planned with an Italian dohc Fiat-Giannini engine.

GLAS (D)

Hans Glas GmbH was an old established manufacturer of agricultural machinery when it started making the Goggo scooter in 1951, following it up with production of the Goggomobil in 1955. Throughout the 1960s, the firm produced a full range of GT and saloon cars. In 1967 BMW acquired Glas and the marque name disappeared in 1968.

GOGGOMOBIL T300/400. 1955-67/1955-69 (prod all types: 280,739). 2-door saloon. R/R, 296cc/395cc (S2 TS). Rather more than a bubble, with room for two children in the back, a differential rear axle, Mini-size wheels, and hydraulic brakes. Four-speed motorcycle-type 'box standard, but some with Getrag preselectors. 250cc type not sold here: imports ceased 1963/4.

GOGGOMOBIL TS300/TS400. 1957-67 (prod: see T300/T400). 2-seater coupé. R/R, 296cc/395cc (S2 TS). Amusing little 970lbs coupé Goggo with same platform chassis and mechanics. Faster than saloons (60mph) but remembered for rather hairy oversteer. Most British-market ones had temperamental Getrag electric preselectors with 'square' dash quadrants, but stock dog-clutch 'box also listed: Imports to 1963 only.

T700. 1954-65 (prod all types: 87,000). 2-door saloon, station wagon. F/R, 688cc (S2 OHV). Conceived as fwd, but produced to conventional layout with beam rear axle, and a rather uninteresting 60-65mph from 30bhp. Never caught on in Britain. Smaller T600 (584cc, 20bhp) not marketed here: nor, unfortunately, were the later Glas 4s and V8s with cogged-belt ohc.

GORDON-KEEBLE (GB)

The Gordon was the product of John Gordon and Jim Keeble. It mated American power and reliability with European styling and chassis. The Gordon never went into production, but in 1964 a revised version, the Gordon-Keeble, went on sale. The price was set too low and the firm failed in 1965, only to be rescued in the same year. It ceased production finally in 1967.

◄**GK1/IT. 1964-66/1966-67 (prod all types: 99). Sports saloon. F/R, 5395cc (V8 OHV).** 300bhp Chevy engine in a tubular space-frame with de Dion back end, Selectaride dampers, all-disc brakes, and four-speed manual only. Bertone's shape still looks good, and the body's rustproof glassfibre. 135mph plus: model designation change merely means a change of sponsor. Nicest of the modern Euro-Americans?

GSM (GB)

This car's origins were in Capetown, South Africa, where Bob van Niekirk and Verster de Witt built the Dart. They brought the car to England and renamed it the Delta, setting up a factory at West Malling, Kent. Undercapitalisation led to the collapse of the firm in 1961, just a year after the car came to England.

DELTA. 1960-64 (prod: n/a). Sports 2-seater, sports coupé. F/R, 997cc (S4 OHV). South African design by Bob van Niekerk which lasted longer in that country than here. Mechanics Ford: tuned 57bhp 105E engine, 100E rear axle with coils instead of semi-elliptics. Coupés had breezeway rear windows like the contemporary Anglia. 100mph and 45mpg claimed: quite a successful club-racer in its day. ►

HEALEY (GB)

Before being absorbed into the BMC empire, Donald Healey produced his own cars at Warwick from 1946 to 1954. The early Riley powered cars were excellent, among the first post-war high performance British vehicles. The Nash Healey was for export only, while the Austin-engined prototype shown at Earls Court in 1952 was later to become the Austin-Healey.

◄**2.4-LITRE WESTLAND ROADSTER. 1946-49 (prod: 64). 4-seater sports tourer. F/R, 2443cc (S4 OHV).** A sensation of its time, with X-braced box-section frame, individualistic streamlined body, and all-coil springing, weighing only a ton, and capable of 105mph, thanks to the beefy high-camshaft Riley engine. Like contemporary Rileys, a bit heavy on the controls, but it's better looking than contemporary Italian creations.

2.4-LITRE ELLIOTT SALOON. 1946-50 (prod: 101). 2-door sports saloon. F/R, 2443cc (S4 OHV). 1948's fastest production closed car (110mph at Jabbeke). Perspex windows save weight and cut costs. Kite-shaped grille elegant and individual, steering is high-geared in the Riley manner, and 28mpg is within reach. For looks, though, choose the later Tickford version.

2.4-LITRE SPORTSMOBILE. 1949 (prod: 23). 4-seater drophead coupé. F/R, 2443cc (S4 OHV). Not their best effort, slab-sided and with a curious offset facia. Mechanics as before: 106bhp Riley engine, trailing link front suspension, and the full hydraulic brakes Rileys didn't yet have. Some 39 2.4s of the early post-war period also fitted with odd bodies (2-door saloon, sports 2-seater) by Duncan.

SILVERSTONE. 1949-50 (prod: 105). 2-seater sports. F/R, 2443cc (S4 OHV). The club-racer's dream: shorter frame, front anti-roll bar, stiffer springing, cycle wings, and a spartan light-alloy body with headlamps tucked away inside the grille. The recessed spare wheel doubles as rear bumper. 10-107mph in top gear quoted. High prices now for a decent one.

2.4-LITRE TICKFORD SALOON. 1951-54 (prod: 224). 2-door sports saloon. F/R, 2443cc (S4 OHV). This one has the late F chassis with Girling brakes, and is certainly the prettiest closed Healey complete with proper boot. It's also put on several hundred pounds *avoirdupois* and won't be as lively as the Elliott, though the ton is still there. Relatively common, so a possibility still at reasonable money.

2.4-LITRE ABBOTT DROPHEAD COUPÉ. 1951-54 (prod: 77). 4-seater drophead coupé. F/R, 2443cc (S4 OHV). Beautiful rag-top, still with the kite-shaped grille and Riley engine/gearbox. Chassis as for Tickford: both cars have lower overall gearing to cope with extra weight, but spacing's the same. More compact than a Riley, but unlikely to be a bargain.

NASH-HEALEY. 1951-54 (prod all types: 506). Sports 2-seater, coupé. F/R, 3848cc/4138cc (S6 OHV). US-only hybrid with SU carburettor Nash Ambassador engine, and Nash three-speed and overdrive 'box with floor change. Early ones with British bodies and horrible grilles; Pininfarina took over from '52, when bigger engine used. The odd mixture of British and US instruments on '51s is almost certainly authentic.

G-TYPE 3-LITRE. 1951-54 (prod: 25). Roadster. F/R, 2993cc (S6 OHV). A hybridised hybrid, or the marriage of an early Nash-Healey roadster to the 106bhp twin-carburettor TB21 Alvis engine/gearbox, which gave four speeds in the traditional manner. Grille neater than on Nash versions, but rather a heavy car, and the ton is hard work. Scarcity the main attraction.

HEINKEL (D)

This ex-aircraft manufacturing firm from Stuttgart enjoyed the bubble car boom in the mid-1950s. In 1958, the last year of German production, the design was sold to Dundalk Engineering in the Irish Republic, and the machine was also made later in England by Trojan. Heinkel sales died off with improvements in the German economy.

CABIN CRUISER/TROJAN 200. 1956-60/1961-65 (prod: n/a). 2-seater convertible. R/R, 174cc/198cc (S1 OHV). Isetta competitor with unitary structure, bell-crank front suspension, hydraulic brakes to the front wheels only, and a simpler front-door arrangement without the Isetta's tiresome joints. Like the Isetta, a four-stroke: bigger engine introduced during 1957. British manufacture by Trojan from 1961. Some four-wheelers made, but these aren't common.

HERON (GB)

Heron Plastics of Greenwich built its first Europa coupé in 1960, having earlier made special bodies for cars such as the Austin Seven. The car finally made limited production in 1962, and Peter Monteverdi used it as a basis for the MBM. After only 12 cars had been sold, however, the firm was wound up.

EUROPA. 1962-1964 (prod: 12). 2-seater coupé. F/R, 998cc/1498cc (S4 OHV). Pretty glass-fibre bodied special that was too cheap and complicated to last despite the assistance of Peter Monteverdi's own '64 Swiss-market version. 115mph (from 1500cc car), de-luxe interior and independent suspension all-round were plus factors but chassis problems and low price ultimately spelled disaster. A good one might be worth keeping.

HILLMAN (GB)

Makers of undistinguished cars early on, Hillman became an important part of the British motoring scene in the heyday of the Rootes brothers' empire. Founded in 1907, the firm was taken over by Rootes in 1928. The cars were always pretty conventional, but at the same time very stylish, a trend continued after World War II with, for instance, the Minx model. The Imp manufacturing facility at Linwood in Scotland was to prove disastrous, and by 1964 the giant Chrysler Corporation had acquired a majority stake in Rootes. The Hillman name disappeared in 1976, prior to the Peugeot takeover in 1979.

MINX PHASE I. 1940-47 (prod: n/a). Saloon, drophead coupé, estate car. F/R, 1185cc (S4 SV). First unitary Minx and first with alligator bonnet: in production through the War for the Services. Semi-elliptic springs, floor change, and Bendix brakes – will do 65mph but handling poor. Nasty 'twin-trim' upholstery, but sliding roofs on saloons. Estate cars very truckish, and usually Commer-badged. ➤

◄ **MINX PHASE II. 1948 (prod: n/a). Saloon, drophead coupé, estate car. F/R, 1185cc (S4 SV).** Apart from waterfall grille, recessed headlamps, revised facia and disc wheels, very like Phase I, and its unibody rusts just as well – or as badly! Plus: hydraulic brakes. Minus: the revolting Rootes 'Synchromatic' four-on-the-column. Most of them were exported, and they're very rare today.

MINX PHASE III/IV/V. 1949/1950/1951-52 (prod: n/a). Saloon, convertible, estate car. F/R, 1185cc/1265cc (S4 SV). The one with the squashed-Plymouth look, and a six-seater at a squeeze. Four lights on saloons and convertibles, plus coil ifs. Phase IV has the bigger 37.5bhp engine and separate sidelamps: so has Phase V, recognisable by some side chromium trim and a proper, floor-mounted handbrake. ➤

◄ **MINX PHASE VI. 1953 (prod: n/a). Saloon, convertible, Californian coupé, estate car. F/R, 1265cc (S4 SV).** 21st anniversary model for Coronation Year. Changes are new oval grille, carburettor hot spot, two-spoke steering wheel and revised combustion chambers. No more noticeable urge, though. The one to look for is the snazzy Californian hardtop in tasteful two-tones, a real baby Plymouth.

MINX PHASE VII. 1954 (prod: n/a). Saloon, convertible, Californian coupé, estate car. F/R, 1265cc (S4 SV). Last of the regular flathead Minxes, though watch it, 1955's Phase VIII Special (saloons, estates, only) is really only a leftover '54 with simplified trim and low-ratio back end. You can tell a VII by the combination of the '53 grille with longer rear wings and a bigger boot. Only convertibles and Californians of any interest. ➤

MINX PHASE VIII/VIIIA. 1955-56 (prod: 93,609 all variants including SV). Saloon, convertible, Californian coupé, estate car. F/R, 1390cc (S4 OHV). Ohv at last, though not for Specials till '56. Suspension revisions plus 15ins wheels; the latest square-dimensioned engine pushes top speed well into the 70s, though it's a trifle thirsty. Phase VIIIA 'Gaylook' (1956 de luxe line) with two-toning and more side chrome. Estate cars made well into 1957.

HUSKY I. 1955-57 (prod: approx 38,000). Estate car. F/R, 1265cc (S4 SV). Best described as a sawn-off, austerity-specification van with seats and windows, only just over 12ft long. Low gearing means brisk traffic pick-up even on 35bhp, but handling ghastly. More economical than most Minxes, but rust has decimated their ranks. Also made as Commer Cob delivery van.

HUSKY II/III. 1958-63/1963-66 (prod: n/a). Estate car. F/R, 1390cc (S4 OHV). The old Husky theme with the mid-56 Minx styling and the new ohv engine. An extra 4ins of length helps the handling a bit, but still only a workhorse. Commer van versions again listed. Series III (late '63) has lower bonnet line and greasing points deleted.

MINX SERIES I/II. 1956-57/1958 (prod: n/a). Saloon, convertible, estate car. F/R, 1390cc (S4 OHV). The Sunbeam Rapier's sculptured styling, wrap-round screen, better looks, and more room. Hydraulically-actuated clutches now, but no Californians, and new-style wagon doesn't arrive till June '57. Austere Special (1957 on) has bucket seats and (thank goodness) floor change. Latticed grilles and Manumatic two-pedal option on Series II.

MINX SERIES IIIA/IIIB/IIIC. 1958-60/1960-61/1961-63 (prod: n/a). Saloon, convertible, estate car. F/R, 1494cc/1592cc (S4 OHV). Facelift with new grille and tail fins, plus floor change, bigger brakes and a semi-automatic option on 1960s. Series IIIB with hypoid rear axle, replaced in July '61 by 1.6-litre IIIC. Convertibles and estates dropped in the summer of '62.

MINX SERIES V/VI. 1963-65/1965-67 (prod: n/a). Saloon. F/R, 1592cc/1725cc (S4 OHV). Last of the '56 shape with the bonus of front disc brakes: 1959's fins are out, but the new razor edge roofline suits the car. Borg Warner is now the automatic option instead of Smiths Easidrive; all synchromesh back (first time since '38) for 1965. Bigger five-bearing engine in Series VI. ➤

◄ **SUPER MINX SERIES I/II/III/IV. 1962/1963/1964-65/ 1966 (prod: n/a). Saloon, convertible, estate car. F/R, 1592cc/1725cc (S4 OHV).** Elongated Minx, initially with 1.6-litre engine, tail fins, and Smiths Easidrive option. Front disc brakes and Borg Warner auto option on Series II, all-synchro 'box on Series III, six-light saloon styling '65, and 65bhp 1.7-litre unit in final Series IV. Only convertibles (March '62-June '64) of any interest.

IMP/SUPER IMP. 1963-76 (prod all types: 440,032). 2-door saloon. R/R, 875cc (S4 OC). The tragedy of our times, or what might have been if it hadn't been three years behind the Mini. Lovely enginę, superb gearbox, but lots of minor troubles including the pneumatic throttle and interior trim held together by self-untapping screws. Super (1965 on) identifiable by chrome rubbing strips and mock grille between headlamps. ➤

◄ **IMP CALIFORNIAN. 1968-70 (prod: see Imp/Super Imp). 4-seater coupé. R/R, 875cc (S4 OC).** Nice little plunging-roof coupé that came along after the worst bugs had been sorted out. The usual 75-80mph and 45mpg, but handling can be funny in the wet, and watch for rust. Sunbeam Stiletto is the same car, but has the Sports engine and really goes like stink.

HUSKY. 1967-70 (prod: see Imp/Super Imp). Estate car. R/R, 875cc (S4 OC). Rare station wagon member of the family, also sold as a van with Commer badging. Quite a lot of room, thanks to the slanted mounting of the 39bhp Coventry-Climax based ohc engine. Probably hairy if driven fast on full load. ➤

HUNTER. 1966-67 (prod: n/a). Saloon, estate car. F/R, 1725cc (S4 OHV). A hardy perennial (it lived to be a Chrysler) with a wedge shape subtly more attractive than the Ford Corsair's: Fordlike strut front suspension, too. 74bhp from the latest five-bearing alloy-head engine. Front disc brakes always standard, with overdrive and automatic options. Lighter than the old Super Minx, and much nicer to drive. ➤

◄ **NEW MINX. 1967-70 (prod: n/a). Saloon, estate car. F/R, 1496cc (S4 OHV).** A dull end for a near-immortal name – just a stripped Hunter with smaller, 60bhp engine and no overdrive option. Servo brakes available (also on Hunter) from May '68, so better to avoid earlier examples of either. Hunters better equipped and generally preferable.

AVENGER. 1970-76 (prod: n/a). Saloon, estate car. F/R, 1248cc/1498cc (S4 OHV). Lived on to become a Chrysler and even a Talbot before its demise in '81. All coil springing (McPherson at the front), rack and pinion steering, and front disc brakes with servo option. Automatic available on up-market editions, including the twin-carb 1.5-litre GT. 2-door saloons and high-performance Tigers 1973, bigger engines from 1974. ➤

HONDA (J)

Unlike so many maufacturers in Europe who turned from motorcycle production to car making early on, Honda only started volume car making in 1962. Until that time, it was the most successful motorcycle maker in the world. Alongside that foray into passenger cars, Honda took the plunge and entered Grand Prix racing, with some success, although not as much as it hoped. 1960s cars were a bit of a joke in western eyes, but since the early 1970s the firm has acquired a reputation for making the Japanese cars most acceptable to European taste, and is now liaising heavily with Austin Rover in a number of areas.

◄ **S600. 1966-70 (UK imports: 1350). Sports 2-seater, sports coupé. F/R, 791cc (S4 DOC).** A little bomb, with a tiny inclined hemi-head, roller bearing engine pushing out 70bhp at 8000rpm, and four horizontal carburettors fed by electric pump. Torsion-bar ifs, servo front disc brakes, and a potential of around the ton. UK-available from '67. Somewhat fragile, but already a cult object.

N360/N600. 1968-74 (UK imports: 1145/7860). 2-door saloon. F/F, 354cc/598cc (S2 OC). Japan's answer to the Mini, only with half the number of cylinders, air cooling, and a beam rear axle. Servo brakes a bonus on the N600, which will top 80 on 45bhp. Both models available with three-speed Hondamatic. N360 not imported after 1970. ➤

HOTCHKISS (F)

Benjamin Hotchkiss, an American, set up this firm in 1867 at St Denis in France to make armaments. The company branched out into car production in 1903 as a result of an arms slump. All early products were medium to large touring cars, but the UK factory established during the Great War supplied engines to W.R. Morris's concern. 1920s cars were fine machines indeed, as were some of the 1930s products. Just before World War II, it acquired Amilcar, but the war was really to kill off Hotchkiss, along with the expensive mistake of producing the Gregoire flat-four, which gave endless teething problems.

◄ **686. 1936-52 (prod: n/a). 2-door sports saloon, 4-door saloon, limousine, 4-seater cabriolet, F/R, 3485cc (S6 OHV).** Post-wars were to all intents and purposes as pre-war cars: however, just to confuse, 1950 cars were renamed 2050s and fitted with new, sleeker coachwork *à la* Talbot GS. Still winning Monte Carlo rallies after 1945, rare and attractive with a really long lasting engine.

2050. 1950-54 (prod: n/a). Saloon, cabriolet. F/R, 3485cc (S6 OHV). Tough Monte Carlo rally winner with a pedigree going back to 1929, briefly back in England in its final form, with vertical coil ifs, auxiliary coil springs at the back, synchromesh or Cotal 'box, and facelifted styling – vee screen and recessed headlamps. Suddenly it's 1935 again, but the scarce 130bhp short chassis Grand Sport is still a desirable classic. ➤

HRG (GB)

HRG was probably the only company that made a point of producing the same design after World War II as it had marketed before it. Founded in 1936 by Ron Godfrey, Guy Robins and E.A. Halford, the firm's first cars were intended to carry on the Frazer Nash tradition, and that they did until 1956, when the firm concentrated on general engineering.

◄ **1100. 1939-50 (prod: 49). Sports 2-seater. F/R, 1074cc (S4 OC).** Wonderful traditional sports car with slab tank, proper instruments, beam axles, quarter-elliptic front springs, and an engine 6ins behind the axle. Singer Nine engine very extensively reworked by HRG, but though you get synchromesh and coil ignition, brakes are still cable-operated mechanicals.

1500. 1939-55 (prod: 138). Sports 2-seater. F/R, 1496cc/1497cc (S4 OC). 1100 with bigger, 61bhp Singer unit, giving 80-plus mph. (Earlier models had 4ED Meadows engines and magneto ignition). Superb steering and early thirties looks are ample reward for a harsh ride. Last 12 cars (WS series, 1953 on) have fractionally larger SM engine, hypoid axles, hydraulic brakes. ►

◄ **1500 AERODYNAMIC. 1946-48 (prod: 30). Sports 2-seater. F/R, 1496cc (S4 OC).** 1500 with full-width, slab-sided body which cuts down drag but has other headaches, including self-destructive scuttle shake and variable weight distribution, thanks to putting the spare wheel opposite the fuel tank at the rear. Some since reconverted to standard bodies, and curiosity value only. Hurgs should look like Hurgs.

TWIN CAM. 1955 (prod: n/a). Sports/racer. F/R, 1497cc (S4 DOC). A totally different HRG, and the last gasp from this Tolworth-based concern. Twin tube chassis, light alloy, full-width bodywork, magnesium wheels and 108bhp version of Singer twin-cam engine. Some evidence that more than just the prototype built. ►

HUMBER (GB)

Another of the Rootes stable, Humber was always at the upper end of the market. Like many Midlands car firms, Thomas Humber's concern made bicycles, until 1898 when an experimental venture appeared, followed by a line of forecars. Up to 1908, there were two factories, one in Beeston, Notts, the other in Coventry. In 1930 Rootes took over. The classic Humber, the Super Snipe, came in the late 1940s, and typified a range of luxurious saloons which were used as official cars at the top end and as superior bank managers' carriages at the bottom. By 1964 the firm had been taken over by Chrysler – indeed, from 1968 on the only Humber produced was an up-market version of the Hillman Hunter, a far cry from the glory days of official limousines. Following the Chrysler sell-out to Peugeot-Talbot the name has gone the way of so many famed British marques – into the bin.

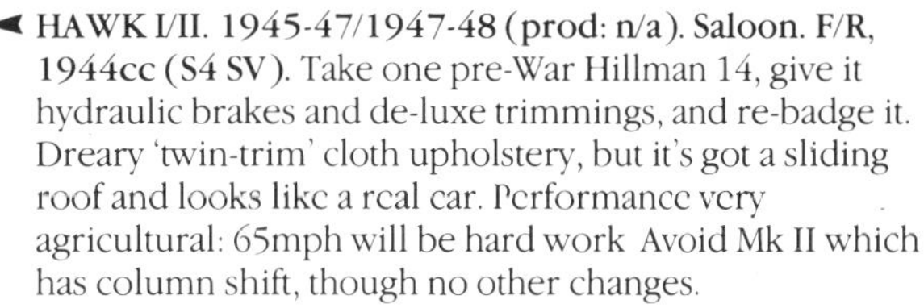

◄ **HAWK I/II. 1945-47/1947-48 (prod: n/a). Saloon. F/R, 1944cc (S4 SV).** Take one pre-War Hillman 14, give it hydraulic brakes and de-luxe trimmings, and re-badge it. Dreary 'twin-trim' cloth upholstery, but it's got a sliding roof and looks like a real car. Performance very agricultural: 65mph will be hard work Avoid Mk II which has column shift, though no other changes.

SNIPE/SUPER SNIPE I. 1945-48 (prod: n/a). Saloon. F/R, 2731cc/4086cc (S6 SV). Six-cylinder Hawks with cruciform-braced frames and disc, not steel-spoke wheels. Snipes use leftover 1936-7 18hp units, and not the 20.9hp type fitted just before the War. Better go for the 100hp Super, which'll accelerate away from a standstill to 80-plus in top. ►

◄ **PULLMAN I. 1945-48 (prod: n/a). Limousine, Sedanca de Ville. F/R, 4086cc (S6 SV).** Civilian version of wartime staff car, with the familiar transverse-leaf ifs and hydraulic brakes. Thrupp and Maberly's razor edge styling attractive, and unlike later Pullmans it's less than 17ft long. 12-14mpg a deterrent. H.J. Mulliner did the rare sedanca with full-flow wings and electric division.

HAWK III. 1949-50 (prod: n/a). Saloon. F/R, 1944cc (S4 SV). Americanised styling, with four-light bodywork, curved screen, and atrocious arcuate instrumentation, though leather and sliding roofs are still with us. Coil ifs a marked improvement, but the dreadful four-on-the-column has come to stay, and retention of the 1.9-litre flathead engine guarantees nil performance. ►

SUPER SNIPE II/III. 1949-50/1951-52 (prod: n/a). Saloon, touring limousine, drophead coupé. F/R, 4086cc (S6 SV). Not such a radical update as the Hawk's though headlamps are in the wings, there's a big rear window, and four-on-the-tree, of course. Transverse front suspension is retained. Tough and reliable, but thirsty. Dropheads (1949-50 only) by Tickford and covetable. Touring limousine from '51.

PULLMAN/IMPERIAL II/III. 1948-53/1950-53 (prod: n/a). Limousine, 7-seater saloon. F/R, 4086cc (S6 SV). 17ft 6in long, and updating as per Super Snipe II, with a two-piece propshaft necessitated by the extra wheelbase. Definitely for vintage-minded morticians. Imperials (from 1950) have no division: Mk III (1951) comes with an all-synchromesh gearbox.

HAWK IV/V. 1951-52/1953-55 (prod all types: 8866). Saloon, touring limousine. F/R, 2267cc (S4 SV). 1949 Hawk with bigger sv engine and higher-geared steering. No other changes on Mk IV, but 70mph now possible if laborious. Reasonably rustproof, but later ohv cars preferable. Touring limousines only on Mk V, which has minor front end styling changes.

SUPER SNIPE IV. 1953-56 (prod: 5286). Saloon, touring limousine. F/R, 4138cc (S6 OHV). First Humber with all its valves upstairs, courtesy the Commer truck range: seven main bearings and 113-116bhp, or 95-100mph. All-synchro 'box, wood facias from April '54, overdrive available from '55, and automatics optional for 1956. Heavy on the hands and don't expect better than 14/15mpg.

PULLMAN/IMPERIAL IV. 1953-54 (prod: n/a). Limousine, 7-seater saloon. F/R, 4138cc (S6 OHV). Last of the Pullmans with the 116bhp Blue Riband engine and all-synchro 'box. Limousines now available with power-operated divisions. Very rare indeed, but a very big car and no fun whatever to drive. Only Imperials ever seen in any shade other than black.

HAWK VI. 1954-57 (prod: n/a). Saloon, touring limousine, estate car. F/R, 2267cc (S4 OHV). A Mk V with 70bhp ohv engine (detuned Sunbeam 90), bigger brakes, and extended rear wing line: estate cars from late '55. Still pretty stodgy (0-50mph takes 15.3secs), but they've still got separate chassis frames and last well. Overdrive, but not as yet automatic option.

HAWK I/II/III. 1957-64 (prod: n/a). Saloon, touring limousine, estate car. F/R, 2267cc (S4 OHV). Unitary construction models with four-on-the-column, American styling, recirculating ball steering, and 110ins wheelbase. Looks like a luxury US compact. Automatic now on the options list. Mk II (1961) with servo front disc brakes: Mk III (mid '62) with minor styling changes and a dual-over-drive option.

SUPER SNIPE I. 1959 (prod: n/a). Saloon, touring limousine, estate car. F/R, 2655cc (S6 OHV). Luxury version of the unitary Hawk with 'square' six-cylinder engine, hydrovac brakes and three-speed 'box. Usual overdrive and automatic options, but this one is a little gutless, so the later 3-litre editions are to be preferred.

SUPER SNIPE II/III/IV. 1960-64 (prod: n/a). Saloon, touring limousine, estate car. F/R, 2965cc (S6 OHV). All the wood and leather you can ask for within, plus a quiet 95-100mph, but this one pitches madly, and handling is generally a weak point. All have servo front disc brakes, but Britain's first (?) quad headlights came on Series III (1961), and Series IV (1963) has a bit more power.

HAWK IV. 1965-67 (prod: n/a). Saloon, Touring limousine, estate car. F/R, 2267cc (S4 OHV). Last of the family, with six-light, more angular styling, deeper 'screen, rear anti-rollbar, and synchromesh on bottom, though the depressing column shift is retained and most people will prefer automatic. Arguably the best looking Hawk.

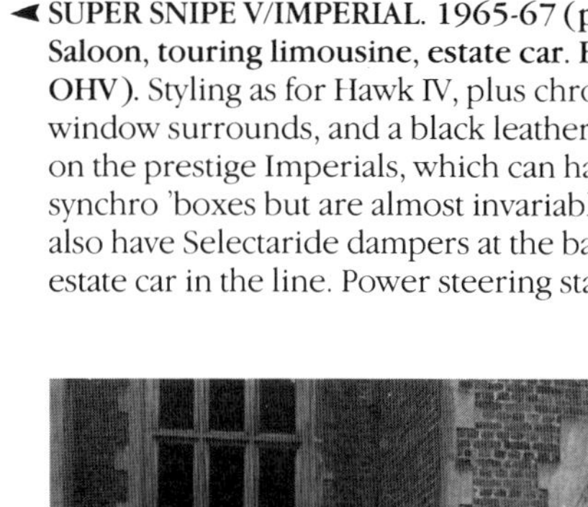

◄ **SUPER SNIPE V/IMPERIAL. 1965-67 (prod: 4055). Saloon, touring limousine, estate car. F/R, 2965cc (S6 OHV).** Styling as for Hawk IV, plus chromium plated window surrounds, and a black leatherette roof covering on the prestige Imperials, which can have four-speed all synchro 'boxes but are almost invariably automatic. They also have Selectaride dampers at the back, but there's no estate car in the line. Power steering standard on all cars.

SCEPTRE I/II. 1963-65/1966-67 (prod: n/a). Saloon. F/R, 1592cc/1725cc (S4 OHV). Curious and not unattractive cross between a Super Minx and a Rapier with the former's 4-door bodyshell and the latter's grille. Quad headlights, dual overdrive, and servo front disc brakes standard: twin carburettors only on some very early Series Is. Automatic option only on the big-engined Series II. ►

◄ **SCEPTRE. 1968-76 (prod: n/a). Saloon. F/R, 1725cc (S4 OHV).** The ultimate in badge engineering, or merely a jazzed-up Hillman Hunter with twin carburettors, quad headlights, twin reversing lamps, and four-speed all synchro 'box with dual overdrive. Maybe some scarcity value, but dubious. No estate cars before late '74.

INVICTA (GB)

A short postwar life was the fate of this firm. By 1950, AFN Ltd had taken over its assets after the failure of the horribly expensive luxury Black Prince model. Before the war, the firm, founded by Lance Macklin and Oliver Lyle in 1925, had made some very fine cars with Henry Meadows power units, but they were always extremely expensive . . .

BLACK PRINCE, 1946-50 (prod: approx 25). Saloon, drophead coupé, various specials. F/R, 2998cc (S6 DOC). Twin overhead camshafts, 12 sparking plugs, three carburettors, twin electric pumps, a 24-volt dynamotor, built-in jacks, all independent torsion-bar springing, and an infinitely variable 'hydro-kinetic turbo transmitter' which reputedly didn't like going into reverse. Superbly elegant, but much too heavy and complex to succeed. Most survivors have been converted to four-speed synchromesh, usually Jaguar. ►

ISO (I)

'Chalk and cheese' sums up Iso's car manufacturing efforts, for in the 1950s it produced the Isetta bubble cars, and then in the 1960s built a range of American V8 powered supercars, including the mighty Grifo. Both were doomed to failure, the bubble cars stopping in 1955, the muscle cars winding down in 1978.

◄ **RIVOLTA. 1962-70 (prod: 797). 2-door sports saloon. F/R, 5359cc (V8 OHV).** Italian equivalent of the Gordon-Keeble with the same Chevrolet engine in a box-section frame with de Dion back end, all-round servo disc brakes, and a top speed of around 140mph. Restrained good looks not always found on Italian supercars. Options include centre-lock wire wheels, five-speed and automatic 'boxes, and air conditioning.

GRIFO/GRIFO 7-LITRE. 1963-74/1969-74 (prod: 414/ 90). 2-seater coupé. F/R, 5359cc/6998cc (V8 OHV). Bizzarrini designed two-seater in a shortened (98in) wheelbase version of the Rivolta chassis with the same power train, and the same automatic or five-speed options. 7-litre versions very rare, but good for some 170mph on 390bhp. Not for purists, but American bits cost less than blue-blooded Italian ones. 1973s and 1974s have Ford engines instead of Chevrolet. ►

◄ **FIDIA. 1969-74 (prod: 192). 4-door saloon. F/R, 5359cc (V8 OHV).** Family version of the Iso theme on a long wheelbase. Limited slip differential standard, as is four-speed all-synchro 'box, though usual transmission options listed. Not as handsome as de Tomaso's rival Deauville. Ford engines from '73.

LELE. 1970-74 (prod: 317). 4-seater coupé. F/R, 5359cc (V8 OHV). Fastback GT to replace the original Rivolta: conservatives may prefer the older shape. For, mechanical spares relatively easy: against, no Club in England, heavy fuel bills, and defunct factory. Ford engines (5.8-litre) from 1973, though at least if you get a late automatic Iso with either unit it won't have that deplorable Powerglide. ►

JAGUAR (GB)

Now one of the truly great marques, yet Sir William Lyons' firm had pretty inauspicious beginnings. The SS (Swallow Sidecar) Company produced 'Jaguar' models before the war, but it was only after 1945 that Lyons changed its name. Throughout the 1950s and 1960s, the firm made svelte sports cars and sporting saloons which provided value for money second to none. Daimler was acquired in 1960, followed by Guy, Coventry-Climax and Meadows, although in 1966 Jaguar merged with BMC to form British Motor Holdings, before being taken over by Leyland in 1968. Jaguar has now regained its autonomy, and in 1984 was floated on the Stock Exchange.

◄ **1½-LITRE. 1938-49 (prod: 12,713 including pre-war). Saloon. F/R, 1776cc (S4 OHV).** Best-selling economy model with the same roomy body and luxury appointments as the sixes. Should return 26mpg and it's got odd refinements like a manual advance-and-retard. Against, a laboured 70mph and negligible acceleration. Pre-war cars are SS-badged and don't have heaters. No dropheads post-war.

2½-LITRE. 1938-48 (prod from 1936: 7222). Saloon, drophead coupé. F/R, 2664cc (S6 OHV). Pure traditional and the same as late-pre-war cars apart from the Jaguar badges and hypoid rear axles. Seven-bearing engine should last for ever, if dural rods have been replaced by steel. Rot in the body frame is a more likely problem. Very few dropheads (1947/8) in our period, and they almost all went for export. ►

3½-LITRE. 1938-48 (prod: 5424 including pre-war). Saloon, drophead coupé. F/R, 3485cc (S6 OHV). The 2½ with some more power and a 90-95mph potential, ◄ though be prepared for a 15mpg thirst. Very elegant, and centre-lock wire wheels are standard equipment. Brakes mechanical and pedal pressure formidable. Cockpit fumes a problem. Unless you're in a real hurry, the 2½'s quite adequate.

MK V 2½-LITRE/3½-LITRE. 1949-51 (prod: 1675/8791). Saloon, drophead coupé. F/R, 2664cc/3485cc (S6 OHV). Charming transitional model with the old pushrod engine, plus XK-type torsion-bar ifs and hydraulic brakes. Restyled body gives better forward vision. Rather spongy feel, but a very forgiving car. Scarcity has boosted saloon prices to three grand odd. Dropheads? Reach for the sky... ►

◄ **XK120 ROADSTER. 1949-54 (prod: 7612). Sports 2-seater. F/R, 3442cc (S6 DOC).** The classic of post-war classics, rare here and hard to find with rhd. 120mph plus a very durable engine, but neither the drum brakes nor the original lighting equipment can really cope. Ali-bodied cars rare: others rust. Many have been heavily updated, so expect to pay handsomely for an original.

XK120 FIXED HEAD COUPE. 1951-54 (prod: 2678). 2-seater coupé. F/R, 3442cc (S6 DOC). Prettiest of the hard tops for our money, if a little claustrophobic. Like the roadsters, available from '52 with a Special Equipment package (high lift camshafts, lightened flywheel, twin exhausts, centrelock wire wheels) and output up from 160 to 180bhp. Still drum braked, of course, and rare even in the USA.

XK120 DROPHEAD COUPÉ. 1953-54 (prod: 1765). 2-seater drophead coupé. F/R, 3442cc (S6 DOC). Rarest of the 120s and introduced late, so it'll have most of the later improvements including the Salisbury back end. Proportions much better than comparable 140s and 150s. In passing, when shopping for 120s, remember that not all cars from California will be rust-free: it rains a lot in northern parts of the Sunshine State!

C-TYPE. 1951-53 (prod: 54). 2-seater sports. F/R, 3442cc (S6 DOC). Basically an XK120 with a spaceframe for a chassis and a specially tuned engine developing 204bhp. It gave Jaguar wins at Le Mans in 1951 and '53, the latter occasion using Dunlop disc brakes to give it a decisive advantage over other competitors. A classic shape, its racing pedigree and rarity make it pricey today.

MK VII. 1951-54 (prod: 20,908). Saloon. F/R, 3442cc (S6 DOC). It's a big car: nearly 2 tons laden and over 16ft long, and rust will have taken its toll. Handling that seemed marvellous 35 years ago feels elephantine today, and 16mpg can be daunting. Overdrive (optional 1954) desirable, but the early two-speed automatic (from 1953) is, mercifully, seldom seen in Britain.

MK VIIM. 1955-57 (prod: 10,061). Saloon. F/R, 3442cc (S6 DOC). As Mk VII, but with all three transmission options, power up to 190bhp, high-lift camshafts, wrap round bumpers, built in horn grilles and fitted foglamps. Overdrive on top only, as per standard Jaguar practice. The brake servo is unpredictable on all Mk VIIs, so watch it.

XK140 ROADSTER. 1955-57 (prod: 3347). Sports 2-seater. F/R, 3442cc (S6 DOC). Big news on 140s is rack and pinion steering, though you can spot the model by its heavier grille and Le Mans-winner's medallion on the boot lid. 190bhp engine standard, 210bhp and wire wheels for special-equipment cars. Only 73 made with rhd, so start saving up now if you want to shop on the home market. ➤

◄ **XK140 FIXED HEAD COUPÉ. 1955-57 (prod: 2797). 2/4-seater coupé. F/R, 3442cc (S6 DOC).** Improvements as for XK140 roadster plus an extended roofline which spoilt the looks in return for a pair of occasional seats or more luggage space. Prettier than the XK150, but the same scuttle, wing and sill rusting problems which'll have had more time to develop. A few (less than 400) late cars with automatic.

XK140 DROPHEAD COUPÉ. 1955-57 (prod: 2740). 2/4-seater drophead coupé. F/R, 3442cc (S6 DOC). Like the fixed-head, a very occasional four-seater though the result is more elegant. Rarest of the three variants, though not in rhd form: 479 as against the handful of roadsters and 843 fixed-heads. Again, a handful of late automatics, though overdrive tends to be the rule. No 140 should have disc brakes. ➤

◄ **2.4-LITRE MK 1. 1956-60 (prod: 19,400). Saloon. F/R, 2483cc (S6 DOC).** All-new compact unitary structure with coils instead of torsion bars at the front, and a trailing disc option from '58. Overdrive always available; automatic (avoid with this model) from 1958. For: 27mpg with careful driving. Against: rust, and plenty of Mk IIs still around.

3.4-LITRE MK 1. 1957-60 (prod: 17,340). Saloon. F/R, 3442cc (S6 DOC). A frightening beast, capable of 115-120mph and of taking off about 20mph short of this. Effectively an up-engined 2.4 with reinforced structure, identifiable by its different grille and cutaway rear wheel spats. All three transmissions available, but go for 1958s or later which will probably (but not certainly) have all-disc brakes. ➤

XK-SS. 1957 (prod: 16). 2-seater drophead coupé. F/R, 3442cc (S6 DOC). Leftover monocoque D-type racing hulls with proper furnishings, windows, hood, bumpers, and no tail fin. The disc brakes and running gear are authentic D, and so is the 250bhp dry-sump engine. There's been a lot of cross-conversion between Ds and XK-SSs, so detail specifications may vary, but you'll need a bag of gold for either. ►

◄ **MK VIII. 1957-58 (prod: 6212). Saloon. F/R, 3442cc (S6 DOC).** Refined Mk VIIM with all that model's splendours and miseries, plus an extra 20bhp which should give you 105mph plus with manual transmission. New grille, single panel curved 'screen, and two-tone finishes available as well. Manual cars now have a proper handbrake lever on the floor. Rare, but a MkIX probably does it all better.

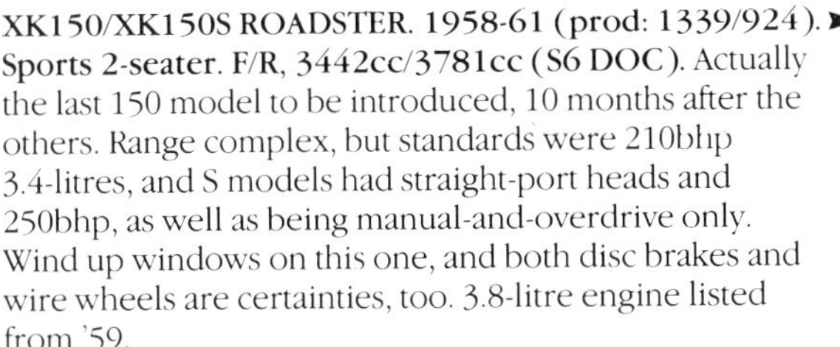

XK150/XK150S ROADSTER. 1958-61 (prod: 1339/924). Sports 2-seater. F/R, 3442cc/3781cc (S6 DOC). Actually the last 150 model to be introduced, 10 months after the others. Range complex, but standards were 210bhp 3.4-litres, and S models had straight-port heads and 250bhp, as well as being manual-and-overdrive only. Wind up windows on this one, and both disc brakes and wire wheels are certainties, too. 3.8-litre engine listed from '59. ►

◄ **XK150/XK150S FIXED HEAD COUPÉ. 1957-61/1958-61 (prod: 4101/349). 2/4-seater coupé. F/R, 3442cc/3781cc (S6 DOC).** Wider, more bulboid occasional four-seaters theoretically available with disc wheels and drum brakes, but these are seldom seen, and what you're likely to encounter is the 'Special' with wire wheels, discs, and twin foglights. All three transmissions available, except on S (1958 on) 3.8s from 1959.

XK150/XK150S DROPHEAD COUPÉ. 1957-61/1958-61 (prod: 2489/193). 2/4-seater drophead coupé. F/R, 3442cc/3781cc (S6 DOC). Development history as fixed-head, ie S from 1958, and 3.8 engines from 1959. On this one the shape is less aggressive than on hard-tops, and you could pay quite a lot less for a good one than for a roadster. Watch those sills, wings and bulkheads, though: all XKs are costly to restore. ►

MK IX. 1959-61 (prod: 10,009). Saloon. F/R, 3781cc (S6 DOC). 220bhp version of the 3.8 engine in the last of the big separate-chassis saloons, plus all-disc brakes and power-assisted steering which makes the IX more manageable than the earlier cars. Usual choice of transmissions, though automatic now in the majority: manuals therefore more expensive. 12-14mpg, alas, and the usual rust problems. ➤

◄ **MK II 2.4/3.4/3.8. 1960-68 (prod: 25,070/28,660/30,070). Saloon. F/R, 2483cc/3442cc/3781cc (S6 DOC).** Disc brakes to make it stop, a wider rear track to help the handling, and a wrap-round rear window to help the vision. By this time automatics are invariably three-speeders. Rust can quickly become terminal, but presentable cars with no inbuilt repair bills are reasonably-priced – less for a 2.4, quite a lot more for a special-equipment 3.8.

E-TYPE 3.8-LITRE ROADSTER. 1961-64 (prod: 7820). Sports 2-seater. F/R, 3781cc (S6 DOC). The true uncluttered shape. Over 140mph and rare in UK (only 760 sold). For: the best looking of the line. Against: no synchro on bottom, most of them will have rusted out. Factory hardtops available, but genuine Lightweights in unmodified form just about impossible to find. ➤

◄ **E-TYPE 3.8-LITRE COUPÉ. 1961-64 (prod: 7670). 2-seater coupé. F/R, 3781cc (S6 DOC).** As roadster, only more about, UK sales being double the open car's. Always less prized, so allowed to rust out sooner. Brakes not really up to everyday motoring at those speeds, and all twin-cam Jaguar sixes burn oil. Well preserved specimens, however, remain immensely desirable properties.

E-TYPE 4.2-LITRE. 1965-68 (prod: 9550/7770). Sports 2-seater, 2-seater coupé. F/R, 4235cc (S6 DOC). Redesigned engine with better bottom end torque and mid-range pickup, plus (at last) synchromesh on first, a/c electrics and more comfortable seats. Radial ply tyres standard from '66 models. Probably the most desirable E from an enthusiast's standpoint, but everything is now 18-years-old at least, so watch for corrosion. ➤

E-TYPE 4.2-LITRE 2+2. 1966-68 (prod: 5600). 2+2-seater coupé. F/R, 4235cc (S6 DOC). Longer by 9ins and with a proper rear door. Rear seats probably less useful than the extra luggage space for two people. Extra height spoils the looks and it isn't any collector's favourite E-type, ergo cheaper than two-seaters. If you like automatic, this is the only six-cylinder E on which you'll get it. ➤

◄ **E-TYPE 4.2-LITRE SERIES II. 1969-70 (prod: 8630/4860/5330). Sports 2-seater, 2-seater coupé, 2+2-seater coupé. F/R, 4235cc (S6 DOC).** Open headlights, rocker switches, collapsible steering column, key starting and heavy raised bumpers (though some early Series '1½' cars happened without these last nasties). Power steering optional (automatic on 2+2 only), plus twin electric fans. Detoxed 171bhp engine is, however, mercifully confined to US-market cars.

E-TYPE SERIES III ROADSTER. 1971-75 (prod: 7990). Sports 2-seater. F/R, 5343cc (V12 DOC). First volume production V12 since Lincoln (1948): 272bhp engine restores performance. Ventilated brakes and wide rims are vital improvements, but new grille imparts a heavy look, power steering is compulsory, and fuel consumption/servicing costs call for deep pockets. Collectable from the moment the last one left Coventry. Last 50 painted black with dashboard plaque to identify the heritage. ➤

◄ **E-TYPE SERIES III COUPÉ. 1971-75 (prod: 7300). 2+2-seater coupé. F/R, 5343cc (V12 DOC).** As for roadster: all cars are on the long 2+2 wheelbase and automatic optional on both types. All but very early cars have Lucas-Opus transistorised ignition, still in its infancy then. Ventilation still a weak point, so on coupé you might consider the optional-extra air conditioning.

MK X 3.8-LITRE. 1962-64 (prod: 13,382). Saloon. F/R, 3781cc (S6 DOC). Coil-spring front suspension, irs, limited slip diff, and unitary construction applied to a big Jaguar. Power steering standard: handling superior to earlier types. Usual three transmission options, though manual/overdrive uncommon and straight manual almost never seen. Large, heavy, thirsty, and it rusts. Later versions preferred. ➤

MK X 4.2-LITRE. 1965-66 (prod: 5137). Saloon, limousine. F/R, 4235cc (S6 DOC). Mk X updated with a synchronised first for manuals, the latest 4.2 engine, and the vastly superior Marles-Varamatic power steering. Only 18 limousines made. Better than a 3.8, but still on the large and heavy side for the enthusiast, as a 17 footer weighing 4200lb.

S-TYPE 3.4/3.8-LITRE. 1964-68 (prod: 9830/15,070). Saloon. F/R, 3442cc/3781cc (S6 DOC). Front end is Mk II with a revised grille, back end is Mk X with twin fuel tanks and irs. Mk X roofline doesn't improve the looks, but it handles better than a Mk II, even if it's heavier. All-synchro 'box standard from March '65. So far tends to attract special-builders rather than collectors, so could be cheaper than the older models.

240/340. 1968-69/1968 (prod: 4210/2630). Saloon. F/R, 2483cc/3442cc (S6 DOC). Cut price Mk II specification with the plastic trim and extra-only foglamps of the last IIs, plus slimline bumpers. 340s (rare) have no engine mods, but a revised cylinder head boosts the little engine's output to a useful 133bhp. If you like Mk IIs and want something that hasn't had so much time to rust out, this one is for you.

420/DAIMLER SOVEREIGN. 1967-68 (prod: 9600/5700). Saloon. F/R, 4235cc (S6 DOC). Making the S-type even more like a Mk X with a quad-headlamp nose. Alternators, limited slip diffs, and dual-circuit brakes standard, though Varamatic pas still extra. Usual choice of transmissions. More manageable than Mk X, but a lot of car. Daimler is pure badge engineering.

420G. 1967-70 (prod: 5763). Saloon, limousine. F/R, 4235cc (S6 DOC). Last and best of the Mk X family with minor styling changes and room for fuel and baggage. Limousine again rare (24 only): you're still carrying 600lbs more than on a 420, and this one is really for executives to be driven in, or for people who can't stand an XJ12's fuel bills.

XJ6 SERIES I/DAIMLER SOVEREIGN. 1969-72 (prod: 78,891/15,139). Saloon. F/R, 2790cc/4235cc (S6 DOC). Admirable, rationalised Jaguar saloon with built-in safety, ie anti-dive front suspension, Adwest rack and pinion power steering, more ergonomic facia. Straight manual very rare: overdrive commoner. Also rare is the 2.8, which suffered from overheating troubles. So far no cult for early ones, so wiser to get a Series II. ➤

JENSEN (GB)

Richard and Allen Jensen made the firm's name as coachbuilders, producing some pretty bodies on, for instance, Standard chassis before venturing into production of their own cars from 1936 onwards. These stylish and comfortable machines used Nash and Ford engines, and were followed after World War II with a prototype with Meadows power unit. It never reached production but the 1950 Interceptor coupé and cabriolet followed in the pre-war tradition, using large Austin engines. The firm built stylish and fast GT cars – after 1963 with Chrysler V8s – throughout the 1960s and '70s. The FF innovation was never really recognised, and the firm hit financial difficulties in 1976, reforming for car manufacture in 1983.

◄ **PW. 1946-51 (prod: approx 15). Sports saloon, 4-door convertible. F/R, 3860cc/4205cc/3993cc (S8/S6 OHV).** Beautiful but heavy classic with hydraulic brakes and all-coil springing (independent at the front). Original short-stroke Meadows Eight was a lemon, so first cars had leftover 1939 Nash 8s instead. Remainder have the Austin A135 unit with hypoid instead of worm-drive back end.

INTERCEPTOR. 1950-57 (prod: 25/52). 4-seater convertible, 2-door saloon. F/R, 3993cc (S6 OHV). Long-legged, high-geared tourer with slab sides and oval grille like a scaled-up A40 Sports (Jensen made those bodies too). Semi-elliptics at the rear, overdrive standard from '52 when saloon added to range. Early ones have hydromech brakes. Recapture vintage-style motoring with all mod cons. ➤

◄ **541. 1954-59 (prod: 225). 2-door sports saloon. F/R, 3993cc (S6 OHV).** All the Interceptor's virtues on a rustfree glass-fibre bodied GT which gives you 115mph plus in the 2.75:1 overdrive. Servo drum brakes on early ones, discs from late '56. The Austin engine's rustic ways suit the car, but the indirects are rustic, too. Rare, but not impossibly expensive.

541R. 1957-60 (prod: 200). 2-door sports saloon. F/R, 3993cc (S6 OHV). Best of the 541s, 123mph and 0-100 in just over 30secs. Wire wheels, disc brakes, rack and pinion steering and Armstrong piston dampers on this one. Uses the ultimate twin-carburettor version of the A135 unit (150bhp reputed) and it really will go. ➤

◄ **541S. 1961-63 (prod: 108). 2-door sports saloon. F/R, 3993cc (S6 OHV).** Longer, wider, and roomier 541, with limited slip diff, and most of the extras now standard – on later ones this spells seat belts, heated rear windows, and electric cooling fan. Maybe rather effete, especially with the standard Rolls-Royce-built Hydramatic. Very few manuals made.

CV8 MK 1. 1962-63 (prod: 70). 2-door sports saloon. F/R, 5916cc (V8 OHV). Chassis and glassfibre body (though not front end styling) ex-541, but now with Chrysler V8 engine and Torqueflite (column-selected). Very fully equipped: Powr-Lok diff, radio, reclining front seats – good for 140mph, but fearsome thirst keeps prices down today. A very few with Chrysler-built three-speed manual 'boxes. No power steering on this one. ➤

◄ **CV8 MK II/III. 1964-65/1965-66 (prod: 250/141). 2-door sports saloon. F/R, 6276cc (V8 OHV).** CV8 developments, still with the ugly slanted quad headlights and manual steering, but now with a bigger 330bhp engine. Mk II has Selectaride rear dampers, and you'll spot a Mk III by its equal-size headlamps, separate flasher units, and dual braking system. For: non-rusting plastic bodies; against: the usual Euro-American thirst.

INTERCEPTOR/SP. 1967-76 (prod: 5472/105). 2-door sports saloon, convertible. F/R, 6276cc/7212cc (V8 OHV). Vignale comes up with a modern body for the Chrysler-Jensen, but watch it, it's all-steel. All with automatic and servo discs. Power steering standard '69, 7.2 engines from '71 in luxury SP (air conditioning, stereo), from '73 in Interceptor. Convertibles from '74. Again, thirst holds prices to reasonable levels. ➤

FF. 1967-71 (prod: 320). 2-door sports saloon. F/4, 6276cc (V8 OHV). 4-wheel drive plus luxury years before the Audi Quattro, with automatic, Powr-Lok diff and power steering thrown in. Dunlop Maxaret anti-lock brakes make this one really safe in the wet. Spot it by its 4in longer wheelbase, brushed metal roof, bonnet scoop, and dual extractor vents in the front wings. Complicated and thirsty.

JOWETT (GB)

Yorkshire's finest car, but then not that many came from Yorkshire . . . Benjamin and William Jowett spent some time building experimental flat-twin engined cars between 1906 and 1913, when the little vehicle entered production. This power unit was destined for a long life, being used in cars until 1953. It was joined by a flat-four engine in 1936, but the marque's most exciting period was after 1945: both the Javelin and Jupiter were technologically advanced by the admittedly backward British industry standards of the day. The R4 sports model joined the line-up at Earls Court in 1953, but by then the firm was in financial trouble and sadly died in 1954.

BRADFORD. 1946-53 (prod: 40,995, including commercials). Estate car. F/R, 1005cc (HO2 SV). It's 1932 again! Good old Jowett flat-twin in a cart-sprung, mechanically-braked chassis, oval facia straight off a 1930 Morris, and only the three-speed synchromesh 'box to remind you of the present. Bouncy ride and flat out at 55mph, but will climb the side of a house. Wagons metal, though sometimes with varnished finish.

JAVELIN. 1947-53 (prod: 22,799). Saloon. F/R, 1486cc (HO4 OHV). Most of them will have rusted by now, but a great car for its day; all-torsion-bar springing, rack and pinion steering, and a bearable four-on-the-column. 80-plus mph, engine inaccessible and drowns in wet weather. Full hydraulic brakes from '52, also the more reliable Series III engine which most survivors have.

JUPITER. 1950-54 (prod: 899 all types). 3-seater convertible. F/R, 1486cc (HO4 OHV). Luxury drophead with swing-up bonnet/wing assembly on a space frame with Javelin mechanics apart from wishbones at the front. Always hydraulic brakes and (alas!) column shift. Mk IA (95 made 1952/4) has luggage accommodation. Too heavy, but nicely finished and drives well. Late-type engine imperative.

JUPITER R4. 1954 (prod: 3). 2-seater sports. F/R, 1486cc (HO4 OHV). Glassfibre-bodied mini-Ferrari *barchetta* weighing less than 1600lbs on an 84-ins wheelbase chassis with semi-elliptic rear springing. Overdrive plus (in 1954!) an electric fan to assist cooling, but it hardly happened at all. Ever seen one?

KIEFT (GB)

Cyril Kieft started making Formula 3 cars in 1950, progressing to produce a number of special racing sports cars in 1953. These were succeeded by the pretty Climax-engined car the following year, but Kieft himself moved into the steel industry in 1955, selling out to Berwyn Baxter: he eventually sold the assets to Burman's, who made Formula Junior cars in 1961, but 'production' ceased shortly afterwards.

◄ **1100 SPORTS. 1954-56 (prod: n/a). 2-seater sports. F/R, 1098cc (S4 OC).** Better known for his 500cc Formula 3 racers, Cyril Kieft produced a Coventry-Climax-powered Le Mans car for 1954. With all-independent suspension and a claimed max speed over 110mph this glass-fibre road going racer was later catalogued at £1560.

LAGONDA (GB)

Another great name in British motoring, and one that is still with us, even though it was bought by David Brown in 1947 and is now part of Aston Martin. Unusually for an English company, it was founded by an American, Wilbur Gunn, in 1906 at Staines. Actually Gunn first built engines and motor bicycles there before branching out into car manufacture. The firm made both light cars and more powerful tourers before 1939, but is best known for fast touring/sports cars. The David Brown takeover enabled W. O. Bentley's last design to enter production. Lagondas were made until 1963, then there was another break until 1974-5 when special Aston-Martin V8-based cars were made. The current Lagonda is a luxury Aston Martin, made since 1978.

2.6-LITRE. 1948-53 (prod: 550). 4-door saloon, drophead coupé. F/R, 2580cc (S6 DOC). W.O. Bentley design with all-independent springing and the engine later adopted by Aston Martin. Inboard rear brakes, but styling messy-traditional, weight and complication excessive, and column shift as well. Mk II (1952) has built-in jacks and minor styling changes. Early specification quoted a Cotal gearbox, but doubtful if any sold with this. ►

◄ **3-LITRE SALOON. 1953-58 (prod: 430 all types). 2-door sports saloon, 4-door saloon. F/R, 2922cc (S6 DOC).** Lagondas got the 3-litre engine before Astons – with over 3500lbs to haul, they needed it. 100mph hard work, and this one's heavy on the hands. Full-width bodies quite handsome. Four-door replaces two-door for '55, when servo brakes also added.

3-LITRE DROPHEAD COUPE. 1953-56 (prod: see 3-litre saloon). 4-seater drophead coupé. F/R, 2922cc (S6 DOC). Much handsomer than its 2.6-litre counterpart (the Duke of Edinburgh used to own one), but heavy to drive like the saloons, and too expensive to sell well. Complexity and weight make it less attractive than a drophead Aston, but if you find one it'll be less expensive, too. ►

RAPIDE. 1961-64 (prod: 54). Saloon. F/R, 3995cc (S6 DOC). Again, Lagondas get the bigger engine before Astons, this time a Touring-styled saloon on a platform frame with dual circuit servo disc brakes and a de Dion rear end with torsion bars. Non-rusting aluminium panels, but they're almost all automatics, and collectors aren't showing a lot of interest. ➤

LAMBORGHINI (I)

The most serious threat to Ferrari's image as *the* Italian supercar. However, like so many of these small manufacturers who aspire to greatness, the path has been difficult. Ferrucio Lamborghini's fortune was made from tractors and air conditioning, and his road cars were a result of an intense desire to out-Ferrari Ferrari. The Miura created a sensation when announced, literally creating the standard by which all supercars were judged, even if build quality could be below par. The 1970s were disastrous with money always tight. In 1972, a 51 per cent stake in the firm was sold, with the rest going in 1974, but it was not until the French Mimram concern took over in 1981 that the firm's finances looked altogether sounder.

◄ **350GT. 1964-67 (prod: 131). 2-seater coupé. F/R, 3497cc (V12 QOC).** Or how to try and outgun Enzo Ferrari. Elegant styling by Touring, a magnificent four-cam V12 engine and all round independent suspension should have made this the finest GT car in the world, but somehow it didn't quite come off – mainly because Lamborghini lost interest and wanted a 2+2 seater. Cue the 400GT.

400GT. 1966-68 (prod: 260 approx). 2-seater coupé, 2+2-seater coupé. F/R, 3929cc (V12 QOC). Dallara's original design – four upstairs camshafts, six dual-choke Webers, five forward speeds (synchro on reverse, too), all-independent springing and a tubular frame. Hairy and noisy, but a lovely shape unspoilt by quad headlamps, not to mention the expected 150-plus mph. ➤

◄ **MIURA. 1966-69 (prod: 475). 2-seater coupé. R/R, 3929cc (V12 QOC).** Usual suspension and four-cam engine, but this time set transversely aft, in a unitary structure. Just about the ultimate in its day, good for 170 if not the claimed 180mph, though later S/SV models are preferred by collectors.

MIURA S/SV. 1969-71/1971-72 (prod: 140/150). 2-seater coupé. R/R, 3929cc (V12 QOC). Over 375bhp now from 4-litres, and that 180mph is within reach of the S. Better finish, power windows, and leather for the British market. The 385bhp SV with wider track and enlarged wheel arches is the ultimate Miura. You'll pay handsomely even for a fairly tired specimen. ➤

ISLERO/ISLERO S. 1968-69 (prod: 125/100). 2+2-seater coupé. F/R, 3929cc (V12 QOC). Cleaned up 400GT, with retractable headlamps, power windows, and air conditioning in the usual tubular frame, plus the usual five forward speeds and limited slip diff. 160mph claimed, and probably there if you go for the S with 350bhp engine.

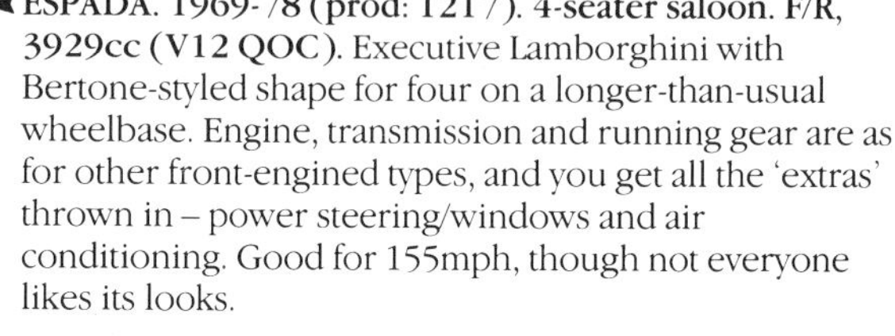

ESPADA. 1969-78 (prod: 1217). 4-seater saloon. F/R, 3929cc (V12 QOC). Executive Lamborghini with Bertone-styled shape for four on a longer-than-usual wheelbase. Engine, transmission and running gear are as for other front-engined types, and you get all the 'extras' thrown in – power steering/windows and air conditioning. Good for 155mph, though not everyone likes its looks.

JARAMA/JARAMA S. 1970-73/1973-78 (prod: 177/150). 2+2-seater coupé. F/R, 3929cc (V12 QOC). Last of the front-engined cars, best described as an abbreviated Espada with the same steel body construction. Semi-retractable headlamps, power windows, and air conditioning available, but no automatic, or power steering. S versions have 385bhp as against 350, but even with the cooking unit it'll top 160mph and hurtle up to the ton in 16.4sec.

LANCHESTER (GB)

One of the pioneer British motoring concerns, Lanchester faded after its acquisition by BSA in 1931 – the armaments and motorcycle firm also controlled Daimler. The Lanchester of 1895 was remarkable in that it was designed as a motor car from the ground-up rather than as a horseless carriage, and the Lanchester brothers' innovatory spirit can be seen in all their pre-1930 products. After that date the cars were fairly characterless, if sound, a trait which could be applied to the postwar products, which were true middle class machines. By 1956 the make had been quietly phased out of production.

LD10. 1946-51 (prod: 3050). Saloon. F/R, 1287cc (S4 OHV). Modernised retired-colonel transportation with coil-spring ifs, mechanical brakes, and the good old fluid flywheel transmission. Leather, though not wood, within, and solidly built. Briggs' original six-light body (to 1949) rusts easily: the later four-light Barker (575 made) better-looking and aluminium panelled, but much rarer.

LJ200/201. 1951-54 (prod: 2100). **Saloon, drophead coupé. F/R, 1968cc (S4 OHV).** Resembles a Daimler Conquest with Lanchester grille. Torsion-bar ifs, hydromech brakes, and one-shot chassis lubrication. Home market LJ200s are wood framed, the export LJ201 all-steel: both rust. Dropheads appeared in colour ads and at Earls Court, but apparently nowhere else. ➤

◄ **SPRITE.** 1955-56 (prod: approx 10). **Saloon. F/R, 1622cc (S4 OHV).** Odd unitary device with Hobbs automatic 'box, slab sides and a four-cylinder derivative of the Daimler Conquest engine. Original four-light prototype looked vaguely Singer, but 'production' cars six-light and too heavy. Money ran out after the first pre-production batch, but one still survives.

LANCIA (I)

Cars from the Lancia factory have always been technologically advanced, yet full of Italian *brio* and flair: to many drivers, that is an ideal combination. The firm was started by Vincenzo Lancia in 1906, and Edwardian products were mainly mid-sized tourers. The firm's reputation was made by the unitary construction Lambda of the 1920s and the amazing little Aprilia of the late 1930s. In the 1950s, Lancia made some stunning cars, but never had a good enough line-up to be competitive with Alfa Romeo or Fiat. The firm made a remarkable recovery in the early 1960s with the Flaminia and Fulvia, but mounting debts forced a sell-out to Fiat in 1969. Since then the Lancia product mix has lacked direction.

APRILIA. 1937-49 (prod: 27,642) **4-door saloon, various specials. F/R, 1352cc/1486cc (V4 OC).** Showing the rest of Europe the way ahead. Unitary construction, all round independent suspension and hydraulic brakes were part of the package, but what set it apart was its excellent interior space. Post '39s had the larger engine, and some of the coachbuilt sportscars are lovely. ➤

◄ **APPIA SERIES I/II.** 1953-55/1955-59 (prod: 20,005/ 22,424). **Saloon. F/R, 1089cc (V4 OHV).** Delightful little car with compact V4 engine (38bhp, Series I; 43bhp, Series II), unitary body incorporating some aluminium panels, and classical Lancia front suspension. Looks like an Aurelia, but mechanically simpler (beam rear axle, conventionally-located 'box, outboard rear brakes). Too expensive ever to catch on here, but a rust-free one would be a desirable property.

APPIA SERIES III. 1959-63 (prod: 55,577). Saloon. F/R, 1089cc (V4 OHV). Last of the standard models with 48bhp and split circuit brakes. Wide barred grille, bigger rear window and enlarged boot don't help the looks, but, like its rivals from Alfa Romeo and Fiat, it's a delight to drive. Again uncommon in Britain. ➤

◄ **APPIA (COACHBUILT) SERIES II/III. 1956-59/1959-63 (prod: 1755/408). Coupé (Pininfarina and Viotti), GTE and Sport (Zagato), cabriolet (Vignale). F/R, 1089cc (V4 OHV).** Floor instead of column shift on these separate-chassis 'specials': 53bhp on second series cars, 60bhp for thirds. The Zagatos apart, they are pretty little machines and rare even in Italy. Never seen with traditional Lancia grilles, and seldom with rhd, either. A potential 85-90mph.

AURELIA B10/B21/B22/B12. 1950-55 (prod: all types 12,705). Saloon. F/R, 1754cc (B10), 1991cc (B21, B22), 2266cc (B12) (V6 OHV). Jano's lovely if complex 60-degree V6 with hemi heads, four-speed synchromesh transaxle and inboard rear brakes, originally a modest 1750, but progressively uprated to 2.2-litres and 90bhp. B12 has this engine and de Dion back end instead of original irs. A lovely car, but expensive to service, and it rusts. ➤

◄ **AURELIA B20-2500GT. 1953-58 (prod: 2568). 2+2-seater coupé. F/R, 2541cc (V6 OHV).** First of the modern GTs, fast and taut-handling, but also a complicated rust-trap. Third to sixth series sold here: outputs 110-118bhp, speeds around 110mph. Fourth (1954) had de Dion rear end, fifth (1956) is detuned with a direct top gear, and sixth is uprated again. Even good ones can be surprisingly cheap.

AURELIA B24 SPYDER AND CONVERTIBLE. 1955-58 (prod: 761). 2-seater sports, 2-seater convertible. F/R, 2451cc (V6 OHV). Came with fourth series, so all will have de Dion rear axles. Fourth (118bhp) the most potent series, but these were also the first catalogued lhd Lancias and you will seldom see a right-hooker Spyder. Spyder has curved one-piece screen, convertible has hinged quarterlights. Both designed and built by Pininfarina. ➤

◄ **FLAMINIA BERLINA. 1957-70 (prod: 3424). Saloon. F/R, 2458cc/2775cc (V6 OHV).** Pininfarina-styled and, thank goodness, no pillarless doors. Short-and-long arm front suspension replaces traditional Lancia arrangements, but handling still excellent. De Dion transaxle still with us, though all but very early cars will have disc brakes. 100mph easy with the bigger engine (1963 on).

FLAMINIA COUPÉ. 1959-67 (prod: 5282). 4-seater coupé. F/R, 2458cc/2775cc (V6 OHV). Pininfarina's shape pleases, and all these'll have disc brakes. Faster than a saloon: early ones have 119bhp, and the 2.8 version (1963 on) is rated at a respectable 140bhp. Power windows too on later cars. Flaminias don't have much following anywhere as yet, and spares can be difficult. ➤

◄ **FLAMINIA GT AND CONVERTIBLE. 1959-67 (prod: 2748 all 'chassis' types). Coupé, cabriolet. F/R, 2458cc/2775cc (V6 OHV).** Sportier models on a short, 99-in wheelbase with disc brakes and limited slip diff. Bodies by Touring, 140bhp three-carburettor engine from '61, and 150bhp from 2.8-litres in '63. Longer-wheelbase GTL also '63. Attractive if complicated cars.

FLAMINIA SPORT AND SUPERSPORT ZAGATO. 1959-67 (prod: 525). 2-seater coupé. F/R, 2458cc/2775cc (V6 OHV). Probably the prettiest of the Zagato Lancias with big air intake on top of bonnet, wrap-round rear window and double-bubble roof treatment. Mechanics are problems as for other Flaminias, but servo brakes are a plus, and with the bigger engine you should manage 130mph. A few made with special 160-175bhp units. ➤

FLAVIA BERLINA 815. 1961-66 (prod: 42,434). F/F, 1488cc/1800cc (HO4 OHV). First of the complex Cemsa-Caproni-based flat-fours, with beam rear axles, and angular styling. Dual circuit servo disc brakes on all, 1.8-litre engine available '63, fuel injection option listed '65. Saloons have column change and usual rust problems: maybe you'd do better with a coupé.

FLAVIA COUPÉ 815. 1962-68 (prod: 19,293). 4-seater coupé. F/F, 1488cc/1800cc (HO4 OHV). Short chassis cars, all with quad headlights and floor change. Highly complicated range, but the Pininfarina coupé's the only one regularly seen here. (You might find a Zagato sport or Vignale convertible though.) Usually with 1800 engine: fuel injection available from '65.

FLAVIA BERLINA 819. 1967-70 (prod: 22,305). F/F, 1488cc/1800cc (HO4 OHV). Restyled and better looking: usually 1800s here. Floor change available, also fuel injection, while LX versions will have (desirable) power steering as well. Some of the last cars even with the 2-litre unit.

FLAVIA 2000 BERLINA/COUPE. 1970-74/1969-73 (prod: 15,025/6791). Saloon, 4-seater coupé. F/F, 1991cc (HO4 OHV). Back to the old shield-shape grille on the saloons, though not on the short-wheelbase coupés. Floor change standard, power steering on LX versions, and fuel injection and power windows also available. Five-speed 'boxes standard on coupé by mid '71, on saloon mid '73.

FULVIA BERLINA. 1963-64/1964-67/1968-73 (prod: 192,097 all types). Saloon. F/F, 1098cc/1216cc/1298cc (V4 OHV). Complicated range, but everything will have a slanted 13deg V4 engine, fwd, and transverse leaf ifs, plus all-disc brakes. Column change on early cars, floor shift on 80bhp GT (1967). 1.3 engine during 1968. 1969 and later models with slightly longer wheelbase and new styling. Five speeds from 1970. Usual rust problems.

FULVIA COUPE/SPORT. 1965-67/1967-76 (prod: 134,035/6170). Coupé. F/F, 1216cc/1298cc (V4 OHV). Delightful little cars with the usual formula of a shorter wheelbase for coupes: the factory body was sold here, but there were also Zagato lightweights (illustrated). Quad headlights and all-disc brakes, of course, plus five speeds from 1971. The last of the real Lancias, with not a drop of Fiat in it.

FULVIA HF. 1966-68/1968-69/1969-72 (prod: 7102). Coupé. F/F, 1216cc/1298cc/1584cc (V4 OHV). This was the full-house, if not quite same-as-works model with tuned engine, alloy panels and plexiglass windows, available UK from late '68, and therefore rhd. 108bhp from the 1.3, but with the definitive 1.6-litre there's 118-130bhp according to tune, a five-speed 'box, and 115mph.

LEA-FRANCIS (GB)

Cars appeared in fits and starts from the Lea-Francis concern, which originally made bicycles. In 1904 the firm made one car design, but it was 1920 before the next model appeared. During the late 1920s, Lea-Francis produced fine small sporting cars, but in 1935 the cash ran out, and reorganisation was needed before another sporting range came out in 1938. Updated versions of the pre-war cars were produced after the war, but they were always expensive, with limited appeal, and by 1952 the firm was in financial trouble. Several abortive attempts, including one in 1960, have been made to revive the name since.

12/14 HP. 1946-48/1946-54 (prod: 3137 inc estate cars). 4-light saloon, fixed head coupé. F/R, 1496cc/1767cc (S4 OHV). Good old 1939 theme with Riley-like twin-camshaft, high pushrod engine. Few 12s made, mechanical brakes to '51, hydraulics thereafter. Torsion bar ifs '49, headlamps recessed into front wings 1951. Coupés made 1947/48 only. Tough cars backed by an excellent spares service.

14 HP ESTATE CAR. 1946-54 (prod: see 12/14 HP). Estate car. F/R, 1767cc (S4 OHV). Solid four-door woody, sometimes sold as a purchase-tax dodging van. Mechanicals as 12/14, only it didn't get ifs until 1951, though hydraulic brakes happened a year later. Runs out of steam at 70mph, and you'll need a good joiner, but it's an excellent job compared with some of the awful bodge-ups by back garden firms fitted to forties Alvises.

14 HP SPORTS. 1947-49 (prod: 129). 2/4-seater sports. F/R, 1767cc (S4 OHV). Streamlined grille and recessed headlamps looked pure heresy in '47, but there's a thirties humped scuttle, and underneath you'll find beam axles and mechanical brakes. Twin-carburettor engine credited with 70bhp-plus pushes this one along at 85mph, and the Special Sports 14 was the basis for the first Connaughts. 12hp 1496cc engine also available.

14/70/18 HP. 1949-52/1950-53 (prod: 162/90). 6-light saloon. F/R, 1767cc/2496cc (S4 OHV). Modern, slab-sided, rather ponderous creation, originally as an export-model 14hp with torsion-bar ifs and hydromech brakes. 2½-litre 95bhp version (1950) had Riley performance if not Riley looks. Hydraulic brakes from 1952.

2½-LITRE SPORTS. 1950-53 (prod: 77). 2/4-seater sports. F/R, 2496cc (S4 OHV). The old Special Sports's 99-in wheelbase, but with torsion-bar ifs and hydromech (hydraulic from '52) brakes. In standard tune it had 100-105bhp, which spells the ton, plus the occasional rear seats lacking on an XK120 or the contemporary Riley Roadster. Another neglected classic, but with a good spares service it could be expensive to buy, too.

LYNX. 1960 (prod: 3). 2-seater sports. F/R, 2553cc (S6 OHV). Only three prototypes of this ghastly looking machine were made. Gone was the 'Leaf' engine, replaced by a Ford Zephyr unit. The original Earls Court car was finished in mauve with gold-plated fittings – enough to put anyone off, which it did, and spelt *finis* for a fine old name.

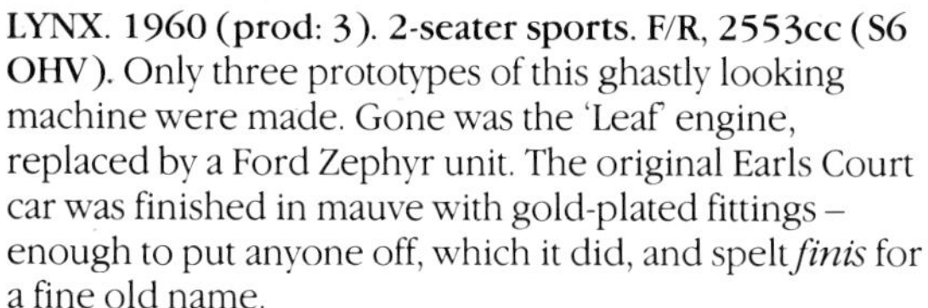

LLOYD (GB)

Production of the Lloyd car, the brainchild of Roland Lloyd, started in Grimsby in 1935 with the 350 model. The car which followed, the 650, built from 1946 on, was far more advanced. It lasted until 1950, but sales were always poor due to the car's high price.

650. 1946-51 (prod: 600 approx). 2/4-seater roadster. F/F, 654cc (S2 TS). Made in Grimsby, but appears German with its front drive, double backbone frame, rack and pinion steering, and all-coil independent suspension. Synchromesh extends to bottom and reverse and full pressure oiling means no messy petroil. Alas, 45mph is hard work. Used no proprietary parts, so spares now extinct.

LMB (GB)

Leslie Ballamy was famed from the 1930s onwards for his improvements to production chassis, especially the fitment of independent front suspensions. In 1960, 100 tubular chassis were laid down, with one model suitable for Ford sidevalve engines. They lasted until 1962, with various proprietary bodies fitted to the cars.

◄ **DEBONAIR. 1960-62 (prod: n/a). 2/4-seater coupé. F/R, 997cc/1340cc (S4 OHV).** Leslie Ballamy's well-known swing axle front suspension (a familiar pre-war Ford conversion) applied to a kit-car chassis with drilled straight side members and coils at the rear. Other mechanics Ford, with a choice of ohv Anglia or early Classic engines. Pretty glassfibre bodywork by E.B. of Tunstall. One or two still exist.

LOTUS (GB)

Now a highly respected car manufacturer and development group – Lotus has prepared prototypes for Toyota and Peugeot, for instance – the firm had very humble beginnings in Colin Chapman's lock-up garage in Hornsey. It is certainly a long way from a tuned Austin Seven to the current Esprit Turbo, but that is how far the company has come since 1952, with many Grand Prix and other racing wins on the way. From the late 1950s, Lotus has produced cars such as the Elite and Elan as well as racing machinery. The company came under the effective control of David Wickens' British Car Auctions in 1983.

VI. 1953-56 (prod: approx 100). 2-seater sports. F/R, 1172cc/1250cc/1508cc (S4 OHV). Beginning of the Seven theme: multi-tubular space frame reinforced by flat light alloy panels, usually unpainted. Specifications to builder's choice (it was sold as a kit only), but brakes and rear axle are Ford, and front suspension is by divided axle and coils. Usual engines Ford (sv Ten, Consul I) or MG (TC/TD). ►

◄ **SEVEN. 1957-64 (prod: 3300 to 1972, all types). 2-seater sports. F/R, 1172cc/948cc/997cc (S4 OHV).** As VI, and still doorless, though civilisation creeping up, and Girling hydraulic brakes standard. Almost any suitable engine will go in, but commonest for street use are the BMC A-type and the small flathead and ohv Fords. With 1172cc Ford engine and twin SUs, a typical Seven weighed 980lbs and managed 83mph.

SUPER SEVEN. 1961-69 (prod: see Seven). 2-seater sports. F/R, 1340cc/1498cc/1599cc (S4 OHV). Improved Seven with flared glass-fibre wings. Chassis and suspension still to the old formula, though front disc brakes standard by 1962. Ultra-spartan, and how fast you go depends on what you can cram under the bonnet. With a Cosworth-tuned 1500 and twin Webers (95bhp), quoted figures were 103mph and 0-50 in 7.4secs. ►

SEVEN S4. 1970-72 (prod: see Seven). 2-seater sports. F/R, 1599cc (S4 OHV). Last of the Lotus-built cars with bodywork (still doorless) in plastic, a horizontal barred grille, disc front brakes, and a dry weight of just over, 1300lbs. With Cortina GT engines you got 100mph and 0-50 in only 6.3secs. Available with rollbar and twin cam engines. Seven (S3) production transferred to Caterham Cars 1973, and still going strong.

XI CLUB/LE MANS. 1956-60 (prod: 270). 2-seater sports. F/R, 1172cc/1098cc (S4 SV/OC). Marginally street only, but quite driveable to the circuit. De Dion rear end with the Climax unit (Le Mans), live axle and coils with the 'cooking' Ford. Weather protection nil, but stabilising tail fins, and front and rear sections lift up for servicing. Coventry-Climax version did 46mpg at a constant 70mph, but that's not what you'll buy it for.

ELITE. 1958-63 (prod: 988). 2-seater coupé. F/R, 1216cc (S4 OC). Splendid unitary glass-fibre coupé with Coventry-Climax engine and Chapman struts at the rear, giving the usual Lotus combination of mph, mpg, and less-than-civilised transportation. Series II (October '60) with revised rear suspension, better trim. 83bhp SE model with close ratio ZF 'box, 1962. Same year's Super 95 has servo brakes. Later ones have fewer bugs.

ELAN SI. 1962-64 (prod: 7895, inc Series 2 and 3). 2-seater sports. F/R, 1558cc (S4 DOC). Top handler of its decade, with pop out headlamps, backbone frame, all-independent springing and discs all round. 1498cc engines of first batch all since changed to later type. Rust-free glass-fibre bodies, but the frames can rust, and though Lotus will supply new ones, it's cheaper to find a sound specimen.

ELAN S2/S3. 1964-66/1966-69 (prod: see Elan S1). 2-seater sports, coupé. F/R, 1558cc (S4 DOC). Same base specifications and general remarks, but S2 with larger front brake calipers, polished veneer facia, centre-lock wheels: only fixed heads before June 1966. S3 has higher final drive ratio plus a close ratio gearbox option. Also a Special Equipment model with 115bhp engine, c/r 'box, and servo brakes.

ELAN S4. 1968-71 (prod: 2976). 2-seater sports, coupé. F/R, 1558cc (S4 DOC). Recognisable by its wide wheel arches to take low-profile tyres, servo brakes (now standard) and rocker-type switches. Watch out for carburettor permutations, such as Strombergs between November '68 and August '69, with a reversion thereafter to Webers, and an eight-port head. ➤

◀ **ELAN SPRINT. 1971-73 (prod: 1353). 2-seater sports, coupé. F/R, 1558cc (S4 DOC).** The hot one, desirable as being younger, but still more so for its 126bhp big-valve engine giving 120mph plus and 0-60 in 6.7secs. Driveline and diff strengthened to take the extra power. Two-tone paint. A few late ones have five-speed 'boxes.

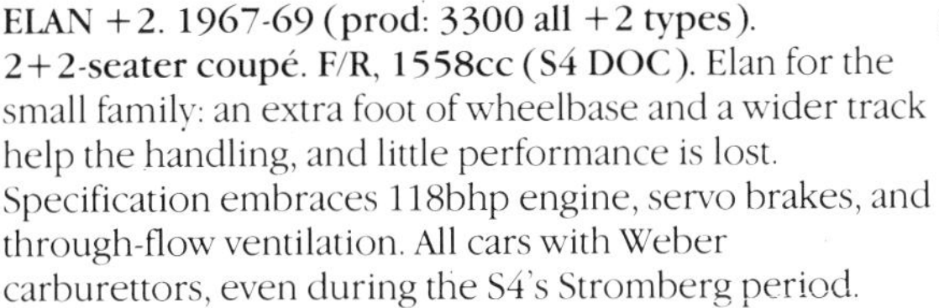

ELAN +2. 1967-69 (prod: 3300 all +2 types). 2+2-seater coupé. F/R, 1558cc (S4 DOC). Elan for the small family: an extra foot of wheelbase and a wider track help the handling, and little performance is lost. Specification embraces 118bhp engine, servo brakes, and through-flow ventilation. All cars with Weber carburettors, even during the S4's Stromberg period. ➤

◀ **ELAN +2S/130. 1971-74 (prod: see Elan +2). 2+2-seater coupé. F/R, 1558cc (S4 DOC).** A long chassis Sprint model with the 126bhp engine and matching driveline mods, recognisable by its silver topped body (this section self coloured, not sprayed as on other Lotuses). Rare 2S/130-5 version has the five-speed gearbox also fitted to late Sprints.

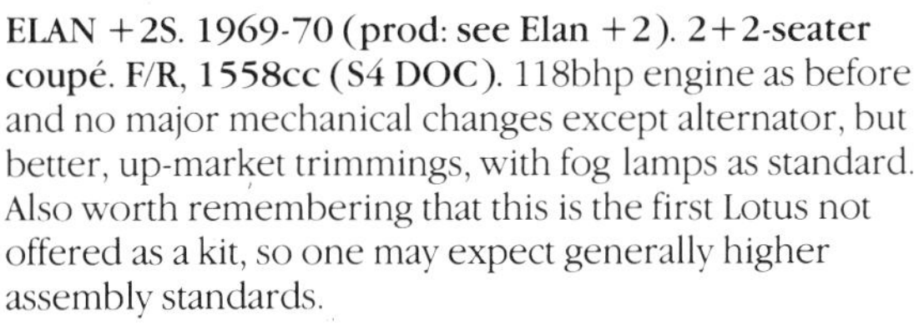

ELAN +2S. 1969-70 (prod: see Elan +2). 2+2-seater coupé. F/R, 1558cc (S4 DOC). 118bhp engine as before and no major mechanical changes except alternator, but better, up-market trimmings, with fog lamps as standard. Also worth remembering that this is the first Lotus not offered as a kit, so one may expect generally higher assembly standards. ➤

EUROPA SERIES 1/2. 1966-69/1969-71 (prod: 9230, inc later Twin Cam cars), 2-seater coupé. R/R, 1565cc (S4 OHV). Mid-engined coupé with Renault 16 engine/gearbox transferred to the other end of an Elan-type backbone. Four speeds, all-coil springing and all disc brakes. Clutch not its strong point, and avoid S1s, on which glass-fibre body is permanently bonded to chassis. S2s also have electric windows. Twin cam Lotus-Ford engine replaces Renault unit from October '71. ➤

MARAUDER (GB)

George Mackie and Maurice Wilks left Rover to set up the Marauder sports car concern in 1950, but by 1952 production had ceased. Spen King was a shareholder in the firm, but costs for the Rover P4-based machines rose faster than the price the firm thought it could sell them for.

◄ **A/100. 1950-52 (prod: 15 both types). 3-seater roadster. F/R, 2103cc/2392cc (S6 IOE).** Mechanical elements of the original Rover '75 P4 in a shorter chassis with setback engine. Some of Auntie's body panels used, also her original hydromech brakes, but not her column shift. Quadruple (!) overdrive an alternative to standard Rover synchro/free wheel. With enlarged three-carb engine, 100mph claimed.

MARCOS (GB)

This small company is still with us and has been making cars since 1959, when Jem Marsh and Frank Costin used a composite chassis and a lower body made of marine ply for their first car. The Mantis model of 1971 was timed badly and the company folded that year, but it has since been reorganised.

GT. 1960-63 (prod: 29). 2-seater coupé. F/R, 997cc/1340cc (S4 OHV). Laminated marine-ply construction, Cuprinol-coated, with wrapround 'screen, gullwing doors, and breezaway rear window. Plastic nose. Herald front suspension. Standard 10 back end, and choice of twin-carb ohv Ford engines. Front disc brakes and mag-alloy wheels optional. Opening windows and recessed headlamps came in 1962. ➤

◄ **1800/1500/1600. 1964-66/1966-67/1967-68 (prod: 99/82/192). 2-seater coupé. F/R, 1783cc/1498cc/1599cc/1650cc. (S4 OHV).** The Dennis Adams shape with near-prone seating and raked 'screen, still with laminated plywood construction. All with front disc brakes and overdrive. De Dion back end on Volvo-powered 1800, others with live axle, coils, and twin-carb Ford engines. 1650 was a Lawrencetune special unit.

MINI-MARCOS. 1965-74 (prod: approx 700). 2-seater coupé. F/F, 848cc/1275cc (S4 OHV). Mini-Jem development, and a glass-fibre monocoque shell designed to take Mini mechanics to any specification the buyer wanted. Both rubber and Hydrolastic suspensions fitted. Made 1975-81 by D and H of Oldham, but now replaced by their own Mini-based Midas. ➤

◄ **3-LITRE/2½-LITRE/3-LITRE VOLVO.** 1969-71/1971/1970-71 (prod: 80/11/250). 2-seater coupé. F/R, 2994cc/2498cc/2978cc (V6/S6 OHV). Six-cylinder steel-chassis cars retaining the Adams shape, with all-coil springing, disc/drum brakes, rack and pinion steering, and overdrive 'boxes. Ford V6 gives 140bhp and 120 plus mph. Alternative units were Volvo's straight-six and the seldom-seen 2.5-litre Triumph. An acquired taste, but they have their following.

2-LITRE. 1970-71 (prod: approx 40). 2-seater coupé. F/R, 1996cc (V4 OHV). Little known variant of the steel-chassis Marcos with Ford V4 engine rated at 85bhp with single Weber carburettor. Other specifications as for 3-litre including options (sunroof, light alloy wheels), but no overdrive. Never sold as well as the sixes. ➤

◄ **MANTIS.** 1971 (prod: 32). 4-seater coupé. F/R, 2499cc (S6 OHV). One of the most bizzare shapes ever to appear from the Adams brothers. Prototype powered by Ford V6, all others by Triumph's 2.5-litre injected engine. Luxurious, even though available in kit form, but sounded the death knell of the company.

MASERATI (I)

Now beginning to find its feet again after a long period in the doldrums, Maserati is a classic example of an Italian make with a reputation founded on quality and very little quantity. Classic racing cars, both in the pre-World War II era and just afterwards, made its name, with only spasmodic road car production (for example road versions of the A6 sports racers) until the early 1960s. Originally founded by five brothers, Maserati was taken over in 1938 by the huge Orsi industrial group, before becoming part of the de Tomaso empire.

◄ **3500GT. 1958-64 (prod: 2000 approx). Coupé (Touring), spyder (Vignale), numerous other specials. F/R, 3485cc (S6 DOC).** First Maserati attempt at a luxury GT. 230bhp and 140-plus mph. Tubular chassis, originally with four-speed 'box and servo drum brakes, but five speeds, front discs and eventually all-disc brakes introduced gradually. Latterly, more powerful fuel-injected engine became standard. Automatic option on the last cars (1964).

5000GT. 1959-64 (prod: 37). Various bodies, mainly by Allemano. F/R, 4935cc/4941cc (V8 QOC). First use of the four-cam V8: a true street model with engine derived from the 450S sports-racer. First few cars have gear-driven camshafts, four Webers, and four-speed 'box. Semi-elliptic rear springs as on all touring Maseratis of the period. All disc brakes and a new engine (chain driven camshafts) with Lucas fuel injection 1961. ZF five-speed 'boxes on most cars, top speed 170mph plus. ►

◄ **SEBRING SERIES I/II. 1962-65/1965-66 (prod: 340/98). 4-seater coupé. F/R, 3485cc/3693cc/4014cc (S6 DOC).** Vignale's quad headlamp four-seater on a 98.4ins wheelbase. Five speeds, disc brakes, fuel injection standard. 260bhp 3.7-litre and 275bhp 4-litre engines gradually introduced. Automatic, air conditioning, limited slip differential in options list.

MISTRAL. 1964-70 (prod: 828/120). 2-seater coupé, spyder. F/R, 3485cc/3693cc/4014cc (S6 DOC). Frua styled two-seaters on a short but square-tubed version of the six-cylinder chassis, with regular specification bodies very like AC's 428. All engines fuel injected. Most cars with 3.7-litre engine, 4-litre from 1967 (and quoted as standard 1968). Automatic and factory metal hardtop (for spyder) available. ►

◄ **QUATTROPORTE. 1964-71 (prod: 760). 4-seater saloon. F/R, 4136cc/4719cc (V8 QOC).** Only Italian four-door luxury saloon in its class. Four Webers, five-speed manual or automatic transmission, and all the usual options. Semi elliptics replace original de Dion rear end 1967. 4.7-engine available from '68 and air conditioning standard on latest cars. In its day the fastest four-door production saloon. Neglected classic that can still be acquired for reasonable money.

MEXICO. 1967-72 (prod: 250). **4-seater coupé. F/R, 4136cc/4719cc (V8 QOC).** Basically Quattroporte mechanics, but without the early de Dion axle, and with Vignale bodywork. Four Webers, choice of cylinder capacity, and the usual power options. Air conditioning standard 1969. 155mph. Improved Ghibli-type ventilated disc brakes on later cars.

GHIBLI. 1967-73 (prod: 119/125). **2-seater coupé, spyder. F/R, 4719cc/4930cc (V8 QOC).** Maserati equivalent of the Ferrari Daytona, with Ghia bodies. Over 170mph and one of the fastest cars of its era. Short chassis, retractable headlamps, and air conditioning. Automatic available. Still semi-elliptics at the back. 4.9-litre engine optional from 1970. Factory hardtop available for spyder.

INDY. 1969-74 (prod: 1136). **4-seater coupé. F/R, 4136cc/4719cc/4930cc (V8 QOC).** Four-seater Vignale body on 102ins wheelbase chassis of traditional Maserati configuration, with four Webers and five-speed all-synchro 'box. Headlamps retractable and power windows standard. Capable of 155-160mph. Usual options include automatic and limited slip diff.

MAZDA (J)

Like so many Japanese volume producers, Mazda is the automotive branch of a large industrial combine, in this case Toyo Kogyo Ltd of Hiroshima. The first vehicles were trucks, built from 1931 onwards, while a prototype car was developed in 1940 but never manufactured. The R-360 coupé of 1960 was the firm's first series production car. Mazda carved a name for itself by following the rotary-engined route, remaining the only major manufacturer to persevere with this form of engine. Today it has something of a reputation as an innovator, as well as being linked with Ford.

1200. 1968-70 (prod: 131,572). **Saloon, station wagon, F/R, 1169cc (S4 OHV).** Small, conventionally engineered Japanese saloon with 68bhp engine, four-speed 'box, semi-elliptic rear springing, and disc/drum brakes. Later developments have ohc or Wankel power. Seldom encountered here in the sixties.

1500. 1966-72 (prod: 121,804). **Saloon, station wagon. F/R, 1490cc (S4 OHV).** A species of near-BMW with five-bearing engine, electric pump feed, and the usual woolly recirculating ball steering. Top speed in the low 90s, front disc brakes and floor change on British market cars available from late '67. Well appointed but undistinguished.

1800. 1968-72 (prod: 39,041). Saloon. F/R, 1796cc (S4 OC). 1500 development with floor change and servo front disc brakes as standard. Bertone's styling not unattractive, and quite a good performer, but again of little interest and very few imported. ➤

◄ **110S. 1967-72 (prod: 1176). 2-seater coupé. F/R, 1964cc (Wankel).** Exciting and unusual 110mph sports car with de Dion rear end, offering 110-115mph on 110bhp. Front disc brakes, radial ply tyres and radio part of the package. Quite attractive, but watch out for early Wankel problems. Sales negligible over here.

MERCEDES-BENZ (D)

Formed in 1926 as an amalgam of the Benz and Mercedes concerns, it is held in awe by many other manufacturers, not only for its engineering integrity but also for its sales successes. The Mercedes of 1901 was epoch making, while Benz was the first volume manufacturer, so the combination of the two was always going to be formidable. In the 1920s and 1930s magnificent sports and racing cars were built alongside very mundane machines. In the 1950s the firm began to move away from more humble cars into its present-day niche of producing up-market executive saloons and coupés.

170SV/SD. 1953-55 (prod: 27,872). Saloon. F/R, 1767cc (S4 SV/OHV). Last of a complicated line dating back to 1936, with hydraulic brakes, swing-axle rear suspension, and traditional styling (exposed headlamps, side-opening bonnet). One of the first Mercedes to be imported post-war. Slow and heavy, but indestructible, especially the SD diesel variant. ➤

◄ **180/180D. 1953-62/1954-62 (prod: 118,234/152,283). Saloon. F/R, 1767cc (S4 SV/OHV), 1897cc/1988cc (S4 OC).** First post-war unitary made, listed in countless variations. OHV petrol and enlarged diesel units from 1959. SV car gutless, and rust will have taken its toll, so best go for later, more sophisticated fours.

190. 1956-61 (prod: 89,808). Saloon. F/R, 1897cc (S4 OC). Improved 180 with the same low-pivot rear springing, all synchromesh 'box with column shift, a servo-brake option, and a 75bhp ohc engine which makes it a better performer than earlier petrol cars. Diesel 190s not sold in Britain. ➤

220. 1951-54 (prod: 18,514). Saloon, fixed head coupé, 2-seater cabriolet, 4-seater cabriolet. F/R, 2195cc (S6 OC). The original 220 with 170S styling apart from its recessed headlamps and fixed bonnet sides, the latter impeding service work. 90mph and 22mpg, but available in UK only from October '53. Rhd almost never seen. Coupés and cabriolets very rare, ergo expensive. ➤

◄ **220A/220S/219. 1954-56/1956-59/1955-59 (prod: 25,937/55,279/27,545). Saloon, cabriolet. F/R, 2195cc (S6 OC).** Six-cylinder cousins of the 180 with same unitary saloon coachwork and suspension. Drum brakes on all, servos standard on 220 from late '55, though not on simplified 219 variant. Hydrak automatic clutch available from late '57. Cabriolets rare and expensive. 220S will do 100mph, but just try to find a rust-free one!

220S/220SE COUPE/CABRIOLET. 1956-59/1958-59 (prod: 3429/1942). 4-seater coupé, cabriolet. F/R, 2195cc (S6 OC). Rare, much fancied, and seldom seen with rhd: fixed heads are of two-light type. All have later S engine and servo brakes. SE (fuel injected) engines offer 115bhp, but too many survivors now have expensive rust problems. ➤

◄ **300A/300B/300C. 1951-57 (prod: 7246). Saloon. F/R, 2996cc (S6 OC).** Germany's first post-war prestige automobile, UK-available from late 1953. Six-light saloon with seven-bearing engine, good for the ton. Usual nasty column shift, servo brakes (desirable) from 1955. Mercedes's own automatic transmission available on C-series (late 1956). Some later examples have 160bhp fuel-injected engines. Becoming collectable.

300 CABRIOLET. 1951-62 (prod: 707). 4-door cabriolet. F/R, 2996cc (S6 OC). Rare ragtop edition (Daimler-Benz called it a Cabriolet D) of the 300 much favoured by presidents of emergent republics, and now a costly item rating way up with the 300S in the specialist market. Mechanics as 300 A/B/C, though the last 65 cars (August '57 on) are to the final D specification. ➤

300D. 1957-62 (prod: 3077). Saloon. F/R, 2996cc (S6 OC). This one's looks are improved by thinner pillars and a wrapround rear window, and all have the fuel injection engine boosting top speed to 105-110mph. Power steering available late '58. Manual gearboxes listed, but British market cars came with three-speed automatic (possible servicing problems). ►

◄**300S. 1952-58 (prod: 760). Roadster, 2-seater cabriolet, 2-seater coupé. F/R, 2996cc (S6 OC).** Spiritual successor to the 540K on a shortened 300 chassis, and costing more when new than a 300SL. Three-carburettor 150bhp engine (175bhp with fuel injection from '55), plus the usual all-synchro 'box. Servo brakes 1954. One for the Maharajahs.

300SL COUPE. 1954-57 (prod: 1400). 2-seater coupé. F/R, 2996cc (S6 OC). The famed Gullwing with inclined, dry-sump engine in a tubular spaceframe. Handling strictly for advanced motorists, maintenance nightmarish, and restoration costs mind-boggling. Plus: floor change instead of the S's column shift, 140mph, and 0-60 in less than 9secs. Minus: lhd only, but a gilt edged investment if you find a really good one. ►

◄**300SL ROADSTER. 1957-63 (prod: 1858). Roadster. F/R, 2996cc (S6 OC).** Mechanics as Gullwing, but with ragtop coachwork (factory hardtop listed). Probably a better buy than the coupé, as it runs a cool 20 per cent cheaper, has had less time to deteriorate, and from March '61 you get all-disc servo brakes instead of drums. Still possible to find good examples.

190SL. 1955-63 (prod: 25,881). Roadster. F/R, 1897cc (S4 OC). Poor man's 300SL with similar shape, plus twin-carburettor edition of the stock 190 unit and floor change for the all synchro 'box. Servo brakes from mid-56, rhd and factory hardtop available. A promenade sports car with rust problems, but no major maintenance headaches, and you get 105mph and 28mpg even if acceleration is poor. Appreciating fast. ►

190/190D. 1961-65 (prod: 130,554/225,645). Saloon. F/R, 1897cc (S4 OC). The good old 180 saloon, now with the latest angular styling, tail fins, a wider track, and more room inside. 190D has 55bhp diesel engine. Automatic available. Front disc brakes August 1963, power steering option on 1964s. ➤

◄ **200/200D. 1965-68 (prod: 70,207/161,618). Saloon. F/R, 1988cc (S4 OC).** Styling essentially as 1961-65 fours, but dual circuit servo disc/drum brakes are standard, and you can have floor shift as an alternative to four-on-the-column. Twin-carb petrol engine gives 95bhp, and even the commoner diesel is good for 80mph. Later cars are better bets, though.

220S/220SE/220SEC. 1959-65/1959-65/1961-65 (prod: 161,119/66,086/15,902). Saloon, coupé, cabriolet. F/R, 2195cc (S6 OC). Second generation unitary 220s with the angular hull of the 190/200 family. Fuel-injected SEs and SECs thirstier and more complicated, but give better mid-range performance. Coupés and cabriolets already expensive, but all have the front disc brakes not found on saloons till the spring of '62. ➤

◄ **300SE/300SEL/300SEC. 1961-65 (prod: 5202/1546/3127). Saloon, coupé, cabriolet. F/R, 2996cc (S6 OC).** Cross pollination of the fuel injected 3-litre six and the 1960 220 hull, with 600-type self levelling air suspension. Automatic standard for Britain, though some cars made with manual and floor change. SEC coupés (four-light) and cabriolets from '62, SEL saloon with 4ins extra wheelbase from '63 (UK 1965). Don't expect better than 13mpg.

230/230S. 1965-68 (prod: 181,365). Saloon. F/R, 2281cc (S6 OC). 220 derivative with bigger 105/120bhp twin carburettor engine. Floor or column change, automatic and power steering on options list, as well as rear hydropneumatic spring compensator. Servo front disc brakes standard. ➤

230SL. 1963-67 (prod: 19,831). Roadster, hardtop coupé. F/R, 2281cc (S6 OC). Luxury injected into a new, softer SL line, capable of 120mph, with a 100mph cruising gait. 150bhp fuel injected engine, servo disc/drum brakes, and automatic and power steering on the options list. Some people prefer them to later SL sixes, so expect to pay accordingly for a good one.

250SL. 1966-68 (prod: 5196). Roadster, hardtop coupé. F/R, 2496cc (S6 OC). The mixture as before, but now with the latest 2½-litre seven-bearing engine. Luxurious, but not significantly faster than a 230SL. Manuals have rather ill-spaced ratios, and the five-speed option's almost never seen, so you may prefer automatic.

280SL. 1967-71 (prod: 23,885). Roadster, hardtop coupé. F/R, 2778cc (S6 OC). Output's up to 170bhp with the bigger seven-bearing motor, and there are disc brakes all round, though these aren't quite the improvement they should be. Suspension considered soggier than on smaller-engined SL sixes, but the later the car the less chance of expensive structural repairs.

250S/250SE/250SEC. 1965-69/1965-67/1965-67 (prod: 74,677/55,181/6213). Saloon, coupé, cabriolet. F/R, 2496cc (S6 OC). Playing the permutations with the latest seven-bearing engine, rare two-door options, and carburettors versus fuel injection. New longer and lower hull with bigger, all-disc brakes, low profile tyres and hydropneumatic rear spring compensator. S with twin carburettors and 130bhp, others have fuel injection and 150bhp. Floor change standard on SEC coupés and cabriolets.

280S/280SE/280SEC. 1968-72 (prod: n/a). Saloon, coupé, cabriolet. F/R., 2778cc (S6 OC). Yet another permutation using the 280SL's bigger seven-bearing engine, though on S versions you get twin carburettors and 140bhp. Coupés and cabriolets (as always) come with fuel injection as standard. Power steering and automatic on options list: so is a very rare five-speed 'box.

300SE/300SEL. 1965-67/1968-69 (prod: n/a). Saloon, coupé, cabriolet. F/R, 2996cc/2778cc (S6 OC). Another 250 permutation using the traditional fuel-injected 3-litre engine, though later long-wheelbase SELs only have the 2.8 unit from the 280SL. All cars with automatic. Coupés and cabriolets are, of course, on short wheelbase. ➤

◄ **300SEL 6.3 1968-72 (prod: 6526). Saloon. F/R, 6330cc (V8 DOC).** How to enjoy that big, thirsty V8 without benefit of a chauffeur and two parking meters, in a long chassis 300 saloon hull. Air suspension and other 600 refinements plus dual-circuit power disc brakes. It'll do 135mph, and length is down to a manageable 197ins, too.

600. 1964-81 (prod: 2677). Saloon, limousine. F/R, 6330cc (V8 DOC). Monstrous car designed to waft Popes and Presidents down the motorway at 120mph. All mod cons including air suspension, automatic, and power steering. The standard article (18ft long, dry weight of 5500lbs) is big enough, but the eight-light Pullman seats nine and is a 20-footer. More exotic than a Phantom V. ➤

◄ **220/220D. 1968-73 (prod: 137,739/366,280). Saloon. F/R, 2197cc (S4 OC).** More semantic complexity from Stuttgart: this one's a four and a lineal descendant of the 180, combining the '65 shape with the latest ohc engine, giving 105bhp in petrol guise and 60bhp as a diesel. All-disc brakes a boon: floor change, automatic and power steering are all options.

250. 1968-72 (prod: n/a). Saloon. F/R, 2496cc (S6 OC). Typical late-sixties saloon of the latest shape with redesigned rear suspension and the familiar seven-bearing six. All disc brakes now standard, five-speed manual, automatic and power steering available. Standard twin-carburettor engine gives 130bhp. ➤

250CE. 1968-72 (prod: n/a). Coupé. F/R, 2496cc (S6 OC). A touring coupé recognisable by its vertical headlamp clusters (also on saloons) and pillarless styling. Not a sports car, though good for 115mph thanks to its 150bhp fuel-injected engine. Floor change standard, automatic and power steering optional. A possible collector's item for the eighties, as rare in Britain. ➤

MESSERSCHMITT (D)

This former aircraft manufacturer based at Regensburg, West Germany, produced oddball machines. The firm actually took over production of the Fend design of small car in 1953, struggling on until 1962. The TG500 (Tiger) model was the most interesting, as it had an excess of power over its ability to put it on the road.

◄ **KR175/KR200. 1953-56/1956-64 (prod: n/a). 2-seater scooter. R/R, 173cc/191cc (S1 TS).** Three-wheeled tandem-seat scooter from famous aircraft firm. UK-available from '55 – but for all that cockpit canopy, they didn't design it. Tubular spaceframe, handlebar steering, and bonded rubber suspension. Later ones ('56 on) have car-type throttle and clutch, Dyna-start and a reversible engine. Great fun, easy to park (99ins long, 48ins wide), and capable of a hairy 60mph.

TG500 TIGER. 1958-61 (prod: 250). 2-seater scooter. R/R, 493cc (S2 TS). Super-bubble with extra rear wheel and hydraulic brakes. The aircooled Fichtel & Sachs twin engine gives 20bhp, hence 75mph. Four speeds, but like the three-wheelers, it's got no synchromesh. Rare anywhere, but a few came to England: one's on show at Beaulieu. ➤

METROPOLITAN (GB/USA)

Variously an Austin, Nash or Hudson, this was conceived by Nash president Bill Mason as a small car for the American market and was made by Austin from 1954 to 1961, with some Hudson versions also built. It was never a huge success, but at one time was the second best selling US import after the Volkswagen.

◄ **1500. 1956-61 (prod: all types: 97,000 approx). 2-seater coupé, 2-seater convertible. F/R, 1489cc (S4 OHV).** Cheeky little two-tone runabout for the ladies made by Austin for American Motors, but UK-available from 1957. Styling's Nash out of Pininfarina, mechanics are BMC B-type (though only three forward speeds). Plus: individual looks, radio and heater as standard. Minus: non-handling of the worst possible kind, and it's a rust trap.

MG (GB)

How are the mighty fallen. Now, MGs are just rebadged – if high performance – Austins, yet in the 1930s and 1950s the name was synonymous with the sports car. The firm started out as the Morris Garage, run by Cecil Kimber. The first MG was just a tuned Morris Cowley, but was followed in 1929 by the trend-setting M-type Midget sports car. In the 1930s the firm produced a whole range of sports and sports racing cars, while after the war the company's products earned many a dollar on the US market. However, while the BMC merger of 1952 made little difference to MG, the take-over by Leyland in 1970 spelt the end of any real development.

◄ **TC. 1945-49 (prod: 10,000). 2-seater sports. F/R, 1250cc (S4 OHV).** Good old thirties traditional with foldflat screen, harsh springing, slab-tank body and 18ins wire wheels (tyres not as easy to find as they used to be). No lhd, so re-imports no problem. 54bhp short-stroke engine an improvement on the pre-war type, but body frames rot. An established classic with an established market price.

TD. 1950-53 (prod: 29,664). 2-seater sports. F/R, 1250cc (S4 OHV). You may not like the disc wheels (perforated on later cars) but bonuses are rack and pinion steering and coil-spring ifs. Mk II (1952) has power boosted to 57bhp, though factory tuning kits could give you over 90bhp even in street form. Most of them exported, so it'll cost as much as a TC. ►

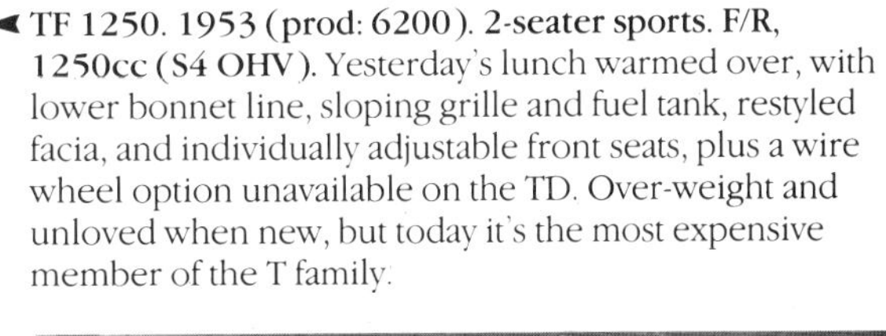

◄ **TF 1250. 1953 (prod: 6200). 2-seater sports. F/R, 1250cc (S4 OHV).** Yesterday's lunch warmed over, with lower bonnet line, sloping grille and fuel tank, restyled facia, and individually adjustable front seats, plus a wire wheel option unavailable on the TD. Over-weight and unloved when new, but today it's the most expensive member of the T family.

TF 1500. 1954 (prod: 3400). 2-seater sports. F/R, 1466cc (S4 OHV). As for TF 1250, but bigger 63bhp engine not only restores the performance, but turns on historians as it's the last proper Nuffield unit to go into an MG. (Parts trickier than for the later BMC B-types, though.) Add 20 per cent to what you're already figuring to pay for a 1250. ►

◄ **YA/YB. 1947-51/1952-53 (prod: 6158/1201). 4-door sports saloon. F/R, 1250cc (S4 OHV).** Would have been 1941's new MG and looks it, with its Morris 8 body panels, cramped body and close-set pedals that won't fit feet over size 10. Chassis is a longer TD with same suspension and steering. YBs have twin leading-shoe brakes and hypoid rear axles. Charming, but runs out of steam at 70mph.

YT. 1948-50 (prod: 877). 4-seater tourer. F/R, 1250cc (S4 OHV). Hybrid YA/TD, with former's chassis and latter's engine, plus somewhat ponderous 1938-style tourer bodywork. Not a great success and export-only; but a good few went to Commonwealth countries, ergo rhd is likely. A surprising number still around in Britain. ➤

◄ **MAGNETTE ZA. 1954-56 (prod: 12,754). 4-door sports saloon. F/R, 1489cc (S4 OHV).** All right, it's an Austin with Austin suspension and Wolseley chassis/body structure and the facia is a horror, but there's a genuine MG grille crowning that alligator bonnet, the rack and pinion steering is very un-Austin indeed, and trim is wood and leather, even if you miss the Y-type's sliding roof. Unrusted ones command respectable prices.

MAGNETTE ZB. 1956-58 (prod: 23,846). 4-door sports saloon. F/R, 1489cc (S4 OHV). As for ZA, but more powerful (69bhp) engine and a higher axle ratio. Varitone models have wrapround rear windows as well as two-tone paint. A few with Manumatic two-pedal control (avoid). Popular in its day, and still well liked, which isn't surprising considering what was to follow. ➤

◄ **MAGNETTE III/IV. 1959-61/1961-68 (prod:15,676/ 13,738). Saloon. F/R, 1489cc/1622cc (S4 OHV).** The good old BMC/Farina theme with twin carburettors, some extra bhp, leather trim, an MG grille, and the odd octagon or two dotted around the scenery. Mk IV (1.6-litres/ 68bhp, automatic option) from August '61. Slightly more 'U' than an Oxford or Cambridge, but better suited to country cabbies than to enthusiasts.

A. 1955-59 (prod: 58,750). 2-seater sports. F/R, 1489cc (S4 OHV). First modern sports MG with twin carb 72bhp BMC B-type engine, coil ifs, and rack and pinion steering. Brakes are drum, if very good drum, heaters are extra, and so are centre-lock wire wheels. 95plus mph and 27-30mpg. Separate chassis a bonus, though there are body rot problems. Factory hardtops listed. ➤

A COUPE. 1956-59 (prod: see A). 2-seater coupé. F/R, 1489cc (S4 OHV). New at '56 London Show, mechanics as two-seater but superior aerodynamic shape makes it fractionally faster, if rather claustrophobic. Currently appreciating very fast as fewer than 6000 As of all types were sold in Britain. We may soon see an influx of left-hookers from California. Everyday users will prefer the disc brakes of later cars.

A TWIN CAM. 1958-60 (prod: 2111). 2-seater sports, 2-seater coupé. F/R, 1588cc (S4 DOC). Chassis and body as stock A, but the engine's a 108bhp twin ohc unit, boosting top speed to 110 plus. Centre-lock wheels and all-disc brakes standard. Has a well-founded reputation as a piston burner and travelling oil leak, and 25mpg will be hard work. If you're lucky enough, though, to find one that has always been properly maintained, snap it up.

A-1600. 1959-61 (prod: 31,601). 2-seater sports, 2-seater coupé. F/R, 1588cc (S4 OHV). 80bhp engine plus disc front brakes spell a slightly better all-round performance. Roadsters have sliding type sidescreens. A-1600 De Luxe is a rare variant with Twin Cam chassis (all disc brakes, and so on) fitted with the pushrod engine, and this is possibly the best A combo of all, if you can find one.

A-1600 MK II. 1961-62 (prod: 8719). 2-seater sports, 2-seater coupé. F/R, 1622cc (S4 OHV). Last is generally best, and in its final form the A has 86bhp, a higher-ratio back axle, and inbuilt seatbelt mounts. There were even a few De Luxes, too, with the 1622cc unit. Alas, you are too late for a bargain, as A prices have effectively doubled in the past few years.

MIDGET MK I. 1961-62/1962-64 (prod: 16,080/9601). 2-seater sports. F/R, 948cc/1098cc (S4 OHV). Austin Healey Sprite II with fancy grille and side chrome trim. Still, however, with drum brakes and quarter-elliptic rear springing. Front disc brakes and wire wheels on some late 948cc cars, but 1100cc GAN2 cars (1962) have the former as standard. Early 1100 units, however, have suspect crankshafts, so watch it.

MIDGET MK II. 1964-66 (prod: 22,601). 2-seater sports. F/R, 1098cc (S4 OHV). More power and a stiffer bottom end, plus winding windows, lockable doors, and (thank heaven) semi-elliptics at the back. By now Midgets are commoner than Sprites, but the magic of the Octagon holds prices up nonetheless.

MIDGET MK III. 1966-69 (prod: 13,425). 2-seater sports. F/R, 1275cc (S4 OHV). The detuned Mini-Cooper S engine boosts output from 59 to 65bhp, but you get only an extra 2mph of straightline speed and acceleration only improves above 40mph. The fixed hood is easier to operate, while endemic problems (wheel arch rust, transmissions) will have had less time to mature. An attractive buy.

MIDGET MK IV. 1969-74 (prod: 86,623). 2-seater sports. F/R, 1275cc (S4 OHV). As Mk III, but with new grille, black sills and windscreen surround, and (alas) those truckish Rostyle wheels: go for the wire option. Rear wheel arches squared off on 1970 models, rounded from '72 cars, which also have better heating, boot/interior lights, bigger fuel tanks, and collapsible steering columns.

1100/1300. 1962-68/1967-71 (prod: 116,827/26,240). 2-door saloon, 4-door saloon. F/F, 1098cc/1275cc (S4 OHV). Faster, noisier and usually two-toned BMC 1100s with twin SU carburettors and MG grilles, plus walnut facias. Improved Mk II model (with either engine) from October '67, though 1300s have single-carburettor units. Two-door 1100s (though not 1300s) were export-only.

B. 1962-67 (prod: 115,898). 2-seater sports. F/R, 1798cc (S4 OHV). Unitary bestseller with more power (95bhp), but still loosely based on the A with front disc brakes. Higher axle ratio plus an overdrive option. Glass-fibre hardtop available from June 1964. Five-bearing engine (late '65) more robust, but slightly less urgeful. Rust a major problem.

BGT. 1965-67 (prod: 21,835). 2+2-seater coupé. F/R, 1798cc (S4 OHV). Almost a GT estate with its big tailgate, and weighs only 160lbs more than a two-seater. Quieter back axle and (of course) five-bearing engine. Most panels common to roadsters, but factory-sourced replacements for early Bs have long since dried up, *ergo* anything with major rust is best left alone.

BGT MK II. 1967-71 (prod: 91,207). 2+2-seater coupé. F/R, 1798cc (S4 OHV). Nice, practical road car, even if it doesn't handle as well as the roadster. Mechanical specifications identical. Typical performance figures are 105mph, 24-29mpg, and 0-50 in 7.8secs, though remember that anything destined for the USA will have a lower compression ratio and a mere 82bhp.

CGT. 1967-69 (prod: 4457). 2+2-seater coupé. F/R, 2912cc (S6 OHV). General remarks as for C two-seater, with lower-ratio back axle on later cars. All-synchro 'box standard, of course, while the car is becoming a cult, *ergo* expensive. Parts peculiar to the C are already scarce, and that engine is not a BMC C-type, but the later seven-bearing unit shared with the Hydrolastic-equipped 3-litre Austin.

B MK II. 1967-71 (prod: 218,870). 2-seater sports. F/R, 1798cc (S4 OHV). All cars now have the GT-type rear axle, synchromesh on bottom, and an automatic (Borg-Warner) option in addition to overdrive. Remarks as per early Bs, though automatic best avoided, and so are the ugly Rostyle wheels standard from 1970. (The alternative wires remained available.)

C. 1967-69 (prod: 4552). 2-seater sports. F/R, 2912cc (S6 OHV). The Austin-Healey replacement that couldn't quite, though 118mph and 22mpg are quite respectable. Styling pure B, and handling a disappointment by comparison with its rivals. Torsion-bar front suspension, and servo brakes not fitted as standard to Bs till 1974. Overdrive, automatic and wire wheels available.

MINI (GB)

Always produced by the British Motor Corporation and its derivative firms, the Mini is one of the all-time classic designs. The front-drive layout was not new when the Mini appeared in 1959; it was just that the car's packaging was so different and so clever. Minis were marketed at first under the Austin and Morris names, the title changing in 1970. The Mini-Cooper was the sporting breed of the car, using a specially tuned engined developed by John Cooper. The Mini is still with us in the 1980s, and is still as much fun.

◄ **MK I. 1959-67 (prod all types: 1,575,756). 2-door saloon. F/F, 848cc (S4 OHV).** The legendary ADO15 with its rubber suspension, east-west engine and sump-mounted four-speed 'box. Originally badged as Austin Seven or Morris Mini-Minor with Austins distinguishable from Morrises by their wavy grille bars and different colours. Super saloons from '61, key starts and Hydrolastic suspension from '64, AP semi-automatic transmission available '65.

MK I COUNTRYMAN/TRAVELLER. 1960-67 (prod: see MK I). 2-door estate car. F/F, 848cc (S4 OHV). Austin/Morris station wagon (note different names), though decorative wood strakes aren't structural, a comforting thought. As the model didn't come out till March '60, there's no point in hunting for really early Mini wagons. Early automatics probably best avoided. For the record, vans first seen May '60, and pickups in January '61. ►

COOPER. 1961-64/1964-67 (prod all types: 44,859). 2-door saloon. F/F, 997cc/998cc (S4 OHV). First sporting Mini, recognisable by its 11 horizontal grille ◄ bars, Super-type body trim, remote control gearshift, and front disc brakes. Twin-carburettor engine gives 55bhp, close ratio gears are standard, and with the original 997cc unit (to 1964) top speed goes up from 70 to 85mph with acceleration to match.

COOPER S. 1963-64/1964-65/1964-67 (prod all types: 191,242). 2-door saloon. F/F, 1071cc/970cc/1275cc (S4 OHV). Famed rally winner, with the first oversquare engine to go into a Mini. 1071cc engine replaced by later types, March 1964. The 1275 is the definitive model, giving 75bhp on a 9.75:1 c/r plus servo front disc brakes and a possible 100mph. It's an oil burner, but who cares? ►

MK II. 1967-69/1969 to date (prod: 510,824 to end 1969). 2-door saloon, estate car. F/F, 848cc/998cc (S4 OHV). Improved Mini with Hydrolastic springing, 11-bar grille, wider rear window, and remote control shift. AP automatic transmission available. 1970 and later models badged as Minis, not Austins or Morrises.

COOPER MK II. 1967-69 (prod: see Cooper). 2-door saloon. F/F, 998cc (S4 OHV). Last of the series, with changes as for standard Mk II, 55bhp engine, front disc brakes without servo, top speed 85-90mph. Subframe problems mean that only late cars are safe buys.

COOPER S MK II. 1967-71 (prod: see Cooper S). 2-door saloon. F/F, 1275cc (S4 OHV). Servo brakes, all the later body and styling improvements including protuberant tail lights. Austin and Morris badging dropped late in 1969. Good ones scarce – they've been raced and rallied to death – but they're also appreciating fast.

1275GT. 1969-80 (prod: n/a). 2-door saloon. F/F, 1275cc (S4 OHV). Mini badged and to Mk II specification, though it's really a Cooper rather than a Cooper S replacement with its 59bhp single carburettor engine and 87mph maximum. Front disc brakes with servo, and optional automatic all housed in later square front Mini Clubman shell. Survived right up to the Metro's introduction, and therefore readily available in good condition.

CLUBMAN. 1969-82 (prod: 413,154 total). 2-door saloon, estate car. F/F, 998cc/1098cc (S4 OHV). Squared-off nose did little for looks or aerodynamics in a controversial move to update the ubiquitous Mini. Dropped after Metro arrived, leaving original Mini shape to survive.

MOKE. 1964-68 (prod: 29,393). 4-seater utility. F/F, 848cc (S4 OHV). An attempt to provide a Jeep-type device. Failed because of imposition of tax, lack of four wheel drive, and above all restricted ground clearance. Now a Mini-cult...

MINIJEM (GB)

After Jem Marcos and his firm had finished building the Mini-Marcos, the production was taken over by Jem Developments from 1966 to 1968, then by Fellpoint Ltd until 1971, and by High Performance Mouldings from 1971 to 1973. It was always sold as a kit. In 1971, the ugly Volkswagen-based Futura 'sports car' was shown.

MKS I/II. 1966-76 (prod: approx 250). 2-seater coupé. F/F, 1275cc (S4 OHV). Very like the Mini Marcos, a glass-fibre monocoque structure with wood floor reinforcement capable of accepting any type of Mini running gear. Improved Mk II (1969) was sold complete with paint and trim, therefore probably a better buy. 110mph and 0-60 in 10 secs. Had a chequered career under numerous sponsors.

MONTEVERDI (CH)

An obscure Swiss manufacturer of exotic cars, started by Peter Monteverdi, BMW agent and creator of MBM competition cars. The first car was a Frua-styled GT exhibited at the 1967 Frankfurt Show, while the Hai was intended to take the firm into the supercar class, but few laid their hands on these mid-engined machines. Cars are still made by the firm, but only a handful per year.

HIGH SPEED 375. 1967-77 (prod: n/a). 2-seater coupé, 4-seater coupé, cabriolet. F/R, 6974cc/7206cc (V8 OHV). Swiss exotic with various V8 Chrysler engines in tubular frames with servo disc brakes and power steering: manual 'boxes not quoted after 1972. Two-seaters (by Frua) to 1972 only, Fissore did the four-seaters. UK imports negligible.

HAI 450SS. 1970-76 (prod: n/a). 2-seater coupé. R/R, 6974cc/7206cc (V8 OHV). Rear-engined coupé with an advertised 170mph. Five-speed 'box, de Dion rear end, and dual-circuit servo disc brakes. No power steering or automatic options. 380bhp engine from '71, restyled front end 1973. Almost never seen in Britain.

MORGAN (GB)

One of the few family-run car firms to have survived for any length of time, the Morgan Motor Co. has now been in existence for 76 years. It all began with H.F.S. Morgan's tricycles, which had excellent performance and were cheap. Four-wheel cars did not appear from the Malvern factory until 1936, and the transition from making three-wheelers to producing only four-wheelers did not come until 1951. Since then, the cars have remained ultra-traditional, with, effectively, only minor improvements in road manners, looks and refinement since before World War II. But therein lies their charm.

F4/F SUPER. 1934-52/1936-52 (prod post-war: 245). 2-seater sports. F/R, 933cc/1172cc (S4 SV). Final, 'civilised' versions of the famous three-wheeler with Dagenham Ford engines, conventional synchromesh 'boxes, and coupled Girling brakes, allied to classical Morgan chassis and suspensions. 1172cc F Super does 75mph and 45mpg. Chain final drive, of course.

4/4. 1936-50 (prod post-war: 1084). 2-seater sports, 4-seater sports, 2-seater drophead coupé. F/R, 1267cc (S4 OHV). Revival of the original 4/4 with specially built ohv Standard 10 engine and Moss separately-mounted gearbox in place of the original ioe Coventry-Climax unit. Mechanical brakes and pressed steel wheels. Styling and mechanics otherwise virtually unchanged from '39.

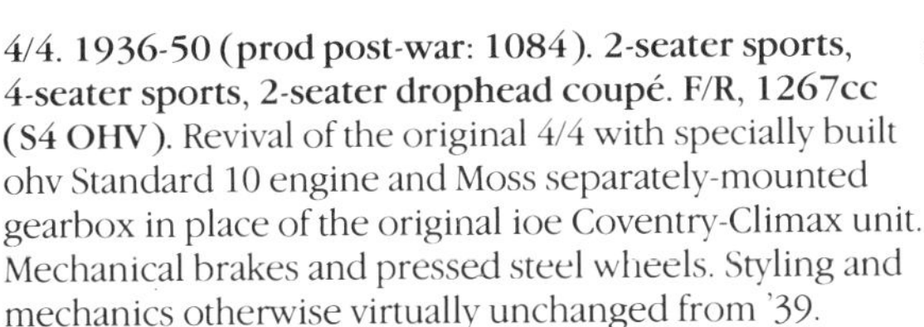

4/4 SERIES II. 1956-60 (prod: 386).. 2-seater sports. F/R, 1172cc (S4 SV). 4/4 revised after a five-year lapse with the latest (1954) Plus-Four styling, 36bhp 100E Ford engine, and hydraulic brakes. 40bhp Aqua-plane-head engine available from '58, wider body 1960. Debits are three speeds only and a rather nasty push-pull gearshift on the dash. Later ohv models preferred.

4/4 SERIES III. 1960-61 (prod: 58). 2-seater sports. F/R, 997cc (S4 OHV). Series II with short-stroke ohv 105E Anglia engine, four speeds (thank goodness) and a better remote-control shift. Still drum brakes, and what would a Morgan be without that famed chassis and sliding pillar front suspension? Spares and service no problem as they're still making the base theme.

4/4 SERIES IV. 1961-65 (prod: 205). 2-seater sports. F/R, 1340cc (S4 OHV). Front disc brakes now, with a more powerful engine from Ford's Classic 315 saloon. No other big changes, but top speed now in the low 80s with 0-50mph in under 12 secs. Later, commoner, Ford power trains might, however, be better buys.

4/4 SERIES V. 1963-68 (prod: 639). 2-seater sports. F/R, 1498cc (S4 OHV). A switch to the Cortina GT engine brings a new all-synchro 'box, plus options of tune of up to 83bhp. All the usual base faults of harsh suspension, flexing bodies, water leaks, plus woodrot on older vehicles, but there's nothing like it except, maybe, some recent Morgan-inspired kit cars. ➤

◄ **4/4 1600. 1968 to date (prod to 1970: 741). 2-seater sports, 4-seater sports. F/R, 1599cc (S4 OHV).** Suddenly we're back in 1955 again with the same sloping grille, the same bodies (four-seaters taken over from the discontinued Plus Four line) and the same mechanics apart from 1962's front disc brakes. Still being made with a choice of Ford CHV or Fiat engines.

PLUS FOUR VANGUARD. 1951-58 (prod: 245). 2-seater sports, 4-seater sports, 2-seater drophead coupé, 4-seater drophead coupé. F/R, 2088cc (S4 OHV). 4/4 replacement with an extra 4ins of wheelbase to take a stock 68bhp Standard Vanguard engine. Hypoid rear axle and hydraulic brakes new on a Morgan. Four-seater dropheads in '55 only, new sloping vertical barred grilles from 1954. TR-engined cars preferable unless you like the traditional radiator. ➤

◄ **PLUS FOUR TR. 1954-62/1963-69 (prod: 3390). 2-seater sports, 4-seater sports, 2-seater drophead coupé. F/R, 1991cc/2138cc (S4 OHV).** High performance TR engines, initially only in two-seaters, in which standardised 1955. TR3 unit (95bhp) 1956, wider bodies 1959, 2.1-litre 105bhp engine listed from July 1962. Front disc brakes optional 1959, standard 1961. All with later radiator grille.

PLUS FOUR SUPER SPORTS/COMPETITION. 1961-69 (prod: 102). 2-seater sports. F/R, 2138cc (S4 OHV). 'Specials' with Lawrencetune Triumph engines (twin SU or Weber carburettors) rated at 115/120bhp. Specifications vary, but you may expect 115-120mph, too. Very desirable. Chassis specification is stock Morgan. ➤

PLUS FOUR PLUS. 1964-66 (prod: 26). 2-seater coupé. F/R, 2138cc (S4 OHV). Glass-fibre coupé with smaller grille and infelicitous styling, the first breakaway from traditional Morgan body construction and the only true closed car ever marketed by the company. Mechanically standard Plus Four with TR engine, twin Stromberg carburettors, and four-speed 'box. Curiosity value only. ➤

◄ **PLUS 8. 1968 to date (prod to 1970: 311). 2-seater sports. F/R, 3528cc (V8 OHV).** Morgan up to date, though it still looks, rides and handles like earlier models! Rover V8 engine gives 161bhp, all-synchro 'box, limited slip differential, and a steel floor replacing the traditional planking. It'll take you to the ton in 19 secs, with a top speed of 125mph. Five-speed gearboxes from 1977 onward.

MORRIS (GB)

This name has now been phased out of British motoring, and it happened in 1983 to a firm which once produced nearly half of Britain's cars. William Morris first manufactured bicycles, but in 1910 he decided to venture into car manufacture, starting production more as an assembler of proprietary parts than a genuine manufacturer. A failure to appoint the right deputies led to a falling market share in the 1930s, and Morris let slip his company to the point of the BMC merger with Austin in 1952. As the Austin men took over, the Morris name became neglected and will not be revived.

8 SERIES E. 1939-48 (prod post-war: approx 60,000). 2-door saloon, 4-door saloon. F/R, 918cc (S4 SV). Pre-war design with bug-eye headlamps, no running boards, and the faithful old 29bhp flathead engine. Four speeds and hydraulic brakes are plus points, the whippy gear lever isn't. Sliding roofs available, but no tourers post-war. Fanciers tend to prefer the 1935-38 cars, so not a very expensive item. ➤

◄ **10 SERIES M. 1939-48 (prod post-war: 53,566). Saloon. F/R, 1140cc (S4 OHV).** The first unitary Morris, so they'll mostly have rusted out by now. Engine served as the TC MG's prototype, and is very tuneable. Handling uncertain in spite of front anti-roll bar. Rounded grille replaces traditional Morris shape from September 1946. Sliding roof optional.

MINOR MM SALOON. 1948-53 (prod all MM series: 176,002). 2-door saloon, 4-door saloon. F/R, 918cc (S4 SV). The baby car *par excellence* of its day, rack and pinion steering, torsion bar ifs, and superb handling. Alas, with the flathead engine it could be seen off by an ohv Fiat *Topolino*. Intrusive wheel arches make it uncomfortable for big-footed drivers. Raised, semi-exposed headlamps mid-'50, four-door saloon from '51. ➤

MINOR MM TOURER. 1948-53 (prod all Minor tourers to 1968: 74,960). Tourer. F/R, 918cc (S4 SV). Successful and very collectable unitary tourer, and if you find a rustfree one with the early-type headlamp installation it'll cost you a bag of gold. Mechanics as saloon. Fixed glass rear window replaced side curtains from 1952.

MINOR SERIES II. 1952-56 (prod: 269,838). 2-door saloon, 4-door saloon, tourer. F/R, 803cc (S4 OHV). BMC influence moves in with the Austin A30 power unit (albeit with SU carburettor) in a Minor hull. Four-doors go ohv from late '52, but other models still being sold with flathead motors well into 1953. More speed and better acceleration, but painfully undergeared, and the 1000 is preferable.

MINOR SERIES II TRAVELLER. 1953-56 (prod all Travellers: 215,331). 2-door estate car. F/R, 803cc (S4 OHV). Aluminium-panelled, wood straked wagon with van-type rear doors on a split-screen Series II 'chassis'. A pretty little car and popular with the ladies, but its 5.375:1 axle makes it even fussier. The woodwork is structural, too, so restoration can come expensive.

MINOR 1000. 1956-62 (prod all types: 544,048). 2-door saloon, 4-door saloon, tourer, estate car. F/R, 948cc (S4 OHV). New 948cc, 37bhp engine (though not its SU carburettor) shared with Austin's A35. 14ins wheels, curved single-panel 'screen; matching, larger rear window and dished steering wheel are other recognition features. Close ratio 'box a great improvement on Series II. From late 1961, flashers replace semaphore trafficators.

MINOR 1000. 1962-71 (prod all types: 303,443). 2-door saloon, 4-door saloon, tourer, estate car. F/R, 1098cc (S4 OHV). More powerful 48bhp engine boosts top speed into the high 70s, but not many significant changes elsewhere. No tourers after '68, and drum brakes only to the end. You pay the earth for low-mileage specimens, but recently prices have taken a knock, and it's surprising how good a saloon you'll find for less than four figures.

OXFORD MO. 1948-54 (prod: 159,960). Saloon, estate car. F/R, 1476cc (S4 SV). Structure, brakes, suspension and steering very largely as Minor, but looks are depressingly American inside and out, the column shift displeases, and the dependable sv engine is also gutless. Usual rust problems. Estate cars (two-door) from September 1952.

OXFORD II/III/IV. 1954-56/1956-59/1957-59 (prod: Series II, 87,341; Series III/IV, 58,117). Saloon, estate car. F/R, 1489cc (S4 OHV). Entirely restyled Oxford, still with four-on-the-column, but now with BMC B-type engine. Offset steering column unpleasing. Series III (available with Manumatic two-pedal drive) has minor styling changes. Series IV made only as all-metal station wagon, minus the strakes of earlier Travellers.

OXFORD V/VI. 1959-61/1961-71 (prod: 87,432/ 208,823). Saloon, estate car. F/R, 1489cc/1622cc (S4 OHV). Yet another name/badge for the good old Farina theme. Drum brakes and unsynchronised bottom gear to the end. Travellers from September '60. 1.6-litre Series VI with automatic option August '61, and a 1½-litre diesel saloon (mainly for export) on the market by March '62. Quite a good rust record, but deadly dull.

SIX MS. 1949-54 (prod: 12,400). Saloon. F/R, 2215cc (S6 OC). Morris's first post-war six, effectively an elongated Oxford with ohc engine, traditional grille, and low-geared cam steering. Fast and reliable, but a poor handler with indifferent forward vision, and expensive to service. Nearly extinct, so some scarcity value.

COWLEY/COWLEY 1500. 1954-56/1956-57 (prod: 17,413/4623). Saloon. F/R, 1200cc/1489cc (S4 OHV). Meaningless revival of a famous name as a stripped Series II/III Oxford, initially with Austin A40 engine. Series IIIs have the bigger engine, fluted bonnet top, and tail fins. The Oxford has little enough following, so let's pass this one up.

ISIS I/II. 1955-56/1956-58 (prod: 8541/3614). Saloon, estate car. F/R, 2639cc (S6 OHV). MS replacement with the same cam steering, Oxford-type structure, and BMC C-type engine, capable of 90mph. Series II with overdrive and automatic options, plus right-hand shift (Morris's first since 1916!) on standard cars. Almost as rare as the MS, but no other particular merit. ➤

◄ **1100/1300. 1962-71/1967-73 (prod all types: 801,966). 2-door saloon, 4-door saloon, estate car. F/F, 1098cc/1275cc (S4 OHV).** Morris had their Issigonis-designed Hydrolastic saloon out a year ahead of Austin. Semi-automatic transmission available from '64, reclining front seat option and Traveller estate car from '66, revised Mk II (first 1300) from October '67. GT variant 1969, but estates only after 1971. Worst problem is rot in the sub-frame.

1800. 1966-75 (prod: 95,271). Saloon. F/F, 1798cc (S4 OHV). Badge engineered Austin announced two years later than Longbridge's version. Automatic available, power steering option September '67. Mk II (March '68) has more power and bigger wheels, though if it's performance you want, try the 1800S (1969) with twin-carb 95bhp engine. ➤

MOSKVICH (USSR)

Iron Curtain countries have made few cars and this was one of the first to come to the notice of westerners. 'Son of Moscow' was basically a pre-war Opel Kadett, built in 1947, with the home grown products taking over in 1956. Most popular in this country was the 412 series.

◄ **407. 1958-64 (prod: n/a). Saloon. F/R, 1357cc (S4 OHV).** Old-fashioned family saloon with high ground clearance, a 30-piece toolkit, seats that fold down into a bed, and (for the British market) inclusive radio and heater. UK-available 1960, but few sold and mostly lhd. Curiosity value only.

408/426. 1964-71 (prod: n/a). Saloon, estate car. F/R, 1357cc (S4 OHV). Restyled with quad headlights and floor change (with an extra forward ratio) for the UK market, but still noisy, a clumsy handler, and under-braked. All the usual Soviet extras, including a radiator blind, and it'll do 80mph. 426 is wagon version. Not much secondhand value when young, and still less now. ➤

412/427. 1969-75 (prod: n/a). Saloon, estate car. F/R, 1478cc (S4 OC). Main change on this saloon/wagon pair is substitution of a five-bearing 80bhp ohc unit which removes the last traces of an Opel ancestry. The brake servo helps, but there are still drums to the end. At 90mph, definitely too fast for chassis. If you want a Russian car, the Lada is preferred. ➤

NOBEL (D)

This peculiar vehicle was called the Fuldamobil in its homeland, and was produced initially by the Elektromaschinbau Fulda GmbH from 1950. It was made under licence by Nordwestdeutsche Fahrzeugbau in Wilhelmshaven from 1954 to 1955 with production in Germany ceasing in 1960. It was built in England by Harland & Wolfe, and abortively by Lea-Francis, for York Nobel Industries.

◄ **200. 1959-61 (prod: 260 approx). 2-seater coupé, 2+2-seater coupé. R/R, 192cc (S1 TS).** Our old friend the Fuldamobil, a lesser egg shape born in Germany, 1950 and last seen in Greece (as the Alta!) 20 years later. British version made by Lea Francis. Three- and four-wheeler versions, plastic body, coupled mechanical brakes, and four-speed 'box with electrically-operated reverse. 126ins long, and they claimed 100mpg.

NSU (D)

Another of the firms in the complicated inter-related pattern of German automotive development. Cars were produced first in 1905, after successful manufacture of motorcycles and bicycles. Small cars sold successfully until Fiat bought the firm's newly established factory at Heilbronn in 1930. NSU opted out of car manufacture, resuming in 1957. The firm startled the motoring world two years later with the first ever production Wankel unit. The Ro80, a medium-sized saloon with Wankel power, was 'Car of the Year' in 1967, but NSU was amalgamated with Audi in 1969, becoming part of the Volkswagen Group. The Ro80 was deleted in 1977, and the NSU died as a marque.

PRINZ I/II/III. 1958-60/1959-60/1960-62 (prod: 94,549 all types). 2-door saloon. R/R, 583cc (S2 OC). Noisy minicar with good brakes, steering, and handling generally considering the rear engine and swing axle. Crash 'box on Prinz I. First two are notchbacks with very cramped rear seats. Prinz III is proper four-seater with styling of the later Prinz 4. ➤

◄ **PRINZ 4. 1961-73 (prod: 570,000). 2-door saloon. R/R, 598cc (S2 OC).** Improved Prinz III with 30bhp instead of 23, the bigger body, a longer wheelbase, and even better handling plus over 70mph from that willing little ohc motor. All-synchro 'box like Prinz II and III. A 12-year run without major change is a good recommendation.

SPORT PRINZ. 1959-61/1961-67 (prod: 20,831 all types). 2-seater sports coupé. R/R, 583cc/598cc (S2 OC). Bertone transforms the ugly duckling into a swan, and it's a pretty little car though neither as fast nor as frugal (75mph, 37/40mpg) as the rival 850 Fiat. The 598cc engine arrived late '61, with front disc brakes from 1965 Rare, and more practical than the original Wankel Spyders.

WANKEL SPYDER. 1964-67 (prod: 2375). 2-seater roadster. R/R, 497cc (W). Built on a Sport Prinz platform with the trailing wishbone rear springing of the four-cylinder cars. Front disc brakes standard and necessary with 95mph on tap. A memorable experience when it first came out, but nobody understood the Wankel's ways then, and you'll be lucky to find a sound engine. Maybe the ohc twin would fit...

1000. 1964-72 (prod: 196,000). 2-door saloon. R/R, 996cc (S4 OC). First of a complete family of all-alloy fours mounted transversely at the rear of a classical NSU structure. All-synchromesh 'boxes with overdrive top. Drum brakes standard, but front discs usual for UK. Rather a harsh ride and noisy like all conventional NSUs. Top speed in the low 80s: later models preferred.

TT/TTS. 1965-72/1967-71 (prod: 63,289/2402). 2-door saloon. R/R, 1085cc/1177scc/996cc (S4 OC). Disc front brakes and 12-volt electrics on these high performance versions: TT gets bigger engine in 1968, with twin carburettors. The 996cc TTS was the hairiest of the bunch, with 70bhp and a potential 100mph. Not much interest as yet in NSU fours.

110/110S/1200C. 1965-67/1967-73 (prod: 230,688 all types). 2-door saloon. R/R, 1085cc/1177cc (S4 OC). The old formula with 8ins more wheelbase and some extra legroom, plus bigger wheels (13ins instead of 12ins). 1.2-litre engine from late '66, but no real differences between the three variants. Choose the 1.2-litre for better acceleration. Thirsty if driven hard.

◄ **Ro80. 1968-77 (prod: 37,204). Saloon. F/F, 994cc (W, 2-rotor).** It's got everything – looks, built in safety, servo disc brakes, power rack and pinion steering, and semi-automatic transmission with full driver control. 110mph too, without excessive thirst. But you've got the old Wankel problem, so drop in a V4 or V6 Ford, which mates easily with the 'box. Originality means preservation rather than use.

OGLE (GB)

David Ogle's industrial design firm had a good reputation, but when he wanted to break into the car field he found he had to build his own. His first design in 1959 was based on a Riley 1.5, with the neat SX1000 coupé following in 1962: but Ogle's death in an SX1000 and its loss-making production saw car manufacture cease the following year. The firm did make some one-off designs afterwards, though.

1.5. 1960-62 (prod: 8). 4-seater coupé. F/R, 1489cc (S4 OHV). Like the early Gilbern, uses a BMC B-type engine. BMC back end with coil springs, semi-spaceframe, and glass-fibre body. Unlike the Gilbern, it features Riley 1.5 (ie Morris Minor) torsion bars at the front. Engine is 68bhp Riley tune. Good looking but hard to find. ►

◄ **SX1000. 1962-64 (prod: 66). 2-seater coupé. F/F, 997cc/1275cc (S4 OHV).** Even prettier than the 1.5, with quad headlights. Platform chassis, plastic body and whatever Mini mechanics the customer supplied, which means 110mph with a full-house Cooper S unit.

SX250. 1962 (prod: 2). 4-seater coupé. F/R, 2548cc (V8 OHV). Giving the SP250 Daimler engine and 'box the chassis and body they deserved – the former a strong box-section job with semi elliptics at the back and all-disc brakes, the latter what later became Reliant's Scimitar coupé. You can still find the Reliant version, however... ►

OPEL (D)

Bicycle and sewing machine manufacture were specialities of the Opel family, who bought the rights to produce the Lutzmann car from 1898. The firm then made Darracq cars from 1902 to 1906 alongside its own designs. By 1928, Opel was the largest car producer in Germany. However, the onset of economic problems in the late 1920s saw the Opel brothers reorganlse as a joint stock company, with majority shareholding going to General Motors. During the 1930s, Opel ranked first among European car producers, and although the marque's image is far more sporting today, it is still getting over hiccoughs caused by an out-of-date model range in the early 1970s.

◄ **KADETT. 1965-71 (prod: 2,311,389 all types). 2-door saloon, 4-door saloon, 2-door fastback saloon, 4-door fastback saloon, estate car, 4-seater coupé. F/R, 1078cc (S4 OHV).** German equivalent of the HB/HC Vauxhall Viva with the same pushrod engine design and rack and pinion steering. All body styles available here (from 1968), all cars in our period with four speeds and drum brakes. Rallye Coupé (twin carbs, 60bhp, 90mph) is the desirable one.

OLYMPIA. 1967-70 (prod: 80,637). 2-door fastback saloon, 4-door fastback saloon, estate car, 4-seater coupé. F/R, 1078cc (S4 OHV). Upmarket Kadett with a different grille, front disc brakes, and the 60bhp twin-carb engine. Usual rust problem with cheap unitaries. Semantics confusing, too, as the Rekord used to be called the Olympia Rekord and you might get mixed up. ►

◄ **REKORD. 1966-71 (prod: 1,280,000 all types). 2-door saloon, 4-door saloon, estate car, 4-seater coupé. F/R, 1698cc/1897cc (S4 OHV).** These have the 105ins wheelbase, complex camshaft-in-head pushrod ohv, five-bearing crankshafts and servo front disc brakes. Permutations in UK (from 1968) not too complex: 1.9-litre engine from 1969. Four speeds standard but pre-1970 automatics will be the less desirable two-speed Powerglide.

COMMODORE. 1967-71 (prod: 156,330 all types). 4-door saloon, 5-seater coupé. F/R, 2490cc (S6 OHV). An extended Rekord with the same wheelbase and a tough seven-bearing six instead of the four. UK-available 1968 in 120bhp standard form with automatic option, usually the later three-speed. 130bhp GS version from 1969, and fuel injected GS/E (150bhp) by 1971. ►

GT 1900. 1968-73 (prod: 103,373). 2-seater coupé. F/R, 1897cc (S4 OHV). Unusual shape with pop-out headlamps and Kamm-type tail which may or may not appeal. Usual five-bearing Rekord engine in 90bhp form, 105-110mph. Automatic available but no rhd, and no luggage room either. Collectable, but for regular use the later Manta could be a wiser choice. ➤

OPPERMAN (GB)

Produced from 1956 to 1959, this 'car' came from Elstree or Borehamwood, not, as its name suggests, from Germany. Low cost and light weight were useful attributes in post-Suez Britain, and the car had superb fuel economy. It was rendered redundant by the appearance of the Mini, as were so many of these small economy vehicles.

◄ **UNICAR. 1956-59 (prod: approx 200). 2-seater coupé. R/R, 328cc (S2 TS).** Rather crude Laurie Bond design with glass-fibre body on a glass-fibre platform, strut type ifs, trailing arms at the rear, and mechanical brakes. Tubular hammock seats peg into the floor. Early ones had 422cc Anzani engines, kits sold from 1958. There are better minicars.

STIRLING. 1958-59 (prod: n/a). 2+2-seater coupé. R/R, 424cc (S2 TS). Poor man's NSU Sport Prinz with the looks the Unicar hadn't, plus hydraulic brakes, and a bored out version of the Excelsior twin giving 25bhp. 70mph and 55/60mpg claimed. Tried with the Steyr-Puch 500 engine, too, but few made in any form. ➤

OPUS-HRF (GB)

Basically a cheap fun car, this delight was produced at first by Rob Walker, the famous race team owner. Standard Ford Popular mechanical components were used with a glass-fibre body shell, the whole thing being marketed by Walker's Corsley Garage in Warminster, Wiltshire. After 1970 Roy Dickenson of Bristol took over the design.

◄ **OPUS. 1966-72 (prod: 250 approx). 2-seater sports. F/R, 997cc/1298cc/1599cc (S4 OHV).** A sort of lowboy T-bucket of Neville Trickett's devising, wit self coloured body resembling a plastic bathtub. Tubular frame, old-school Ford Pop front axle, 105E Anglia brakes, Mini wheels, and any Ford mechanics you wanted. Said to cost £300 on the road if you made it yourself. Hairy anyhow, as one might expect with only 8cwt.

PANHARD (F)

One of the true pioneers of motoring, but sadly a fading force by the late 1950s as sales declined. However, even the later cars, with amazing performance from their two-cylinder engines, were full of mechanical ingenuity. Originally the firm was Panhard et Levassor, founded in 1889, with a car running for the first time in 1891. The car's design was much copied, and in the heroic age of motor racing Panhards were a genuine force. After 1918 Panhard specialised in medium and large touring cars, with nothing startling until the ugly Dynamique of 1937. After 1945 the firm built utility cars, but it was taken over by Citröen in 1965, with the last true Panhard produced in 1967.

◄ **DYNA 120/130. 1950-53/1951-53 (prod: 45,000 all types 1946-53). 4-door saloon, estate car, cabriolet. F/F, 745cc/845cc (HO2 OHV).** Fastest of the old-school Gregoire-based alloy flat-twins, with hydraulic brakes, and crash 'boxes on earlier ones. Fast (70-75mph) and exciting, but said to be good at selecting two gears at a time. Much more fun than Minors, 4CVs, and *Topolino*, but hardly any in Britain.

DYNA JUNIOR. 1952-55 (prod: 2000 approx). 2-seater roadster. F/F, 845cc (HO2 OHV). Mechanics as 120 saloon, but always synchro 'box, and box-section frame with tubular cross members. Ugly little beast, but 13cwt and a 40bhp twin-carb engine should spell early Spridget performance, and there's even more with the optional 60bhp supercharged version. ►

◄ **PL17. 1959-64 (prod: 130,000 approx). 4-door saloon. F/F, 845cc (HO2 OHV).** All-steel version of aluminium Dyna 54 (1954), almost never seen here. 75mph and 40mpg for six people, but looks controversial and no rhd till '59. Tigre of 1961 (twin choke carb, 60bhp) is the best one. All-synchro 'box 1963.

24CT. 1964-67 (prod: 24,962). 2+2-seater coupé. F/F, 845cc (HO2 OHV). Ugly little car with quad headlamps and the 60bhp Tigre motor, speeds in the 90-100mph class. Floor change on all, and all-disc brakes from '65. Detuned (24C) and full four-seater (24B) version not sold here. Parts difficult to impossible. ►

PARAMOUNT (GB)

The brainchild of two Derbyshire enthusiasts, W. A. Hudson and S. Underwood, the Paramount was first shown to the press in 1950. By 1951, manufacture had been taken over by the Meynell Motor Co, before being carried out by Camden Motors, who formed Paramount Cars (Leighton Buzzard) Ltd. The car's price was too high, and by 1956 Paramount was finished.

◄ **TEN/1½-LITRE. 1950-56/1954-56 (prod: n/a). 4-seater tourer, 2-door saloon. F/R, 1172cc/1508cc (S4 SV/OHV).** Sporty rather than sporting: chequered career began in Derbyshire and ended at Leighton Buzzard. Twin tube frame, hydromech brakes, and twin 7½-gallon wing-mounted tanks on late ones giving a 400-mile range. Engines and gearboxes stock Ford (Prefect, Consul) but floor change always standard. Saloons from '55. Bedfordshire cars have BMW-style grilles.

PEEL (GB)

'Little more than a chair in a box on wheels', the original Peel was the only vehicle to be produced for sale in the Isle of Man. It was made from 1962 to 1966, and an electric model was tested in 1965. The firm subsequently made the glass-fibre bodied Viking until 1967.

VIKING. 1965-67 (prod: 50 approx). 2/4-seater coupé. F/F, 848cc (S4 OHV). Manx-built sports saloon conversion for Minis of glass-fibre with internal steel structure bridging front and rear subframes. Buyers provide the paint and the Mini mechanics, and presumably hairier Cooper engines could be fitted. Appearance spoilt by tailfins. Peel also built a 50cc 'bubble' with DKW moped engine. ►

PEERLESS (GB)

Built from 1957 to 1960 at Slough, the Peerless mated rugged mechanical components to a four-seater GT bodyshell. John Gordon, later of Gordon-Keeble, was involved in the design, which had a successful run at Le Mans in 1958 but suffered from roughness in both its performance and its detail finish.

◄ **GT. 1957-60 (prod: 325). 4-seater sports saloon. F/R, 1991cc (S4 OHV).** Bernie Rodger design with TR2 engine, gearbox and front disc brakes, in their own tubular frame with de Dion back end. Pretty, if not very comfortable, glass-fibre body. Overdrive available, good for 105mph and handled well. Reappeared later on the Warwick, and catered for by an active club.

PEGASO (E)

Mainly engaged in truck production, this Spanish manufacturer in 1951 produced an immensely complex V8-engined high performance sports car. Only 125 Pegasos were built between 1951 and 1958. Surprisingly for such a sporting car, the Pegaso was rarely raced and never fared well even when entered in competition.

◄ **Z102/103. 1951-56 (prod: 100 approx). Various. F/R, 2472cc/2816cc/3178cc (V8 QOC).** Staggering noise machine: four gear driven upstairs camshafts, dry sump lubrication, five-speed all-indirect *crash* transaxle of de Dion type, inboard rear brakes and the most complicated steering linkages ever seen. With the 3.2 engine and twin blowers, 285bhp said to be available. A plug-eater, but also the ultimate in fifties exotica.

PEUGEOT (F)

One of the giants of European car manufacture – it now controls Talbot (*née* Chrysler) and Citröen – was founded way back in 1889. During its early years, from 1906 to 1910, there were two firms: Lion Peugeot run by Robert Peugeot, and the main manufacturer. In 1910, this family rivalry finished with the formation of SA des Automobiles et Cycles Peugeot. Through the inter-war years, the firm produced a range of competent and worthy cars, and this trend was continued after 1945. Recently, however, the firm has hit a winner with its 205 model and has a fine range and reputation.

203. 1948-60 (prod: 685,828). Saloon, cabrio-limousine, estate car, coupé, convertible. F/R, 1290cc (S4 OHV). Tough family saloon with indestructible hemi-head engine and even less destructible worm drive back end. Nasty column shift and rather over-geared, but quite a few have sliding roofs. Some interest in France already. Only saloons and wagons (latter on lengthened wheelbase) sold here, from 1954. ►

◄ **403. 1955-67 (prod: 1,119,460 all types). Saloon, estate car. F/R, 1468cc (S4 OHV).** 203 theme enlarged with the Pininfarina touch: bigger, roomier, tougher and slightly faster. Wagons from 1956 on usual extended wheelbase. Geared up top gives effortless cruising, but column shift has very odd action. Used to be quite common, but rust has taken its toll.

403 CABRIOLET. 1956-61 (prod: see 403). 4-seater convertible. F/R, 1468cc (S4 OHV). Rare version, standard chassis specs with worm drive and so on, but seldom seen here and almost never rhd. The French are already putting 'em by. Other 403 variants (stripped 403/7 with 203 engine, 403D diesel, both 1960 introductions) not sold over here. ►

404/404D. 1960-75/1963-75 (prod: 2,385,802/ 366,335). **Saloon, estate car. F/R, 1618cc/1948cc (S4 OHV/OHV Diesel).** 403 development with worm drive still, also live-axle-and-coil rear suspension, but Pininfarina's razor edge styling. Five-bearing engines (1964 on) a bonus, servo front disc brakes (saloons from '69) equally desirable. 96bhp fuel injection engine available UK 1965, automatic options from '66 models. ►

◄ **404 COUPE/CABRIOLET.** 1962-69 (prod: 6837/ 10,387). **4-seater coupé, 4-seater convertible. F/R, 1618cc (S4 OHV).** Rare, attractive, full four-seaters. Improvements and options as 404 saloon, but no automatics or diesels available. Listed UK from '65 though rhd uncommon, and 96bhp fuel injection engine standard here. Already making money in France.

204. 1965-77 (prod: 1,387,473). **Saloon, estate car. F/F, 1130cc (S4 OC).** Transverse engine, upstairs camshaft, and servo disc/drum brakes in an attractive 85mph saloon with McPherson struts at the front end. Over 80mph on 58bhp, but later 304 probably a better buy. Diesel versions don't reach Britain until 1975. ►

◄ **204 COUPE/CABRIOLET.** 1966-70 (prod: 42,765/ 18,181). **2+2-seater coupé, 2-seater cabriolet. F/F, 1130cc (S4 OC).** Again rather pretty (convertibles especially), but these can be found with rhd and late ones won't have as much time to rust as older types. Engines untuned, but as on saloons you get floor instead of column shift from '69. Sunroof option on coupés.

304. 1969-80 (prod: 1,178,425 all types). **Saloon, coupé, estate car. F/F, 1288cc (S4 OC).** Same diecast alloy engine as 204, and same layout, but styling's based on the conventional-drive 504. Sunroofs still available on saloons and coupés. Diesel versions not listed in UK, but go for the high-performance 304S model (69bhp) starting '73. ►

504. 1969-82 (prod: 2,836,237 all types to 1981). Saloon, estate car. F/R, 1796cc (S4 OHV). Last of the rear drive Peugeots with hypoid bevel rear end (at last), all-disc brakes with servo, and a useful extra 3½ins of wheelbase as compared with 404s. Automatic and fuel injection options, but no estate cars till '71, when bigger engines (2-litre petrol, 2.1-litre diesel) also offered.

504 COUPE/CABRIOLET. 1970-74 (prod: see 504). 4-seater coupé, 4-seater cabriolet. F/R, 1796cc/1971cc (S4 OHV). Mechanics as 504 saloon, but fuel injection standard with 103bhp, ergo top speeds around the 105 mark. 2-litre engine, 1971. Automatic available 1972, not usually seen in Britain. From 1975, the first French model to fit the joint Peugeot-Renault-Volvo V6 motor.

PIPER (GB)

Originally, Piper offered a range of sports racing, GT coupé and Formula 3 cars designed by Tony Hilder from its Hayes, Kent, base, but was best known for its stylish GTT coupé, which was developed by a separate company run by Brian Sherwood in Wokingham, Berkshire. After Sherwood's death in 1970, the firm was reorganised, and produced cars until 1974.

GTT/P2. 1968-74 (prod: 100 approx). 2-seater coupé. F/R, 997cc/1298cc/1599cc (S4 OHV). Ultra-low racebred coupé (glass-fibre of course): square tube spaceframe, Triumph Herald front end, front disc brakes, engines and other mechanics Ford, though at least one car with Alfa Romeo engine. P2 (1971) with longer chassis and reinforcing outriggers. '72s and later quite luxurious (pop-up headlamps, tinted glass, sunroof). There's a club for the *marque*.

PORSCHE (D)

While Ferdinand Porsche was responsible for many immortal vehicles before 1939, including the Volkswagen, the first car to bear his name was designed by son Ferry and long-time associate Karl Rabe. It was built in 1948 by the Porsche engineering consultancy, which had been set up in 1930. The company has had few major upheavals, although in 1971 various members of the Porsche family were removed from the firm's day-to-day running, and continuity is today provided by the fact that the 911, with the same rear engined location as the original cars, is still in production. Moreover, Porsche is one of the foremost automotive design organisations.

356. 1950-55 (prod: 7627). Coupé, cabriolet. R/R, 1287cc/1290cc/1488cc (HO4 OHV). The VW-based sports car that corners 10mph faster than its competition. UK sales start late '53, so expect twin leading-shoe brakes, all-synchro 'boxes and 12-volt electrics on anything you buy here. 1100 unit not marketed in Britain, 1290 unit replaces 1287 during '54. Most powerful variant is the 1500 Super (70bhp).

356A. 1955-59 (prod: 21,045 all types). Coupé, cabriolet, hardtop coupé. R/R, 1582cc (HO4 OHV). Panoramic windscreen, stiffer front suspension and a steering damper (important) the main changes. 1300s in Germany, but UK sales limited to 60bhp standard 1600, and 75bhp Super, latter with roller bearing crankshaft. Supers do over 100mph and 0-60 in 15.3secs. ►

◄ **356A SPEEDSTER. 1955-58 (prod: see 356A). 2-seater roadster. R/R, 1582cc (HO4 OHV).** The lovely, if stark, one with shallow barchetta-style screen that all the replicar-merchants reproduce on stock VW floorpans. The real McCoy is hard to find. On all 356s, watch for rust inside the front wings, and remember that not all Porsche owners knew how to cope. An awful lot of them will have been rolled, so take a good look around.

356A CARRERA. 1955-58/1958-59 (prod: 700 all types). Coupé, cabriolet, hardtop, speedster. R/R, 1498cc/ 1588cc (HO4 4OC). For advanced students only: the chicken hearted stay with *Damen* types and pushrods. Twin gear driven camshafts per block, dry sump lubrication, roller bearing crank, and dual ignition with eight plugs. 120mph with the 1½-litre version, more with 115bhp and 1.6 litres from 1958. ►

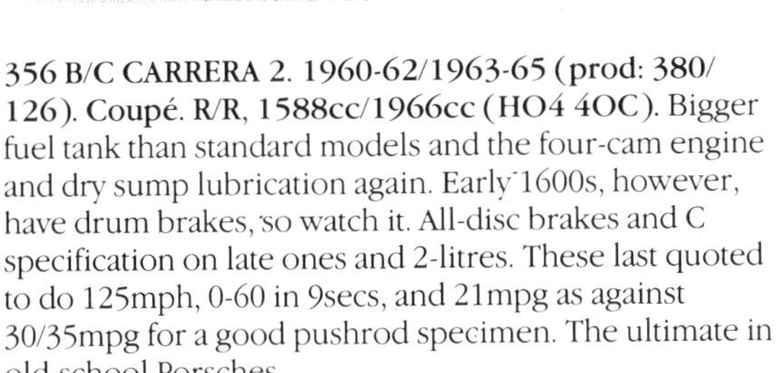

◄ **356B. 1959-63 (prod: 30,963). Roadster, coupé, cabriolet, hardtop. R/R, 1582cc (HO4 OHV).** Just a little better than last time with twin dual-choke carburettors and smaller (15ins) wheels, though steering gear's still VW. 1600s only, from the 60bhp *Damen* up to the Super 90, which'll give you close on 110mph with a 0-60 acceleration time heading towards 10secs.

356 B/C CARRERA 2. 1960-62/1963-65 (prod: 380/ 126). Coupé. R/R, 1588cc/1966cc (HO4 4OC). Bigger fuel tank than standard models and the four-cam engine and dry sump lubrication again. Early 1600s, however, have drum brakes, so watch it. All-disc brakes and C specification on late ones and 2-litres. These last quoted to do 125mph, 0-60 in 9secs, and 21mpg as against 30/35mpg for a good pushrod specimen. The ultimate in old-school Porsches. ►

356C. 1963-65 (prod: 16,668). Coupé, cabriolet, hardtop. R/R, 1582cc (HO4 OHV). ZF instead of Volkswagen steering, compensating transverse-leaf spring at the back and all-disc brakes, plus more power, 75bhp cooking, 95bhp in Supers. Probably the best 356 touring buy, as by this time the press on regardless brigade will have been shunting new 911s instead.

911/911L. 1964-67/1967-68 (prod: 78,872 all types to 1973). Coupé, targa. R/R, 1991cc (HO6 DOC). Original and basic 911, with two triple-choke carburettors and dual-circuit discs all round. Weber carbs replaced Solexes from April '66. Semi-convertible Targas introduced April 1967, Sportomatic four-speed semi-automatic option new in UK on '68s, but five-speed manual standard on all these.

911S. 1966-69/1969-71 (prod: see 911/911L). Coupé, targa. R/R, 1991cc/2195cc (HO6 DOC). High compression engines, ventilated disc brakes, five-speed 'boxes, no Sportomatic option. Forged alloy pistons. 160bhp with 2-litres and carburettors, 170bhp with fuel injection (1968), and 180bhp with 1969's bored out type and fuel injection. From '68 with longer wheelbase, flared wheel arches, wide rim wheels, and optional gas strut front suspension.

911T. 1967-69/1969-71 (prod: see 911/911L). Coupé, targa. R/R, 1991cc/2195cc (HO6 DOC). Tamest of the family, detuned carburettor engine (110bhp, 2-litre; 130bhp 2.2-litre). Specification changes at end of '68 for '69, which included ventilated disc brakes. Four-speed 'box standard, though five-speed and Sportomatic available.

911E. 1968-69/1969-71 (prod: see 911/911L). Coupé, targa. R/R, 1991cc/2195cc (HO6 DOC). Touring specification with longer wheelbase, gas struts to front, wide rims, flared arches. 2.2-litre engine (155bhp), with magnesium alloy crankcase 1969, also quartz halogen headlamps as on other 911s by then. All Es, of course, have fuel injection.

912. 1965-69 (prod: 30,745). Coupé, targa. R/R, 1582cc (HO4 OHV). Really a 911 with four-cylinder engine (the old one from the 356) and same combination of MacPherson struts and torsion bars at the front. Targa option '67, dual circuit disc brakes August '67, longer wheelbase on '69s. Five-speed option to '67, but no automatics. Rather staid and overlooked by collectors as yet. ➤

POWERDRIVE (GB)

Produced by Powerdrive Ltd at Wood Green in North London, this was another of the late-1950s crop of economy cars. It survived until 1958, when it reappeared with modified glass-fibre bodywork as the Coronet, this particular car lasting until 1960. Low road tax, insurance and fuel consumption were the attractions.

◄ **ROADSTER. 1956-58 (prod: n/a). 3-seater roadster. R/R, 322cc (S2 TS).** David Gottleb-designed three-wheeler with twin-tube frame, American-style body, motorcycle-type 'box, and coil-spring ifs. Steel and aluminium, and too heavy. Villiers and Anzani engines tried. Reappeared in '58 as glass-fibre bodied Coronet. Lion mascot about the only collectable element.

RELIANT (GB)

Established in 1935 by T. L. Williams, the firm did not make any vehicles for private use until the three-wheeler of 1952, which was powered by Reliant's version of the Austin Seven engine. A four-wheeler followed in 1962, but the firm is best known for its elegant GTE sporting estate model.

REGAL I-VI. 1952-62 (prod: n/a). Tourer, 2-door saloon. F/R, 747cc (S4 SV). Van-based three-wheelers with old-school Austin 7 engines, and coupled hydraulic brakes. Saloons and rounded glass-fibre bodies from '56, curved screens and first synchro (!) 1957. Mks V-VI (1959 on) have three-speed 'boxes, earlier cars four speeds. Handling peculiar and ride awful, but does it matter, at 55mph and 50mpg? ➤

◄ **REGAL 3/25, 3/30. 1962-67/1967-72 (prod: n/a). 2-door saloon, estate car. F/R, 598cc/701cc (S4 OHV).** Old theme updated with Reliant's own diecast engine and rustproof glass-fibre bodies incorporating a 105E Anglia-type breezeway rear window. Roomier than the Austin-powered types, though the gearbox hump remains in front. Estate cars and bigger engine from late '67.

SABRE. 1961-63 (prod: n/a). 2-seater sports, coupé. F/R, 1703cc (S4 OHV). Odd, ugly beast with odder, leading-arm front suspension, front horns styled into overriders, front disc brakes, rack and pinion steering, and all synchro 'box by ZF. Twin-carb Consul engine gives 73bhp, ergo an easy 90mph. Kamm-tailed coupé variants from June '62. ►

◄ **SABRE SIX SE2S. 1962-64 (prod: 77). 2-seater sports, coupé. F/R, 2553cc (S6 OHV).** Restyled front end and (on '64 cars) a satisfactory wishbone front suspension. 109bhp Ford engine with electric fan cooling: triple overdrive optional. Usually ZF 'box. 110mph and 0-60 in 12.2secs. So far neglected by the collectors, so snap one up quickly.

SCIMITAR SE4A. 1964-66 (prod: 296). 3-seater coupé. F/R, 2553cc (S6 OHV). Ogie's SX250 productionised by Reliant with Ford mechanics, and once again rustfree glass-fibre bodywork as on Sabres. Centre-lock wheels, choice of Ford or ZF 'boxes with optional overdrive. Trailing-arm suspension and a better ride came in 1966, but whichever one you choose, it's a winner on looks. ►

◄ **SCIMITAR SE4B/SE4C. 1966-70/1967-70 (prod: 590/117). 3-seater coupé. F/R, 2994cc/2495cc (V6 OHV).** In, Ford's new V6, a stiffer chassis (ergo better handling) and more speed and acceleration. Even the rare 'economy' 2½-litre gives you 110mph. Out, wire wheels (except at extra cost) and the option of a ZF 'box. All Scimitar coupés are, however, sleepers to watch.

SCIMITAR GTE. 1969-86 (prod: 5687 to Nov 1981). 2-door estate car. F/R, 2994cc (V6 OHV). The car that set the GT wagon mode, and still looks right, though for beauty, give us a coupé any day. Manual, overdrive or automatic available, all have servo front disc brakes, and all are glass-fibre, so no rust problems. Restyled 1976, 2.8-litre engine from 1980. Earlier SE5 models most desirable. ►

REBEL/REBEL 700. 1965-67/1968-72 (prod: n/a). 2-door saloon, estate car. F/R, 598cc/701cc (S4 OHV). Very basic four-wheeler using Regal's engine and back end, with estate car option and bigger 31bhp power unit from '68. Drum brakes and no synchro on bottom gear, but 60mph and 60mpg possible. A runabout for wives suffering from a surfeit of Minis? ➤

RENAULT (F)

Now state-owned and financed (and making huge losses), this firm was once master-minded by the autocratic Louis Renault, whose first design was produced in 1898: by 1913, it was responsible for producing around 20 per cent of French cars. Between the wars, Renault products were uninspired compared to those of rising star Citroën. Since nationalisation in 1945, it has produced some truly great designs, such as the 4CV and the 5. Its reputation lies mainly in small and medium cars, although there have been attempts to produce executive type cars, as well as a major effort to break into the US market by purchasing a stake in American Motors.

◄ **JUVAQUATRE. 1938-50 (prod: n/a). 4-door saloon. F/R, 1003cc (S4 OHV).** Opel Kadett with a Parisian accent and all-transverse springing, independent at the front. Post-war models (all four-door) have hydraulic brakes. Not generally sold here, but quite a few rhd cars put together at Acton for re-export. Light commercial derivatives (Dauphinoise) with ohv engines made up to '61.

4CV. 1947-61 (prod: 1,105,543 all types). 4-door saloon, 4-door convertible. R/R, 760cc/747cc (S4 OHV). Original rear-engined type with rack and pinion steering, hydraulic brakes, and all-independent suspension. Three speeds only, rolltop convertibles rare: on 19-22bhp not really dangerous, unlike later developments. 747cc engine 1950, restyled front end and bigger boot '54, pressurised cooling '55, Ferlec clutch option (avoid) from 1956. ➤

◄ **4CV R1052 SPORT. 1952-56 (prod: see 4CV). 4-door saloon. R/R, 747cc (S4 OHV).** The hairy one, with stiffer crank, light alloy head and conrods, dual-choke carburettor and so on. Up to 42bhp available, with speeds in the low 80s. Five-speed crash 'box option 1953, but the few cars sold in Britain were four-speeders. Unlikely to find one that hasn't rusted out, but could be fun if you do.

FREGATE/DOMAINE/MANOIR. 1952-60 (prod: 168,383 all types to 1958). Saloon, estate car. F/R, 1997cc/ 2141cc (S4 OHV). All-independently sprung, unitary, Vanguard-challenger with noisy all-indirect 'box (direct top on '56 and later preferred). UK-available from '54, Domaine/Manoir wagons and 2.1-litre engines 1956, hypoid rear end '57, Transfluide automatic option '58. Spares now unobtainable. ➤

➤ **DAUPHINE. 1956-68 (prod: n/a). Saloon. R/R, 845cc (S4 OHV).** France's first two-million seller, and effectively an updated and roomier 4CV with enough brake horses to make it lethal. Few left: they were rust traps. Ferlec clutch option '57, variable rate suspension from 1960, four-speed 'box (desirable) from '61, and all-disc brakes from '64. A performer in its day with an honest 45mpg.

DAUPHINE GORDINI. 1957-68 (prod: n/a). Saloon. R/R, 845cc (S4 OHV). *Le sorcier* extracted 38bhp from the little three-bearing four, and all Gordinis are four-speeders, reach 75mph, and are nearly as frugal as the standard article, though as alarming and as rustprone. 1962 Rallye version (1093cc, 55bhp) never imported though it should sort the men out from the boys. ➤

➤ **FLORIDE. 1959-62 (prod: n/a). 4-seater coupé, 4-seater convertible. R/R, 845cc (S4 OHV).** First of the sporty Renault coupés, with Dauphine Gordini mechanics, four speeds, variable rate springing, and those alarming swing axles at the back. Drum brakes and an unsynchronised bottom gear. A nice little fun-car in its day, and beginning to appreciate, but go for the later Caravelle.

CARAVELLE. 1962-63/1963-68 (prod: n/a). 4-seater coupé, 4-seater convertible. R/R, 956cc/1108cc (S4 OHV). Improved Floride, nearly a full four-seater, all-disc brakes this time, and tougher, 51bhp five-bearing engine. From September '63 with bigger unit, synchro on bottom, and a genuine 90mph. Still cheap, but rust-free survivors are beginning to attract attention. ➤

4/4L. 1962-63/1963 to date (prod: n/a). Estate car. F/F. 747cc/845cc (S4 OHV). Engaging little fwd hack with sealed cooling and all-torsion-bar suspension: handling curious and there's a nasty push-pull gearshift. 845cc unit standard in Britain from late '63, four-speed all-synchro (preferred) from '68, 12-volt electrics standard 1971. Later cars are better appointed and will have had less time to rust.

8. 1963-67 (prod: n/a). 4-door saloon. R/R, 956cc (S4 OHV). Has the Floride's rear-mounted radiator, ergo more room than on a Dauphine: other bonuses are five mains, sealed cooling, and all-disc brakes. Automatic available, but there's really nothing to commend the early 8 to collectors. Try the 1100 version.

8-1100. 1964-72 (prod: n/a). 4-door saloon. R/R, 1108cc (S4 OHV). More power and synchro on all gears with this one: better still, it's only been out of production 14 years and you might find an uncorroded specimen. Restyled with longer nose and boot 1965, rectangular headlamps from 1967. Watch for semantic problems (see under Renault 10).

8 GORDINI. 1965-70 (prod: n/a). 4-door saloon. R/R, 1108cc/1255cc (S4 OHV). Lowered suspension, a brake servo, twin dual-choke carburettors, and 95bhp on a 10.5:1 compression give you more performance (if not the handling) than a full-house Cooper S plus plenty of room for four people. Later cars with the 1300 engine and five-speed 'box are even faster. How about 0-50mph in just over 7.5 seconds?

10. 1970-71 (prod: n/a). 4-door saloon. R/R, 1289cc (S4 OHV). Confusion here, as in France the designation is also applicable to longnose R8-1100s from '66! What was sold in Britain as a 10 boasts the five-bearing, 48bhp 1300 engine, four forward speeds, and the combination of 85mph and 35-40mpg. Handling better than on older 8s, but steering rather dead.

6. 1968-80 (prod: n/a). Estate car, F/F, 845cc (S4 OHV). ➤ Bigger, faster, better appointed 4, always with four speeds, but still with that dashboard gearshift. Again an excellent hack, but no point in buying an old one. Go for the 1100 edition (1971 onwards) with 43mpg and front disc brakes. 6s available in UK from October, 1969.

◄ **16. 1965-1979 (prod: 1,846,000 all types). 5-door saloon. F/F, 1470cc/1565cc (S4 OHV).** Early hatchback and still one of the best – tons of room, very reliable, reasonable rust record, and stable in crosswinds if a little tricky on winding roads. Disc front brakes, four-on-the-column, and suspension similar to the 4's. Automatic available with bigger engine, 1970. This unit standard from '71.

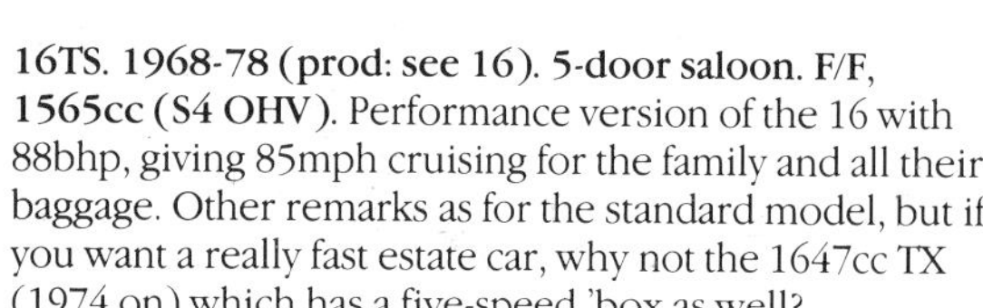

16TS. 1968-78 (prod: see 16). 5-door saloon. F/F, 1565cc (S4 OHV). ➤ Performance version of the 16 with 88bhp, giving 85mph cruising for the family and all their baggage. Other remarks as for the standard model, but if you want a really fast estate car, why not the 1647cc TX (1974 on) which has a five-speed 'box as well?

◄ **12. 1969-80 (prod: n/a). 4-door saloon, estate car. F/F, 1289cc (S4 OHV).** Very roomy family saloon with fair-to-good handling, and excellent economy (32-35mpg driven hard). Automatic available, though Gordini version (1565cc, 113bhp) not marketed here. If you want more than 85mph, go for a later (1972) TS version.

RILEY (GB)

By 1945 the great days of the Riley had passed – these were in the 1920s and early 1930s, when the Riley Nine revolutionised saloon car design, and when the marque established a superb racing record to back up its quality medium-size sporting products. Founded in 1898, Riley lost its independence when the Nuffield Organisation took over the financially shaky firm in 1938. Immediate postwar products managed to retain Riley individuality, but thereafter the cars became just badge-engineered versions of contemporary BMC products. The marque died, some would say for the best, in 1969.

◄ **1½-LITRE RMA. 1946-52 (prod: 10,504). Sports saloon. F/R, 1496cc (S4 OHV).** A 'real' Riley from Nuffield with classic twin-camshaft high-pushrod engine, elegant fabric-topped bodywork, torsion-bar ifs, and hydromech brakes: only early ones have opening screens. 75mph, but heavy on the hands at traffic speeds. One or two dropheads made 1946. Dark blue badge distinguishes this one from the 2½-litre.

1½-LITRE RME. 1952-55 (prod: 3446). Sports saloon. F/R, 1496cc (S4 OHV). Improved RMA with open propeller shaft, hypoid axle, full hydraulic brakes and bigger rear window. 1954-55 cars have streamlined sidelamps, no running board, curious rear wheel spats, and foglamps as standard. Chassis solid enough, but watch for body rot on all RM saloons. ►

◄ **2½-LITRE RMB. 1946-52 (prod: 6900). Sports saloon. F/R, 2443cc (S4 OHV).** The splendid 1937 Big Four engine (90bhp) in a lengthened RMA chassis (mechanics identical) with light blue diamond badge. From 1948, power up to 100bhp, which spells 95mph and 80-85mph cruising. Still a long-legged cruiser, but very heavy on the hands in traffic.

2½-LITRE RMC. 1948-50 (prod: 507). 3-seater roadster. F/R, 2443cc (S4 OHV). US market offering with the 100bhp engine, a 20-gallon tank, and cowcatcher bumpers. Lowered bonnet line helps looks, and 'screen folds flat, but column shift's a liability, so try to find one of the late home-market versions with floor change. Some with two bucket seats: this one is faster than the saloon. ►

◄ **2½-LITRE RMD. 1948-51 (prod: 502). 4-seater drophead coupé. F/R, 2443cc (S4 OHV).** Standard 1948 mechanical specifications with floor change and hydromech brakes, but attractive four-light coachwork, plus the twin leading shoe anchors at the front first used on roadsters. Desirable, but if you want a cheap driveable RM, better opt for a saloon. A fair proportion sold on the home market.

2½-LITRE RMF. 1952-53 (prod: 1050). Sports saloon. F/R, 2443cc (S4 OHV). 2½-litre with the RMF treatment – hypoid axle, all-hydraulic brakes, and so on. Most of them finished in metallic tones. Unlike the later 1½-litres, though, RMFs don't suffer from lowered gear ratios and performance is unaffected. 20mpg obtainable in normal driving conditions. ➤

◄ **PATHFINDER. 1953-57 (prod: 5152). Sports saloon. F/R, 2443cc (S4 OHV).** For, the splendid old twin-cam Riley engine, right-hand shift, a separate chassis. Against, the rest of it is Wolseley, including the cam steering, though the torsion-bar front end's an RM legacy. Servo brakes this time, but not very flexible. Go for late ones with overdrive and without the rear coil suspension. Automatic available from '56.

2.6. 1958-59 (prod: 2000). Sports saloon. F/R, 2639cc (S6 OHV). If you want a 6/90 Wolseley with a U-radiator, this is it. Both have twin-carb C-type engines and overdrive/automatic options – the Riley, however, has four extra brake horses, wider section tyres, bucket front seats, and a rev counter. Scarce and unromantic – decadence value only. ➤

◄ **1.5 1957-65 (prod: 40,577). Saloon. F/R, 1489cc (S4 OHV).** Also a Wolseley, but a much better one, thanks to Morris Minor-type suspension and steering. Twin SUs boost output to 68bhp, and don't forget it did well in its day on the circuits. With 85mph on tap, an uncorroded specimen would be an entertaining and usable cheap buy.

4/68 & 4/72. 1959-61/1961-69 (prod: 10,940/14,151). Saloon. F/R, 1489cc/1622cc (S4 OHV). BMC-Farina yet again, this time a mix of MG performance (twin SUs, 66bhp with the 1½-litre engine) and Wolseley luxury (burr walnut veneer, and so on). Most of them two-toned: this became the standard finish from June '62. 4/72 (Oct 1961) has 1.6-litre engine and automatic option. Definitely not 'magnificent motoring', whatever the catalogue said. ➤

ELF I. 1961-62 (prod: 30,912 all Elves). 2-door saloon. F/F, 848cc (S4 OHV). Mini with a bustle boot, tailfins, and a smattering of wood veneer in odd places. Untuned engine, and not clear why it cost more than its Wolseley stablemate. Always rare, hence mild curiosity value. ►

◄ **ELF II. 1962-69 (prod: see Elf I). 2-door saloon. F/F, 998cc (S4 OHV).** Cooking 1 litre engine in luxury Mini, with Hydrolastic suspension and diaphragm clutch in '64, and automatic option later. Quite an amusing basis for an amateur Custom, but not much else.

KESTREL 1100/1300. 1965-68/1968-69 (prod: 21,529). 4-door saloon. F/F, 1098cc/1275cc (S4 OHV). Rebadged MG 1100, with the usual twin SUs, walnut veneer, and rev counter. 1300s and later 1100s ('69 on) with automatic option. 1300s have all-synchro 'boxes as standard. 1969s preferable, as these have close-ratio gears and 70bhp Cooper S engines. ►

ROCHDALE (GB)

This company started making aluminium bodies for racing cars in 1948, turning to production of glass-fibre bodyshells in 1952. The firm's first manufacturing venture, the monocoque Olympic prototype, appeared in 1959. The Lancashire company, run by Harry Smith and Frank Butterfield, ceased to manufacture cars in 1968, moving instead into the industrial glass-fibre field.

◄ **OLYMPIC I. 1960-62 (prod: 150). 2-seater coupé. F/R, 1489cc (S4 OHV).** Glass-fibre unitary kit with Riley 1.5 mechanics and twin-carb engine, though with a live axle-and-coil set up at the rear. Built in crash hoop at windscreen level, and good for the ton on a weight of 13cwt. Some with occasional rear seats.

OLYMPIC II. 1962-68 (prod: 250). 2-seater coupé. F/R, 1498cc (S4 OHV). Lighter, cleaned up Olympic with Ford Cortina engine, front disc brakes, and coil and wishbone front end courtesy Triumph. Body is a semi hatchback with twin fuel tanks, and there's better underbonnet access. Over 110bhp with Cortina GT unit, though some fitted with BMC power. ►

RODLEY (GB)

Another short lived baby car from the 1950s, although the Rodley Automobile Company's effort did look more serious than some of its competitors. Production was supposed to reach 50-60 per week, but very few were made in the car's short production life of just over a year, and the Leeds firm disappeared in 1955.

◄ **750. 1954-55 (prod: n/a). 4-seater convertible. R/R, 747cc (V2 SV).** JAP-engined minicar from Leeds, with angular rolltop coachwork *à la Topolino*, three-speed motorbike gearbox driving by chain to differential back end, cable-operated brakes, and chain steering. It may have been 'the cheapest four-wheel car in Britain', but who's ever seen one? Not I.

ROLLS-ROYCE (GB)

One of the most prestigious car manufacturers in the world. All pre-war products were superbly made and highly refined, even though the engineering may have been a little staid. A US manufacturing venture folded in 1931, the year the firm acquired Bentley Motors. Postwar products have retained the dignity of their predecessors. Rolls-Royce Motors Ltd was formed in 1971 following the bankruptcy of the company which also operated the aero-engine side of the business.

SILVER WRAITH 4¼-LITRE. 1946-51 (prod: 1144 all swb). Sports saloon, touring limousine, limousine, Sedanca de Ville, numerous specials. F/R, 4257cc (S6 IOE). Short 127in wheelbase, overhead-inlet engine, dual-choke Stromberg carburettor, centralised chassis lubrication, and hydromech brakes with that wonderful servo. All bodies bespoke, which means rustfree ali panels, but no off-the-peg spares. All manual 'boxes, but left-hookers will have column shift. ►

◄ **SILVER WRAITH 4.6-LITRE. 1951-53 (prod: see Silver Wraith 4¼-litre). Sports saloon, touring limousine, limousine, Sedanca de Ville, numerous specials. F/R, 4566cc (S6 IOE).** Rare development of the family with big-bore engine and dual-choke carburettor again. Automatic only from late '52, and uncommon. Some lovely bodies, especially H.J. Mulliner's Sedanca and Hooper's touring limousine, though Park Ward's saloons tend towards the bulboid. Dropheads scarce and very expensive.

SILVER WRAITH LWB. 1951-55/1955-59 (prod: 639 all types). Various, mainly formal. F/R, 4566cc/4887cc (S6 IOE). A heavy car on a 133in wheelbase, and the biggest Royce you could buy in the fifties, ergo ponderous and strictly to be driven in. Automatic optional from late '53, standardised during '54. 4.9-litre engine from mid-'55. Can sometimes be found for less money than a top-condition standard steel, but really best kept for wedding hire. ►

SILVER DAWN. 1949-51/1951-52 (prod: 760 all types to 1955). Standard steel saloon. F/R, 4257cc/4566cc (S6 IOE). Mk VI Bentley with detuned engine and the U-bonnet/radiator. Stromberg carburettor to '51, Zenith thereafter with the big-bore unit. Export only, and rhd scarce: once again column shift on all left-hookers, thus the later R-type derivative preferred. Special bodies very seldom seen.

SILVER DAWN. 1952-55 (prod: see 1949-52 models). Standard steel saloon, drophead coupé. F/R, 4566cc (S6 IOE). This one's a detuned R-type Bentley, almost invariably with the Hydramatic 'box standardised during 1953. Dropheads scarce, but though this model was UK-available it's much in demand, and you can still pay the earth. Beware of Bentley conversions, sometimes quite well done.

PHANTOM IV. 1950-56 (prod: 16). Various. F/R, 5675cc (S8 IOE). Just about the last straight-eight announced, though the B80 engine had military and commercial applications and spares are available. Strictly for Crowned Heads or their republican equivalents. Manual transmission and steering, unless the original VIP owner had it converted. Enormous, immensely heavy, and just about the ultimate collector's status symbol – if you can't lay hands on a Bugatti Royale, that is.

PHANTOM V. 1959-68 (prod: 832). Limousine, various specials. F/R, 6230cc (V8 OHV). Makes a lwb Wraith look tiny with its 12ft wheelbase, 2¾-ton weight, and 20ft from bumper to bumper. Four-speed automatic and some necessary power steering, though you'll never drive it yourself. Drum brakes, but always of dual-circuit type. Some quite pretty Sedancas and sports saloons were fitted to this chassis.

PHANTOM VI. 1968-78/1978 to date (prod: 332). Limousine, various specials. F/R, 6230cc/6750cc (V8 OHV). Possibly the most expensive catalogued car in the world, in spite of which it is still made with drum brakes. Much too big for most people, and secondhand price depends largely on the fame/notoriety of the original owner. Older type engine and four-speed Hydramatic retained until '78, though such points are pretty well academic.

SILVER CLOUD I. 1955-59 (prod: 2231). Standard steel saloon, drophead coupé. F/R, 4887cc (S6 IOE). Total rationalisation, or only the bonnet/radiator assembly distinguishes it from a Bentley, though with new six-port head the ton is obtainable. Electrically controlled dampers and automatic standard, but power steering (a must) optional only, and not fitted at all before 1956. Best of the Clouds for regular use as it's quite fast enough, more frugal, and far easier to maintain than the V8s. ►

◄ **SILVER CLOUD I LWB. 1957-59 (prod: 121). Standard steel saloon. F/R, 4887cc (S6 IOE).** An extra 4ins of wheelbase plus a division, and Park Ward body plates though it's only a conversion. Usually power-steered, but rather unwieldy, and no reason beyond rarity to choose it instead of the standard model. Rear chassis rust a problem on all Clouds, in addition to the usual body headaches.

SILVER CLOUD II SWB/LWB. 1959-62 (prod: 2417/299). Standard steel saloon, drophead coupé. F/R, 6230cc (V8 OHV). First of the V8s, power steering and four-speed Hydramatic on all. As on later SC1s, air conditioning is available, but for use in Britain this is merely an added complication. Long chassis cars are all saloons. 115mph on tap, and comes cheap right now, but sixes and SC IIIs are better buys, unless you have a drophead, and one comes up on this chassis. ►

◄ **SILVER CLOUD III SWB/LWB. 1962-65 (prod: 2044/253). Standard steel saloon, drophead coupé. F/R, 6230cc (V8 OHV).** Quad headlamps the main difference from Series II, but the V8 bugs have been sorted out by now, and cars have had less time to rust, ergo higher prices. Once again beware of Bentley conversions: skilled fakers can cope with bonnet problems, but a 'B' chassis prefix gives the game away.

SILVER SHADOW I. 1965-70/1970-76 (prod: 16,717). Saloon. F/R, 6230cc/6750cc (V8 OHV). Unitary construction, disc brakes, all-independent self-levelling suspension, automatic and power steering – the lot. Higher geared steering and three-speed Hydramatic '68, air conditioning standard '69. 6.7-litre engine from July 1970. 1974 cars ride much better on wide-profile tyres, and the last ones have low-compression power units and electronic ignition. ►

SILVER SHADOW I LWB. 1966-70/1970-76 (prod: 2776). Saloon. F/R, 6230cc/6750cc (V8 OHV). For those who like to be driven, but can't afford a Phantom VI. Development history as for short-chassis cars, though both versions also come with central door locking from Sept '70, radial ply tyres from August '72, and quadraphonic tape on '75s and '76s. No real reason for preferring the lwb cars, though, except that with the unitary construction there are no longer any specials. ➤

◄ **SILVER SHADOW I COUPE/CONVERTIBLE. 1965-70/1966-70 (prod 606/505). 2-door coupé (Mulliner Park Ward), 2-door coupé (Young), drophead coupé. F/R, 6230cc/6750cc (V8 OHV).** All right, they're chopped sedans, but so well done you wouldn't know until the rust sets in. Mechanical mods as for early standard cars, but all the two-doors had the 6.2-litre engine. Convertible still very expensive. Young-bodied cars hard to find – only 35 built.

ROVER (GB)

Although another of those middle-class British makes, Rover has stood the test of time better than most. Like Riley, Rover started its manufacturing activities by making bicycles, before producing a car in 1904. Until the late 1930s, the firm always made some small cars, but it then changed direction by manufacturing mid-range cars, notable among these being the postwar P4 series and the larger P5 machines. The P6 series marked another change of direction, with an eye-catching shape and excellent engineering bringing in new, younger customers. In 1966 Rover lost its independence, becoming part of British Leyland, but since then has emerged, along with Austin, as a prominent marque in the British industry.

TEN. 1939-48 (prod: 2640 post-war). Saloon. F/R, 1389cc (S4 OHV). Traditional thirties design with a pleasant remote-control floor change. Free wheel, underslung frame, mechanical brakes, automatic chassis lubrication, and lots of wood and leather. Dignified, but with less than 40bhp to haul 25cwt, the Ten's best kept for summer pottering. ➤

◄ **TWELVE. 1937-48 (prod: 4840 post-war). Saloon, sports saloon, sports tourer. F/R, 1496cc (S4 OHV).** More power, more room, better stylistic proportions on this one, plus two alternative body styles. Tourers (1947 only) are very rare and pretty cars with fully disappearing hoods. Disc wheels on Rovers from mid'39, though in other respects pre-war models are identical. Caution, though – '37s and '38s don't have synchromesh.

FOURTEEN. 1939-48 (prod: 1705 post-war). Saloon, sports saloon. F/R, 1901cc (S6 OHV). This four-bearing six comes with built-in jacks, but otherwise it's the same old formula capable of a quiet 70mph even if acceleration is not its strong suit. 1937-38 cars are lookalikes but have smaller, 1.6-litre engines. Solid chassis, but watch for woodrot, and luggage accommodation is not spectacular. ➤

SIXTEEN. 1937-48 (prod: 4150 post-war). Saloon, sports saloon. F/R, 2147cc (S6 OHV). Bored out 14 on the same wheelbase with the same mechanical specifications and bodies, ideal for refined, leisurely motoring up to 70-75mph. All '47s and '48s have heaters as standard (this goes for lesser Rovers as well), but matched windtone horns are fitted only to sports saloons. ➤

◄ **60/75 P3. 1948-49 (prod: 1274/7837). Saloon, sports saloon. F/R, 1595cc/2103cc (S4/S6 IOE).** The shape's much the same, but only the inlet valves are still upstairs, brakes are hydromech, fuel is fed by electric pump, and there's some long-overdue coil-spring ifs. The bows-down attitude doesn't help the looks, but the traditional free wheel is still there. Dropheads very rare, but saloons still relatively inexpensive.

75 P4. 1950-54 (prod: 43,677 all types). Saloon, Pininfarina coupé, Pininfarina drophead coupé. F/R, 2103cc (S6 IOE). You won't believe it now but 'Auntie' represented screaming heresy in 1950 with her slab sides, column shift, and cyclop's eye spotlamp (though this last was dropped early '52 with the revised grille design). Hydraulics (1951 on) preferred to hydromech brakes, floor shift on '54s. Pininfarina's specials (1953-4) made only in penny numbers. ➤

◄ **60. 1954-59 (prod: 9261). Saloon. F/R, 1997cc (S4 IOE).** Auntie economy-model with the Land-Rover engine, not really the fuel miser one might expect it to be. All cars have the odd cranked floor change, and other improvements as 75. Most four-cylinder addicts prefer the later 80, so this one could be cheap. But despite the separate chassis, there are rust problems, especially around the sills.

75 P4. 1955-59 (prod: see 75 1950-54). Saloon. F/R, 2230cc (S6 IOE). 75 updated with short-stroke, higher-revving engine and three-piece wrapround rear window. Bucket seats from '56, raised front wing line and wing-mounted sidelamps '57, two-tone colours available from '58. Unless you're a freewheel addict, you'll go for '57's overdrive option. ➤

90. 1954-59 (prod: 35,891). Saloon. F/R, 2639cc (S6 IOE). 90bhp and 90mph (just) plus all the other year-by-year improvements. Reasonable fuel consumption, though heavy on the hands. Go for the '56 and later with vacuum servo brakes. Overdrive option (without freewheel) from '57, and some of the last straight four-speeders don't have freewheels either. ►

◄ **105R/105S. 1957-58/1957-59 (prod: 3499/7201). Saloon. F/R, 2639cc (S6 IOE).** Later styling (wrapround rear window, front wing ridges) plus twin-carb, 108bhp engine. S is a desirable car with overdrive, two-tone paint, twin fog lamps, servo brakes, and the ton available. Avoid the R with its complex, Rover-built two-speed-plus-overdrive automatic. Even the makers found two seasons of this quite enough...

80. 1960-62 (prod: 5900). Saloon. F/R, 2286cc (S4 OHV). 77bhp Land-Rover-based engine with all valves upstairs spells 80-85mph and 27mpg, plus surprising smoothness. All Aunties now feature wider rims, key starting, and servo front disc brakes. The late fours were never very popular, and what big money there is always goes on the sixes. ►

◄ **100. 1960-62 (prod: 16,621). Saloon. F/R, 2625cc (S6 IOE).** New seven-bearing, pump-cooled engine nearly as powerful as the old 105S despite its single SU carburettor. Overdrive standard: other improvements as for 80. 90-plus mph, and a refined carriage commanding respectable money if there's no rust.

95/110. 1962-64 (prod: 3680/4612). Saloon. F/R, 2625cc (S6 IOE). Still plenty of leather and wood about in Auntie's old age, and good 110s with 123bhp engine, overdrive, electric screenwashers and rim trims are sought after. 95 has 102bhp unit and no overdrive. Engines generally go very high mileages with little trouble, but repairs come expensive. ►

3-LITRE MK I/MK IA. 1959-62 (prod: 20,963). Saloon. F/R, 2995cc (S6 IOE). Hefty unitary barge beloved of British officialdom. Drums on very early ones, but usually servo front discs. Automatic available, but overdrive standard on stick shift versions from May '60. Usual slow steering, so go for power option (October '60 on). Mk· IA's (late '61) improvements include a standby extra electric fuel pump. ➤

◄ **3-LITRE MK II. 1962-65 (prod: 15,676/5482). Saloon, 4-door coupé. F/R, 2995cc (S6 IOE).** An extra 20bhp, lowered suspension, and a nicer gearshift, with a choice of manual/overdrive or automatic. All the last ones have power steering. Coupés are low-slung and handsome, but you can't wear a hat in the back. They also command money, but watch it, all 3-litres are potential rust-traps.

3-LITRE MK III. 1965-67 (prod: 3919/2501). Saloon, 4-door coupé. F/R, 2995cc (S6 IOE). Power steering now standard, and Mk III is recognisable by its new radiator badge and continuous side-chrome strip. Reclining front seats and better contours to the back ones are bonuses for tired tycoons. If, however, you're in a hurry, go for the later V8s. ➤

◄ **2000/2000SC. 1964-72 (prod: 327,808 all types). Saloon. F/R, 1978cc (S4 OC).** Out with the old image and in with a new Citroën-shape: 90bhp ohc engine, hydraulic clutch, all-synchro 'box, servo disc brakes all round, and de Dion rear end. A brute to work on, and rough at low speeds, but cruises in the high 80s and will turn in 30-32mpg. Automatic (avoid) available from October '66, nicer dashboard and nastier crosshatch grille from '71.

2000TC. 1966-72 (prod: see 2000). Saloon. F/R, 1978cc (S4 OC). More chrome and sedate wheels (ugh!) but the extra carburettor boosts output to 124bhp and you get a rev counter. Handling excellent, no automatic-option. '71 changes as 2000SC, but early 2000 'boxes were on the stiff side, and the improved '69 version is preferred. Mechanics last well, the structure rusts. ➤

3.5-LITRE. 1968-75 (prod: 11,501/9099). Saloon, 4-door coupé. F/R, 3528cc (V8 OHV). The ultimate in ministerial barges, and Rover's first use of the light-alloy, ex-Buick V8. The 160bhp under your right foot gives you 108mph and 0-50mph in under 9secs, even with the compulsory automatic. Power steering and Rostyles standard. Not as yet very collectable. ➤

◄ **3500. 1968-75 (prod: 79,057). Saloon. F/R, 3528cc (V8 OHV).** Marriage of a 2000 hull and the light-alloy V8. 1971 styling improvements apply here as does a power steering option. Manuals (17,000 odd only from '72) more fun and less thirsty, but the 'box wasn't quite man enough for this engine, and you'd be safer with automatic.

RANGE-ROVER. 1970 to date (prod: 96,331 to end 1981). Station wagon. F/4, 3528cc (V8 OHV). Today's essential adjunct to tweeds, hunting crops and four-wheel horse-boxes, as yet unbeaten at its own game. Servo disc brakes, permanent four-wheel drive, dual-range four-speed 'box, mostly rust-free alloy panels and a separate chassis, adding up to 100mph and 14mpg. No power steering before '80, and they've only just got around to four doors and an automatic option. Why buy secondhand? New ones are terribly expensive. ➤

RUSSON (GB)

An attempt to make a minicar with a reasonable amount of passenger room, the Russon was built at Stanbridge, Bedfordshire for just two seasons. Odd looks, rudimentary specification and negligible performance conspired to kill it, as it was as expensive as most early 1950s small family saloons.

◄ **MINICAR. 1951-52 (prod: 15). Open 3-seater. R/R, 250cc (S2 TS).** Roomy little dachshund of a car with twin-tube frame, tiny wheels, all-coil independent springing, rod-and-cable brakes, and three-speed motorbike-type 'box. Not unpleasing looks and the makers claimed 50mph and 65mpg. Alas, it cost as much as a Ford Anglia new, though if you found one it'd probably come a lot cheaper today.

SAAB (S)

The Svenska Aeroplan AB first made aeroplanes, but after 1945 it branched out into car manufacture with the Model 92, introduced in 1952. Always idiosyncratic, early Saabs had two-stroke engines and aerodynamic styling, and gained a great reputation in rallying. Convention came in 1967 with the first four-stroke cars. In 1968, the firm merged with the old established Scania Vabis truck company and made its odd Sonnet sports coupé: today it makes the slightly unconventional 900 series as well as the excellent 9000, part of a joint product involving Lancia, Fiat and Alfa Romeo.

◄ **96. 1960-68 (prod: 218,000). 2-door saloon. F/F, 841cc (S3 TS).** Sweden's teardrop-shaped rally winner, with 38bhp DKW-type longitudinal engine, three-on-the-column, a freewheel, and a total absence of wind noise. UK-available from '61, four-speed 'boxes during '63, dual-circuit brakes '64, some late ones with discs at the front. Handling less than forgiving, and petroil lubrication a nuisance.

95. 1959-68 (prod: 32,000). Estate car. F/F, 841cc (S3 TS). Engaging little wagon with the dress circle seats, so to speak, facing backwards, ideal for keeping the kids quiet. Development history as 96: from '65 both types have longer noses, frontal radiators, and 40bhp engines. Two-stroke Saabs not imported after '67. ►

◄ **SPORT/MONTE CARLO. 1962-66 (prod: n/a). 2-door saloon. F/F, 841cc (S3 TS).** Cashing in on Erik Carlsson's rally victories, or a super-96 with front disc brakes, triple carbs, four-speed all-synchro 'box, and full-pressure lubrication so you can forget all about petroil mixes. Nearly 90mph, but a daunting 22mpg. Monte Carlo (1966) has a higher axle ratio and a/c electrics, these last featuring on the final 95s and 96s.

96/95 V4. 1967-69/1968-79 (prod: 329,000/78,500). 2-door saloon, estate car. F/F, 1498cc (V4 OHV). Goodbye to two-strokes: the old familiar shape's now powered by a 65bhp German Ford V4 unit. Monte Carlo performance allied to 28/30mpg. Split-circuit disc/drum brakes, but the gearshift's still on the column, and they retained the freewheel to the end. Only recently defunct, so you should be able to find a low-mileage specimen. ►

◄ **SONNET. 1966-74 (prod: 10,219). 2-seater sports. F/F, 841cc/1498cc (S3 TS/S4 OHV).** Saab's attempt to build a sports car for the American market – and a successful one too. The first 258 had the Monte Carlo two-stroke engine, thereafter the V4. Low drag shape (0.32 Cd) made 100mph just possible. Sleeker styling from 1970 with the Sonnet III, identifiable by concealed headlights.

99. 1968 to date (prod: 88,500). 2-door saloon, 4-door saloon. F/F, 1709cc (S4 OC). First appearance of the overhead-cam Triumph-designed engine. Usual dead axle and coils at the rear, but all-disc brakes and floor shift. Gearbox under engine, *à la* Triumph 1300. Available UK 1969, four-doors 1970. Automatic and fuel injected versions not available here with '69/'71 1.7-litre motor. ➤

SCOOTACAR (GB)

A bizarre vehicle produced by Scootacars Ltd in Leeds, whose parent company was Hunslets, famous for making locomotives. Inspiration for the car, it is claimed, was that a Hunslets director's wife wanted something smaller and easier to park than her Jaguar . . . so they made a car for her. Hunslets pulled the plug in 1964.

◄ **COUPÉ. 1957-65/1962-65 (prod: 1000 approx all types). 2-seater coupé. R/R, 197cc/324cc (S1/S2 TS).** Odd little tri-scooter, 81ins long and 51ins wide, featuring single chain-driven rear wheel, all-coil springing, four-speed positive-stop 'box, front hydraulic brakes, and T-bar steering. 50mph with Villiers single, twins faster, but only about 10 made. There's a club for the breed.

SIATA (I)

Basically a tuning firm, Siata had been modifying cars, mainly Fiats, since 1926, and made its first production vehicle, the Amica, in 1949. Most Siatas were Fiat-derived, including some handsome V8-engined Vignale bodied coupés, and the firm lasted until 1970, pooling resources with Abarth from 1959 to 1961.

SPRING. 1968-75 (prod: n/a). 2-seater sports. R/R, 843cc (S4 OHV). Siata's swan-song on a Fiat 850S floorpan dressed up with square-tailed roadster coachwork and a mock-MG grille. Engine tuned the way the customer wanted it, and front disc brakes on later cars. None made 1971-72, but back again in '73 with Orsa badging. ➤

SIMCA (F)

Never quite able to challenge the dominance of Renault and Citroën in the popular car market in France, Simca was founded in 1934 by H. T. Pigozzi to manufacture Fiat cars under licence. After the war, the first entirely Simca-designed product appeared, the Aronde, and such was its success that the firm started on a policy of acquiring other makes, taking over Unic in 1951, Ford France in 1954 and Talbot in 1959. In 1958 Chrysler acquired a minority stake in the company, which had become a controlling interest by 1963, preceding the change of name in 1970 to Chrysler France SA. The name is no longer used.

ARONDE. 1951-55/1956-60 (prod: 1,014,355). Saloon, estate car, hardtop coupé. F/R, 1221cc/1290cc (S4 OHV). French-speaking cousin of the Millecento Fiat – looks better, handling inferior, rust potential about the same. Available UK from late '53. Smaller (14in) wheels '55, 1.3-litre engine '56. 57bhp big-valve version available '57, 1959s restyled with fancy grilles and wrapround rear windows. Only hardtops of any interest. ➤

◄ **ARONDE. 1961-63 (prod: 260,504). Saloon, estate car, hardtop coupé. F/R, 1290cc (S4 OHV).** A tough five-bearing engine applied to an ageing theme with the '60 restyle and auxiliary coil springs at the rear. Almost all UK imports are saloons. Montlhéry (and Monaco hardtop) with 62bhp: cheap Etoile and Elysée have only 52bhp, though still good for 75-80mph.

ARONDE OCEAN/PLEIN CIEL. 1957-62 (prod: 11,560). 2-seater coupé, 2-seater cabriolet. F/R, 1290cc (S4 OHV). The only collectable Arondes: in France you think in thousands rather than in hundreds of francs. Attractive Facel bodies with wrapround screens, 'performance' engines standard: 57bhp in '61, and 70bhp on the last ones. Go for the '61s and '62s with five mains. Not usually rhd, and UK-available from 1960 only. ➤

VEDETTE. 1955-62 (prod: 166,895). Saloon, estate car. F/R, 2353cc (V8 SV). Former French Ford with chassis design akin to early Consul/Zephyr family, plus that depressing little flathead V8 with roots going back to '36. On UK market from '56. Ferlec clutch option '58, overdrive also available from '59. Nothing much to recommend it. Ariane (Vedette hull, Aronde engine) mercifully not sold here.

1000. 1962-78 (prod: 1,642,091 all saloons). 4-door saloon. R/R, 944cc (S4 OHV). Undistinguished little beast with north-south rear engine and all-independent springing. Not a good handler, and drum brakes in basic form, but quite fair performance and good economy. 52bhp engine standard for UK '68, semi-automatics available from '66, but they revised the rear suspension in '73, so go for a modern one.

1000 COUPE. 1962-67 (prod: 10,011). 2+2-seater coupé. R/R, 944cc (S4 OHV). Bertone has transformed the ugliest of ducklings into a pretty NSU Sport Prinz lookalike. All-disc brakes, 52bhp, and a potential 90mph. Available UK from '64, but only with left-hand drive. Abarth breathed on these early coupés to good effect, but we'd suggest the later 1200S as a better bet.

1000 GLS/SPECIAL. 1969-78 (prod: see 1000 saloon). 4-door saloon. R/R, 1118cc (S4 OHV). They got it right in the end, though we still say that post-'72 versions are better. Standard 1969-70 cars offer 49bhp and 80mph, and front disc brakes standardised for UK in the latter year. There are, however, nicer small rear-engined saloons – Fiat, Hillman and Renault, for instance.

1200S. 1967-71 (prod: 14,741). 2+2-seater coupé. R/R, 1204cc (S4 OHV). The old Bertone coupé updated with a high-compression, bored-out motor giving 80-85bhp, and well over the ton. Dual circuit servo disc brakes, but again no right hook available. If the standard article isn't fast enough, Radbourne Racing used to market Abarthised editions which could be fun.

1300. 1963-66 (prod: 275,626). Saloon, estate car. F/R, 1290cc (S4 OHV). Simca are 'marking' Fiat again with a better-looking rival, though this time the handling's not notably inferior and the appointments are better. Live axle and coils at the rear, floor shift for UK (but with tiresome reverse gate on pre '66 cars). Also new for '66, estate cars and front disc brakes. ►

◄ **1500. 1963-66 (prod: 162,183). Saloon, estate car. F/R, 1475cc (S4 OHV).** Same excellent five-bearing engine in Fiat-like hull identifiable from 1300 by absence of vertical grille bars and presence (even in '63) of discs at the front. Offers 90-95mph and 27mpg. Estate cars from '65, automatic option '66, gearshifts as on 1300.

1301/1501. 1967-76 (prod: 637,263/267,835). Saloon, estate car. F/R, 1290cc/1475cc (S4 OHV). Last of the conventionally-engineered Simcas and good, solid family saloons if you can find one that's rust-free. Bigger boots, longer bonnets, and better ventilation. Servo brakes on 1501 from '69 and new grilles applied to 1501 from '70. 1301 doesn't get restyled front end until '73. ►

◄ **1100. 1968-79 (prod: 1,833,485 to end 1976). 3-door saloon, 5-door saloon, estate car. F/F, 1118cc (S4 OHV).** Simca's answer to the Fiat 128 (it happened first, in fact) with east-west engine, all-torsion-bar springing, front disc brakes, and rack and pinion steering. One of the first cars with this body configuration. Some late ones Chrysler-badged, and vans Dodge-badged to make it more complicated. A nice little car, but it rusts, so don't bother with older specimens.

1204. 1970-72 (prod: see 1100). 3-door saloon, 5-door saloon. F/F, 1204cc (S4 OHV). Tweaking a *traction*, or the 1100 with a detuned 1200S power unit at the other end, sporting a pair of dual-choke Webers, a brake servo, an electric fan in the cooling system, and some fancy paint and trim. 90-plus mph, but again, they offered a 1.3-litre development from '73, so why worry with aged specimens? ►

SINGER (GB)

This West Midlands-based car manufacturer was yet another which began by making bicycles. Its best days were from the mid-1920s to the late 1930s – in 1928, the firm was ranked third behind Morris and Austin in private car sales. While many of the firm's postwar products were innovative by conservative British standards, they were always too expensive to be competitive with those of conglomerates such as BMC. In 1956, the firm was saved by Rootes, who used the Singer name for de luxe Hillmans. The Chrysler takeover of 1965 presaged the death of the Singer name.

◄ **NINE ROADSTER. 1939-49 (prod: 2500 post-war). 4-seater sports tourer. F/R, 1074cc (S4 OC).** Mid-year '39 introduction and a pale shadow of the old Le Mans Nine, with its wide ratio three-speed 'box and mechanical brakes. The tough three-bearing engine, however, gives 36bhp and runs up to 5000rpm. Hard to find here as most of them were exported.

NINE ROADSTER 4A. 1949-50 (prod: 3390). 4-seater sports tourer. F/R, 1074cc (S4 OC). Still the same in appearance with its rod-operated brakes and 16ins pressed-steel wheels, not to mention the beam front axle; SU carburettor gives way to a Solex and there's now a much-needed extra forward ratio. Pretty little pre-war hangover, though for performance try the later SM Roadster. ►

◄ **NINE ROADSTER 4AB. 1951-52 (prod: 1000). 4-seater sports tourer. F/R, 1074cc (S4 OC).** Still good old trad with its cutaway doors, foldflat screen, classical radiator and '38-type engine, but with overriders, telescopic dampers, disc wheels, hydromech brakes, and coil-spring ifs. Much prettier than an A40 Sports, but 70mph will be hard work. 4AC had de-bored 1.2-litre SM-type engine.

SUPER TEN. 1938-49 (prod: 10,497 post-war). Saloon. F/R, 1194cc (S4 OC). Uprated pre-war design with 36bhp ohc engine, though on this one you get four speeds and a floor-mounted remote-control shift. Luggage accommodation limited, but screen opens. As good or bad as any old-fashioned family Ten. Brakes are hydraulic and you can spot post-war ones by their vertical-barred grilles. ►

◄ **SUPER TWELVE. 1947-49 (prod: 1098). Saloon. F/R, 1525cc (S4 OC).** Another pre-war car back after a lapse in 1945/6. Plated radiator shell, disc wheels and projecting boot on this one. Hydraulic brakes and beam front axle. Quite well finished, but never common. This engine, not the later SM-type, incidentally, slots into 1500 HRGs.

SM1500. 1949-50/1951-54 (prod: 17,382). Saloon. F/R, 1525cc/1497cc (S4 OC). Underrated, solidly built family saloon on a proper chassis, full hydraulic brakes, ifs, and pressurised cooling, but oh dear!, those slab sides, not much better with the two-tone paint of later cars. Short-stroke engine from '51, twin-carb 58bhp option from '53. Last ones have circular instruments and bigger rear windows. ➤

◄ **SM ROADSTER. 1951-55 (prod: 3440). 4-seater sports, tourer. F/R, 1497cc (S4 OC).** 4AB model with the short-stroke SM engine, hydromech brakes and the old familiar late thirties styling. The 58bhp twin-carb engine (optional '53 on) at least gives it some urge. Export only till late '53, so hard to find in Britain. At best, a charming period piece...the French love it.

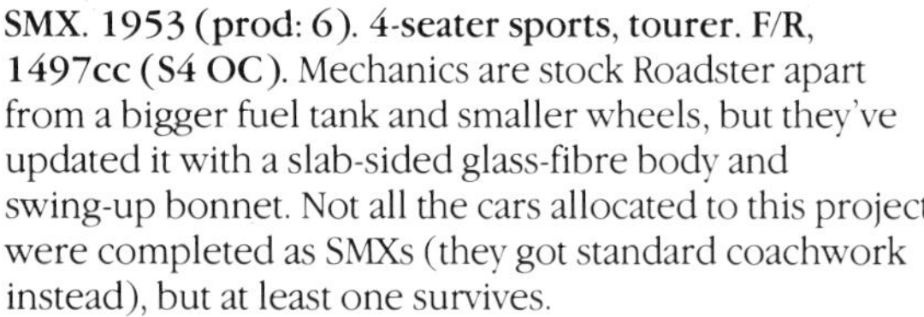

SMX. 1953 (prod: 6). 4-seater sports, tourer. F/R, 1497cc (S4 OC). Mechanics are stock Roadster apart from a bigger fuel tank and smaller wheels, but they've updated it with a slab-sided glass-fibre body and swing-up bonnet. Not all the cars allocated to this project were completed as SMXs (they got standard coachwork instead), but at least one survives. ➤

◄ **HUNTER. 1954-56 (prod: 4772). Saloon. F/R, 1497cc (S4 OC).** Keeping the SM shape going with a traditional radiator grille, leather seats, walnut dash and inclusive *de luxe* equipment (screenwash, twin horns, horse's head mascot). Twin carbs and floor change available, also stripped S variant (1956) without the fancy trimmings. Twin-cam 75bhp version never got beyond the prototype stage.

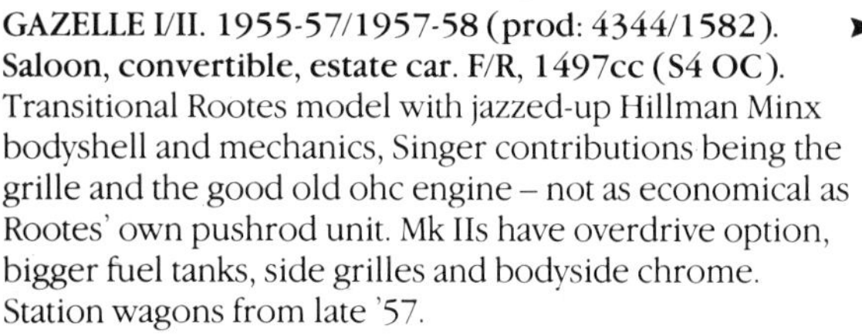

GAZELLE I/II. 1955-57/1957-58 (prod: 4344/1582). Saloon, convertible, estate car. F/R, 1497cc (S4 OC). Transitional Rootes model with jazzed-up Hillman Minx bodyshell and mechanics, Singer contributions being the grille and the good old ohc engine – not as economical as Rootes' own pushrod unit. Mk IIs have overdrive option, bigger fuel tanks, side grilles and bodyside chrome. Station wagons from late '57. ➤

GAZELLE IIA/III/IIIA/IIIB. 1958/1958-59/1959-60/1960-61 (prod: 43,545). Saloon, convertible, estate car. F/R, 1494cc (S4 OHV). Exit the Singer engine, enter the good old pushrod Minx unit. Mk III has better front seats, Mk IIIA gets the mandatory tailfins, a twin-carb 64bhp engine, floor change, and a Smiths Easidrive automatic option. Mk IIIB contributes a hypoid rear axle, but we're back with a single carburettor once more. ➤

◄ **GAZELLE IIIC. 1961-63 (prod: 15,115). Saloon, convertible, estate car. F/R, 1592cc (S4 OHV).** Another Minx variant, this time with enlarged single-carburettor motor and a choice of three transmissions: column shift still offered for export. Convertibles dropped February '62, estate cars a month later. The only Minx-engined Gazelles of any interest are the ragtops.

GAZELLE V. 1963-65 (prod: approx 20,000). Saloon. F/R, 1592cc (S4 OHV). Revised package, still the old familiar formula, but now with razor-edge roofline, wider rear doors, and front disc brakes. The '65 models have synchromesh on first (Hillmans had this in 1935!), a diaphragm clutch, and a floor selector for automatic versions. With overdrive, a Gazelle's more fun than a Minx, but that's not saying much! ➤

◄ **GAZELLE VI. 1965-67 (prod: 1482). Saloon. F/R, 1725cc (S4 OHV).** Last of the old 1956-shape Gazelles with the new, excellent five-bearing engine and a grille that doesn't swing up with the bonnet. Single-choke carburettor, and the usual three transmission choices, though the automatic (as on Mk V) is a Borg-Warner product.

VOGUE I/II. 1961-62/1962-64 (prod: 27,149). Saloon, estate car. F/R, 1592cc (S4 OHV). This time they've stuck a Singer grille and upmarket trim on a Super Minx. Manual, overdrive and Easidrive available, giving 80mph from 62bhp. Mk IIs have Borg-Warner automatic, disc front brakes, individual front seats and higher gearing, ergo are better buys. Estate car introduced May '62. ➤

VOGUE III. 1964-65 (prod: n/a). Saloon, estate car. F/R, 1592cc (S4 OHV). Six-light styling like a miniature Humber Hawk gives better all-round vision, while engine's uprated to Sceptre/Rapier levels, giving 78bhp and some performance. Also new, a synchromesh bottom gear and reclining seats. There were never any Vogue convertibles, by the way, though such a style was available on Super Minxes into '64.

VOGUE IV. 1965-66 (prod: 10,329). Saloon, estate car. F/R, 1725cc (S4 OHV). It had to happen – the 1.7-litre five-bearing engine married to a Singer Vogue. Output up again to 85bhp, and appointments way above the Minx class, plus usual transmission options. Rust problems, of course, afflict the whole family, especially inside the scuttle. Not a very interesting specimen.

CHAMOIS. 1964-70 (prod: 40,700 approx). 2-door saloon. R/R, 875cc (S4 OC). Up-market Hillman Imp with wide-rim wheels, better finish, a smattering of walnut veneer, and external side trim, plus a horizontal barred grille at the front to identify the make. Quad headlights from '69, though Moto Baldet offered such a conversion as early as November '64.

CHAMOIS SPORT. 1966-70 (prod: 4149). 2-door saloon. R/R, 875cc (S4 OC). The Imp family went pretty well on 39bhp, but this one has the 55bhp twin-carb sports engine and reclining seats. (Incidentally – they tended to collapse on early Imps, as I remember.) Servo brakes only on the first cars, quad headlamps from '69. Rarest and most desirable of this sub-group.

CHAMOIS COUPE. 1967-70 (prod: 4971). 4-seater coupé. R/R, 875cc (S4 OC). The pretty little slantback Californian with Singer badges. Cooking engine standard though there's no reason why anyone shouldn't up-rate it into a baby GT. Usual Imp faults, but remember, the auto-choke and pneumatic throttle died early in '65 and won't be found on many Singers.

◄ **NEW GAZELLE. 1967-70 (prod: n/a). Saloon. F/R, 1496cc/1725cc (S4 OHV).** Arrow derivative corresponding to the last of the Minxes. Front disc brakes, but servos not available till May '68, and you need one. Bigger engine with automatics: 1500 unit reserved for manual transmission. Unlikely to become collectable.

NEW VOGUE. 1966-70 (prod: n/a). Saloon, estate car. F/R, 1725cc (S4 OHV). Once again an Arrow with MacPherson front end, full-flow ventilation, and 80bhp engine. Headlamps are rectangular and you've the usual three transmission choices. Estate cars from May '67 (they went on selling Vogue IVs prior to this) and the desirable servo brake option 12 months later. ►

SKODA (CZ)

The first Skodas came out in 1925 after the firm had acquired the Laurin & Klement works – it had earlier made Hispano-Suizas under licence. Early products were conventional, but the mid-1930s saw a range of more advanced offerings. Products since World War II, when the firm became state owned, have tended to be staid and low priced.

◄ **440/445. 1954-57/1958-59 (prod: 84,792). 2-door saloon, estate car. F/R, 1089cc/1221cc (S4 OHV).** Classical, tough Czech design with tubular backbone frame, hypoid back end, swing-axle rear suspension, four-on-the-column, and Fiat-like ohv engine. Front and rear windows interchange on saloons. UK-available 1957, by which time there's synchro on second. The 445 with bigger engine, higher gearing, 1958. Wagons in '59 only.

450/FELICIA/FELICIA SUPER. 1958-59/1959-64/1959-64 (prod: 15,864 all types). 4-seater convertible. F/R, 1089cc/1221cc (S4 OHV). 440/445 with twin carbs – and floor change, plus a ragtop body. New name and choice of engines 1959, though 1.2-litre Super not sold in Britain till '63. Same 15ins wheels as saloons, glass-fibre hardtop optional, but usual problems with rear-end breakaway. ►

◄ **OCTAVIA/OCTAVIA SUPER. 1959-64 (prod: 227,258). 2-door saloon. F/R, 1089cc/1221cc (S4 OHV).** Improved 440 recognisable by one-piece grille in place of old three-piece type. Coils and wishbones replace the old transverse-leaf front end, but we've still got swing axles at the back and a column shift. Heater, screenwash, reclining seats standard for UK, but 1.2-litre Super not sold here till '63.

OCTAVIA TS. 1961-64 (prod: 2273). 2-door saloon. F/R, 1221cc (S4 OHV). Marriage of the Octavia's chassis/body with the Felicia's twin-carburettor 55bhp engine (standard versions have 47bhp), floor change, and a claimed 87mph. Only a handful sold in Britain, 1963-4. Curiosity value. ➤

◄ **OCTAVIA COMBI. 1961-71 (prod: 50,193). Estate car. F/R, 1221cc (S4 OHV).** Simple, austere wagon with Octavia mechanicals, column shift, and 47bhp engine, plus the usual drum brakes and 15ins wheels. Good ground clearance, while late examples have unchromed grilles. Not imported after 1969 and not very interesting.

1000MB/1000MBG/1000MBX/S100. 1965-69/1967-68/1967-68/1970-77 (prod: 1,239,327 all types). 2-door saloon, 4-door saloon. R/R, 988cc (S4 OHV). Semantic problems here, but all are early rear-engined types with all-synchro 'box, reclining bed seats, radiator blind, and that unfortunate swing-axle rear suspension which doesn't help handling. All four-door except MBX, this and MBG having 52bhp twin-carburettor engines. S100 redesignation (1970) also marks introduction of front disc brakes. ➤

◄ **1100MB/S110. 1968-69/1970-77 (prod: 323,848). 4-door saloon. R/R, 1107cc (S4 OHV).** More power, but drum brakes on 1100MB series, though MkII version (2969) has restyled front end and bigger rear window. Also on S110s are four-speed wipers: ground clearance high for a car of this class and good fuel economy, but handling still a very weak point.

S110R. 1970-80 (prod: 56,902). 2+2-seater coupé. R/R, 1107cc (S4 OHV). Pretty little car with 52bhp engine and 90mph potential: the rest of it's stock Skoda, apart from the split-circuit disc/drum brakes, with servos on later cars. In its day it was a cheap alternative to the 850S Fiat coupé: performance about the same, and the last ones won't have had much time to rust. ➤

STANDARD (GB)

R. W. Maudslay's company had modest beginnings in 1903, but by 1906 was marketing Britain's first inexpensive six-cylinder models. The firm specialised in medium range cars through the 1920s, but it was a small car, the Nine, which helped to circumvent increasing financial problems in 1928. In 1945, the firm acquired Triumph, and during the 1950s stopped making small cars. Its most famous model was the Vanguard, which sold well and provided the powerplant for the Triumph TR2. After the Leyland takeover of Standard Triumph in 1961, the Standard name was quietly dropped.

◄ **8 HP. 1945-48 (prod: 53,099 post-war). 2-door saloon, tourer, drophead coupé, estate car. F/R, 1009cc (S4 SV).** Update of '39 best-seller with same transverse-leaf ifs and Bendix brakes, though post-war ones recognisable by four-speed 'box and absence of bonnet louvres. A choice of two ragtop styles and all 8 HPs offer 60mph and 40mpg. Estate cars ('48 only) not on general sale.

12/14 HP. 1945-48 (prod: 9959/22,229). Saloon, drophead coupé, estate car. F/R, 1609cc/1766cc (S4 SV). The '39 notchback Super 12 with ifs, again minus the pre-war bonnet louvres: 14 (unlike its pre-war equivalent) uses 12 chassis, was originally an export-only item. Neither goes nor stops brilliantly, but well equipped with leather trim, opening 'screen, and so on and very reliable. 14s good for 70mph. Estate version used mainly as service van by Ferguson tractor dealers. ►

◄ **VANGUARD PHASE I. 1948-52 (prod: 184,799). Saloon, estate car. F/R, 2088cc (S4 OHV).** Tough six-seater hack (its styling aped the Plymouth) with wet-liner engine, all-synchro three-speed 'box, hydraulic brakes, coil ifs, and a separate chassis. Prototype's 1.8-litre engine never produced commercially, convertibles (by Imperia) in Belgium only. Rear wheel spats '50, overdrive option during that year, new grille and lower bonnet line on '52s.

VANGUARD PHASE II. 1953-55 (prod: 81,074). Saloon, 2-door estate car, 4-door estate car. F/R, 2088cc (S4 OHV). Same chassis and indestructible power train, but saloons now of notchback type with extra overhang, also more headroom and luggage space. Hydraulic clutch, left-hand column shift (also on Phase I from 1950). Handling as awful as ever, but better than 30mpg with optional overdrive. ►

VANGUARD PHASE II DIESEL. 1954-55 (prod: 1973). Saloon, estate car. F/R, 2092cc (S4 OHV). Britain's first catalogued diesel private car, stiffer and heavier frame, and electrically operated overdrive standard on second and top. Otherwise a stock Phase II. 65mph is hard work, but 50mpg possible with gentle driving. Look for these in Wales: the Port Talbot steelworks had a big fleet of them. ➤

◄ **VANGUARD III. 1956-58 (prod: 37,194). Saloon, estate car. F/R, 2088cc (S4 OHV).** The Vanguard goes unitary, with forward-mounted engine and a roofline 3½ins lower: it's also lighter and higher-geared, which spells more mph and mpg. Usual overdrive option, screenwash and heater standard. De luxe models have bigger brakes and hooded headlamps.

VANGUARD SPORTSMAN. 1956-57 (prod: 901). Saloon. F/R, 2088cc (S4 OHV). Meant to be a Triumph Renown replacement, hence the globe badge. MG-Farina style grille, 90bhp twin-carb engine, crossflow cooling, front anti-roll bar and 10ins brake drums. Dual overdrive standard, likewise jazzy two-toning inside and out, and two-speed wipers. Does 90mph and has considerable curiosity value, but a bit perilous in the wet. ➤

◄ **VIGNALE VANGUARD. 1958-61 (prod: 26,276). Saloon, estate car. F/R, 2088cc (S4 OHV).** Michelotti's touches are mainly confined to a new grille and aluminium wheel discs, though the options list now embraces automatic and even four-on-the-floor. Always drum brakes, though the last 210 cars have an updated Vanguard 6 'chassis' specification (longer rear springs, higher gearing).

8. 1953-60 (prod: 136,317 all types). 4-door saloon. F/R, 803cc (S4 OHV). Rival for the A30 and Minor with 26bhp three-bearing engine, unitary construction, coil ifs and hypoid rear end. Early ones very basic with negligible trim, sliding windows only, internal access to boot. Winding windows on De Luxe '54, on all from May '55. Super (1956) is better equipped, and Gold Star (1957) has *triple* overdrive. ➤

10. 1954-60 (prod: approx 172,500 all types). 4-door saloon. F/R, 948cc (S4 OHV). Engine grows up earlier than BMC's A-type: also on Tens you get a plated grille in place of the 8's 'bomb crater', drop windows, and external-access boot. Phase IIs (1957 on) have plated side trim, are available with two-pedal Standrive (caution!) and/or overdrive. Quite a performer for its day, but handling not a strong point. ➤

◄ **10 COMPANION. 1955-61 (prod: see 10). Estate car. F/R, 948cc (S4 OHV).** Four-door wagon, a bit truckish as to trim, but roomy. Mechanics as saloon, with mechanical improvements as they come. Both models also produced in Triumph-badged TBE form for the US market, 1957-60 (prod: 9907 saloons; 7351 Companions). Specs for these the same, the lhd apart.

PENNANT. 1957-59 (prod: 42,910). 4-door saloon. F/R, 948cc (S4 OHV). Mechanically a 1958 Ten with 37bhp engine, but with hooded headlamps, lengthened front and rear wings, and side-chrome arranged to split up the two-tone paintwork. Better instrumentation and remote-control gearshift. Standrive and overdrive available. Some examples still being supplied for export in 1960. ➤

◄ **ENSIGN. 1957-61 (prod: 18,852). Saloon. F/R, 1670cc (S4 OHV).** An economy-model Vanguard with the same hull and overall dimensions, but with smaller 60bhp engine and more austere trim. Four-on-the-column standard. Rare Mk II (991 cars, 1961) has the Vanguard 6's chassis mods. The RAF bought many Ensigns.

ENSIGN DE LUXE. 1962-63 (prod: 2318). Saloon, estate car. F/R, 2138cc (S4 OHV). More semantics than anything else, or getting rid of the Vanguard label and suggesting a luxury that the word 'standard' denies. Otherwise it's just a Vanguard with the latest over-bored engine (75bhp), and four-on-the-floor. Overdrive and front disc brakes available, the latter usually fitted. ➤

VANGUARD LUXURY SIX. 1961-63 (prod: 9953). Saloon, estate car. F/R, 1991cc (S6 OHV). Vignale Vanguard with longer rear springs, higher gearing, and more luxurious trim, plus a smooth, 80bhp twin-carburettor 'six' giving 90mph. Four transmission options – three-on-the-column, four-on-the-floor, overdrive or automatic. Front disc brakes available from July '61. Most people will prefer the later Triumph 2000 with the same engine.

STEYR-PUCH (A)

Steyr made some interesting cars before 1939, some of them designed by Ferdinand Porsche, but home-grown models were dropped in favour of Fiat assembly from 1949 onwards. Fiat production was the firm's staple, albeit with its own engine design. The firm now produces four-wheel-drive vehicles as part of Steyr-Daimler-Puch.

650 TR II. 1964-68 (prod: n/a). 2-door saloon. R/R, 660cc (S2 OHV). Austrian-made Fiat 500 hull, but with Steyr's own high-compression 40bhp air-cooled twin engine, synchro 'box, and swing-axle rear end. Roll-back roof over front seats. Incredibly noisy, but in effect a 'Cooperised' Fiat, which rushes up to 60 in under 16 secs and will do 85mph. Very few imported.

SUNBEAM-TALBOT (GB)

Sunbeam-Talbots were essentially luxury fast touring versions of Hillman and Humber models, being produced in London from 1938 to 1945, and then at the Ryton plant from 1946 to 1954. The '90' model had a fine reputation in rallying, but after 1954 the Sunbeam-Talbot name disappeared from the Rootes inventory.

TEN. 1939-48 (prod: 4719 post-war). Sports saloon, sports tourer, drophead coupé. F/R, 1185cc (S4 SV). Traditional Minx in a party frock first seen in '36 with different styling as the Talbot Ten. Bendix brakes and beam axles, fancy wheel discs conceal ordinary easy-cleans, and underslung back end spells poor ground clearance. Floor shift, but feels and drives like an overweight Minx.

2-LITRE. 1940-48 (prod: 1124 post-war). Sports saloon, sports tourer, drophead coupé. F/R, 1944cc (S4 SV). Ten with longer bonnet which improves looks, but windtone horns and foglamps standard on this one, which also inherits hydraulic brakes from the Humber Hawk with the same engine. But 56bhp really isn't enough to give this one much urge: comparable with the 1½-litre Jaguar.

80. 1948-50 (prod: 4000). Sports saloon, drophead coupé. F/R, 1185cc (S4 OHV). Attractive facelift of the 10/2-litre theme with recessed headlamps, single-panel curved 'screen, rear wheel spats, and an extra 6bhp thanks to an ohv conversion of the Minx engine. Twin leading shoe hydraulic brakes at last, too; good for 70mph. The less said of the facia and the 'synchromatic' column shift, the better.

90. 1948-50 (prod: 5493). Sports saloon, drophead coupé. F/R, 1944cc (S4 OHV). Identical to the 80 apart from 2-litre, 64bhp ohv engine which spells over 75mph. Four-light dropheads very pretty, and separate chassis robust, though watch the sills and the wheel arches, common sources of trouble. Beam front axle spells a pretty rough ride, so go for later 2.3-litre versions and ifs.

90 MK II. 1951 (prod: 1000 approx). Sports saloon, drophead coupé. F/R, 2267cc (S4 OHV). Obvious identification features are the air intakes flanking the still-traditional grille, but underneath you find a reinforced frame, a hypoid rear axle, and coil-spring ifs, not to mention an ohv derivative of the latest Humber Hawk engine which gives you 80/85mph. Sliding roofs still standard on saloons.

90 MK IIA. 1952-54 (prod: 6381). Sports saloon, drophead coupé. F/R, 2267cc (S4 OHV). Rallying experience with earlier 90s has given this one better steering and bigger brakes, plus ventilated disc wheels and deletion of those tiresome rear-wheel spats. 1954 models have higher c/r and 77bhp engines. Last cars to be badged as Sunbeam-Talbots, but if you find an earlier lhd export model that'll wear plain Sunbeam badges, too!

SUNBEAM (GB)

The heyday of Sunbeam was in the 1920s, when the marque produced fine touring and sporting cars, as well as being the first British manufacturer to win a Grand Prix. The firm was originally John Marston Ltd, which had produced japan and tinware, with the first car coming in 1899. Sunbeam-Talbot-Darracq was formed, but this collapsed in 1935, and Sunbeam was purchased by Rootes. No cars were made between 1937 and 1953, but Sunbeams after that date continued the sporting heritage. After the Chrysler takeover in 1964, the name faded away, finally going for good in 1974.

MK III/MK IIIS. 1955-57/1957 (prod: 5249 both types). Sports saloon, drophead coupé. F/R, 2267cc (S4 OHV). Always plain Sunbeams. 90 developments with an overdrive option, slotted wheel discs, and three rectangular bonnet portholes each side. Best of the bunch, though no dropheads after '55. Later saloons often in two-tone paintwork. Mk IIIS (30-40 saloons converted by Castles of Leicester) has overdrive, floor change, straight-through exhaust, and high-compression head.

ALPINE MK IIA. 1953-54 (prod: 3000 approx all 2.3-litre Alpines). Roadster. F/R, 2267cc (S4 OHV). Stiffened 90 chassis with two-seater open body, manual choke/ignition advance, high compression 80bhp engine, louvres to bonnet top, straight-through silencer and geared-up steering. Overdrive available, but column shift, alas, compulsory. Always Sunbeam badged, and not cheap, though good 90s still can be. A little on the heavy side for a two-seater.

RAPIER I. 1955-57 (prod: 6901). 2-door sports saloon. F/R, 1395cc (S4 OHV). Hillman Minx hardtop derivative with Minx-style grille, single Stromberg carburettor (two Zeniths, '57), front anti-roll bar, key starting, sporty facia, and sporty looks – though not, unfortunately, handling to match. Column shift still, but overdrive standard. Usual rust problems, later models preferred.

RAPIER III/IIIA. 1959-61/1961-63 (prod: 40,000 approx both types). 2-door sports saloon, convertible. F/R, 1494cc/1592cc (S4 OHV). Minx evolution on a more exalted plane, with front disc brakes and hypoid rear axle on Mk III. The Mk IIIA (April '61) gets the latest 1.6-litre, 80bhp engine with a better overall performance, though maximum speed's still only about 90mph as against 80-85 for Mk I.

ALPINE MK III. 1955 (prod: see Alpine IIA). Roadster. F/R, 2267cc (S4 OHV). Improvements for Mk III saloon, but both now have the 80bhp engine, anyway. Overdrive and flashers standard: detachable, sliding-panel-type side curtains retained. Good ones are not cheap, but watch those wheel arches again. Sunbeams of this type are catered for by an excellent club.

RAPIER II. 1958 (prod: n/a). 2-door sports saloon, convertible. F/R, 1494cc (S4 OHV). Bigger engine, more power, higher axle ratio, bigger brakes, floor change, and back to a recognisably Sunbeam (or, more strictly, Talbot) grille. Stiffer springing makes it nicer to drive, but ratios still on the agricultural side. Overdrive now extra.

RAPIER IV. 1963-65 (prod: n/a). 2-door sports saloon. F/R, 1592cc (S4 OHV). Smaller, wider wheels, no grease nipples, revised (better) gearing, and an engine redesign with bigger valves, lighter flywheel, and a single dual-choke carburettor. Other improvements include a diaphragm clutch, a brake servo, and (on '65s) synchro for all four gears. Recognisable by its unhooded headlamps and five-bar side grilles. ►

◄ **RAPIER V. 1965-67 (prod: n/a). 2-door sports saloon. F/R, 1725cc (S4 OHV).** Final flowering of the old Rapier hardtop (Mk IIIAs were the last convertibles) with the latest 85bhp five-bearing engine, and a/c instead of d/c electrics. Styling unchanged from Mk IV: even the tail fins are still around. Handling still a bit hoppity, but you can motor up into the mid-90s, not to mention 0-50mph in under 10 seconds.

ALPINE I. 1959-60 (prod: 11,904). Roadster. F/R, 1494cc (S4 OHV). Short-chassis, open Rapier derivative; low line means loss of the Talbot grille. 83bhp twin-carb engine, front disc brakes, hypoid rear axle, and the inevitable tail fins. Overdrive optional. Rear 'seats' for the legless only, but good for nearly 100mph and 26mpg. ►

◄ **ALPINE II. 1960-63 (prod: 19,956). Roadster. F/R, 1592cc (S4 OHV).** More power from a bigger and more robust engine, also better ride and interior trim. Options list includes overdrive, wire wheels, detachable hardtop. Reliable and simple fun cars which haven't yet started to appreciate, but Minx ancestry, of course, spells rust problems.

ALPINE III. 1963 (prod: 5863). Roadster, GT hardtop. F/R, 1592cc (S4 OHV). Compound single Solex replaces twin Zeniths. Other improvements: a stiffer front end, telescopic rear dampers, a brake servo, and twin rear tanks giving a longer range. New hardtop is roomier, but despite being detachable there's no hood. There's also a slightly detuned engine and a walnut dash. ►

ALPINE IV. 1964-65 (prod: 12,406). Roadster, GT hardtop. F/R, 1592cc (S4 OHV). Smaller tail fins on this one, while GT and Roadster now share same engine tune, and there's a new, single-bar grille. Floor-selected automatic listed as well as the usual overdrive. Synchromesh bottom gear on '65 models. Even without tinworm, it could well be yours for less than you'd think. ➤

◄ **ALPINE V. 1965-68 (prod: 19,122). Roadster, GT hardtop. F/R, 1725cc (S4 OHV).** Up to a genuine 100mph now, with the enlarged five-bearing Minx engine rated at 92bhp, and back with twin carburettors once more. Alternators standard, and so are twin reversing lamps on '67s and '68s. Automatic rare, but you won't want it, anyway.

HARRINGTON ALPINE SERIES A. 1961 (prod: 150). 2+2-seater coupé. F/R, 1592cc (S4 OHV). Attractive Alpine II conversion by Hove coachbuilder with extended glass-fibre roof. More headroom and baggage space than on the factory-bodied hardtop, plus a woodrim steering wheel and an electronic rev counter. Hartwell-tuned versions available with up to 100bhp, so you can have both looks and real go. ➤

◄ **HARRINGTON ALPINE SERIES B. 1962-63 (prod: 250). 2+2-seater coupé. F/R, 1592cc (S4 OHV).** Spec's again Alpine II, but this one is even better looking, with the entire original upper works sawn off to make a full fastback – and you lose those tail fins! Full-length side chrome trim, overdrive standard, plus usual options, including wire wheels and 105mph in stock form. A few C-specification cars also converted from Alpine IIs, but differences mainly in interior trim.

VENEZIA. 1963-64 (prod: n/a). 4-seater coupé. F/R, 1592cc (S4 OHV). Touring of Italy did this one, hence the tubular frame and aluminium panels. The rest of it's Humber Sceptre, including the windscreen and the 101ins wheelbase. 88bhp single-carburettor engine, overdrive, front disc brakes, and hooded quad headlights. Not normally sold in Britain, but they have been seen... ➤

TIGER I. 1964-66 (prod: 6495). Roadster. F/R, 4260cc (V8 OHV). Poor man's Cobra, or a stiffened-up Alpine chassis-body with rack and pinion steering. Mk III's twin fuel tanks, a limited-slip differential option, and that same American Ford 260 motor (164bhp) as fitted to the first AC Cobras – and married, once again, to Ford's four-speed all-synchro 'box. It offers 120mph, 0-60mph in 9secs, and 20mpg. UK-available March '65.

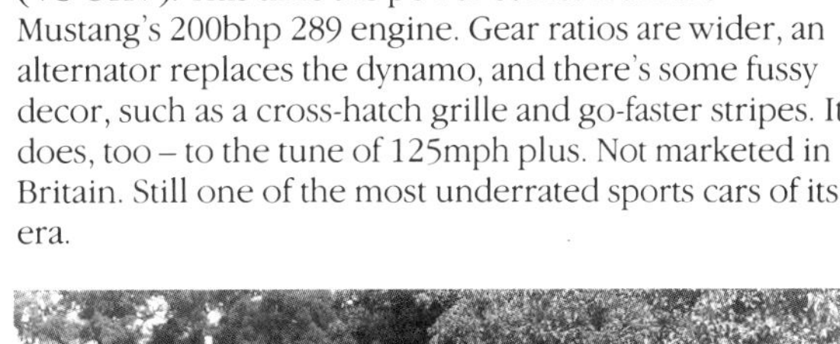

TIGER II. 1967-68 (prod: 571). Roadster. F/R, 4727cc (V8 OHV). This time the power comes from the Mustang's 200bhp 289 engine. Gear ratios are wider, an alternator replaces the dynamo, and there's some fussy decor, such as a cross-hatch grille and go-faster stripes. It does, too – to the tune of 125mph plus. Not marketed in Britain. Still one of the most underrated sports cars of its era.

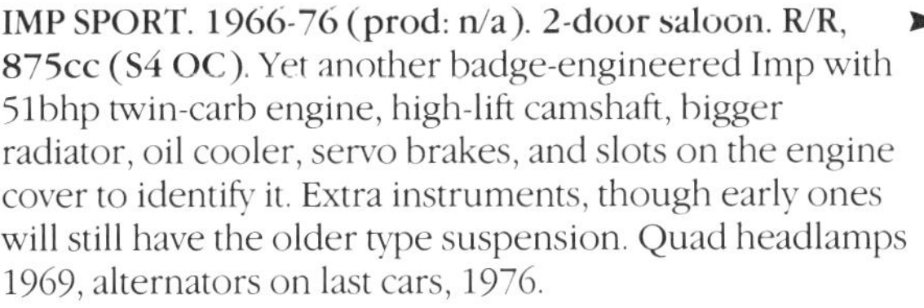

IMP SPORT. 1966-76 (prod: n/a). 2-door saloon. R/R, 875cc (S4 OC). Yet another badge-engineered Imp with 51bhp twin-carb engine, high-lift camshaft, bigger radiator, oil cooler, servo brakes, and slots on the engine cover to identify it. Extra instruments, though early ones will still have the older type suspension. Quad headlamps 1969, alternators on last cars, 1976.

STILETTO. 1967-72 (prod: n/a). Coupé. R/R, 875cc (S4 OC). Sister to the Hillman Californian, but with 51bhp engine, servo brakes, late-type suspension, quad headlamps, padded facia, leather steering wheel rim, black vinyl roof, and radial ply tyres. Watch it, though: in some export markets all Imps were Sunbeam-badged, and this included ordinary Hillmans.

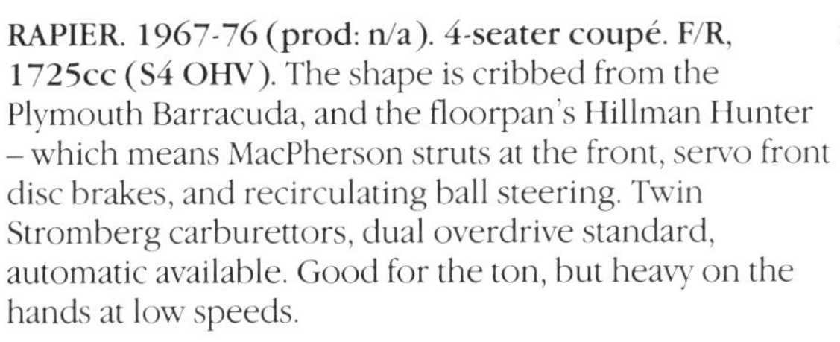

RAPIER. 1967-76 (prod: n/a). 4-seater coupé. F/R, 1725cc (S4 OHV). The shape is cribbed from the Plymouth Barracuda, and the floorpan's Hillman Hunter – which means MacPherson struts at the front, servo front disc brakes, and recirculating ball steering. Twin Stromberg carburettors, dual overdrive standard, automatic available. Good for the ton, but heavy on the hands at low speeds.

RAPIER H120. 1969-76 (prod: n/a). 4-seater coupé. F/R, 1725cc (S4 OHV). Same old pillarless fastback (it's not a hatchback, by the way) with 105bhp Holbay tuned motor, twin Webers, close-ratio 'box, higher final drive ratio, and such sporty trim as a boot-lid spoiler and a matt black grille. Wide-rim Rostyles standard. Not a sports car, for all its 106mph and 0-60 in just over 11 secs. ➤

ALPINE. 1969-76 (prod: n/a). 4-seater coupé. F/R, 1725cc (S4 OHV). Even less of a sports car, this one: it's just a stripped, austerity fastback Rapier. The quad headlamps and power front disc brakes are inclusive, but the overdrive's extra. There's only one carburettor, tyres are cross-ply, and all the fancy trim is deleted. Nothing to recommend it from the collector's standpoint.

SWALLOW (GB)

The Swallow Coachbuilding Co (1935) Ltd was sold by Jaguar during World War II and became part of the giant Tube Investments organisation: its sports car was destined mainly for the American market. It used Swallow's spare capacity and was produced until 1955, cessation presumably being because TI supplied some sports car makers, yet was making a rival product.

DORETTI. 1954-55 (prod: 250 approx). Roadster. F/R, 1991cc (S4 OHV). TR2 mechanical elements transplanted complete into Swallow's own tubular frame with slab-sided double-skinned open bodywork offering a lot more comfort than a TR. Overdrive available. For: it looks different and most Triumph parts fit. Against: it's heavier and less accelerative than a TR. It could, however, come less expensive in the market-place... ➤

TALBOT-LAGO (F)

Although Talbot-Lago itself dates only from 1935, its roots go back to 1896 and the first Darracq car. After the 1920 formation of Sunbeam-Talbot-Darracq, Darracq cars became known as Talbots in Europe and Darracqs in England to avoid confusion with the British Talbot firm. Major Anthony Lago took over Darracq's Suresnes works after the 1935 STD collapse and set to producing a new line of six-cylinder cars with sporting ambitions. After 1945, the firm's race cars were successful, but car sales were crippled by high taxation and shaky finances, and it was absorbed by Simca in 1959.

◄ **GRAND SPORT 26CV. 1947-56 (prod: n/a). Coupé, cabriolet. F/R, 4482cc (S6 OHV).** In its day, the ultimate *grand routier*, with 190bhp (later 210) from the big high-camshaft 'six' with its triple Strombergs. Centre-lock wire wheels, transverse-leaf ifs, and hydraulic brakes not found on contemporary Delahayes. Wilson preselector 'box could present servicing headaches today. There are some lovely bodies by Saoutchik and Figoni, and the standard coupé's a beauty, too.

14CV/AMERICA. 1954-57/1957-58 (prod: approx 80). 2+2-seater coupé. F/R, 2491cc/2580cc (S4/V8 OHV). Pretty little coupé using the chassis and body of the big GS, but now with ZF all-synchro four-speed 'box, and smaller engines. 110-115mph with the five-bearing Talbot four, 125mph with the America's BMW V8. Body detailing sometimes a bit rough: Talbot were nearly broke by then. A few of the last cars (avoid) had the Simca-Ford flathead V8.

TORNADO (GB)

Tornado was one of the leaders in the kit-car field, making its glass-fibre bodied products at Chipperfield and Rickmansworth from 1957 to 1963. Bill Woodhouse's firm eventually ceased car manufacture to concentrate on such activities as central heating, although there were later, abortive, attempts to revive Tornado car production.

TYPHOON. 1958-62 (prod: 400). 2-seater, 4-seater, Sportsbrake. F/R, 933cc/1172cc (S4 SV). Kit cars using flathead Ford mechanicals in a tubular frame with all-coil springing, independent at the front. Remote-control gearshift for stock Ford three-speed 'box, glass-fibre bodies. Sportsbrake is an odd ancestor of Reliant's Scimitar GTE.

TEMPEST. 1960-62 (prod: 15 approx). 2-seater, 4-seater, 2-seater coupé, 4-seater coupé, Sportsbrake. F/R, 997cc (S4 OHV). The Typhoon idiom modified to take more modern 105E Ford mechanics, though Herald or BMC A type units will fit. Front suspension and brakes are Triumph: steering is rack and pinion. Bodies essentially as for Typhoon.

THUNDERBOLT. 1960 (prod: 1). Coupé. F/R, 1991cc (S4 OHV). Planned to take the Tempest's range of bodies in a wider-track chassis with 15-gallon tank, plus Ford ifs and a Zephyr rear end. Ford Consul engine advertised as alternative to TR Triumph. Claimed 108mph, and kits advertised till '62, but the one built was said to be unmanageable.

TALISMAN. 1962-64 (prod: 186). 2-door sports saloon. F/R, 1340cc/1498cc (S4 OHV). Neat little glass-fibre four-seater on usual tubular ladder frame with all-coil springing, rack and pinion steering, and Triumph collapsible column. Ford engines/gearboxes (Classic, Cortina) available in any tune from 55 to 85bhp. Like all Tornados, sold in kit form. ➤

TOURETTE (GB)

This peculiar device was built by Carr Bros of Purley, Surrey, during 1956, before being taken over by a new firm, Progress Supreme Co Ltd. It produced the least expensive 'car' on the British market: the vehicle was inspired by the German Brutsch Mopetta.

◄ **3-WHEELER. 1956-57 (prod: 30 approx). 2-seater. R/R, 197cc (S1 TS).** Egon Brütsch-inspired little egg with single, chain-driven rear wheel. Glass-fibre bodywork over tubular frame: front wheels, brakes, hubs and stub axles are Messerschmitt. Uncoupled mechanical brakes, and you can have it in any colour so long as it's ivory. Non-reversible engine option in catalogue for customers under 17!

TOYOTA (J)

Japanese manufacturers seem to have taken the world by storm in a very short time: Toyota is no exception, as it made its first car only in 1935, having previously specialised in textiles. Early postwar production was low, with only 700 cars made per month in 1955, but that figure had risen to 50,000 per month in 1964. The mid-1960s saw production of off-road vehicles alongside executive saloons and ordinary small cars, as well as the absorption of Daihatsu and Hino into the corporate fold. With the exception of its recent products and the 1966 2000GT, most of its cars have been competent but dull.

CORONA 1500. (prod: 1,788,000 approx all types 1965-72). Saloon, estate car. F/R, 1490cc (S4 OHV). First Toyota sold in Britain, recognisable by its slant grille and quad headlamps. Square-dimensioned pushrod engine gives 74bhp, but engineering unspectacular – four-speed all-synchro 'box, hypoid final drive, semi-elliptic rear springs, a/c electrics. Two-speed wipers and electric washers standard for UK, also front disc brakes from '68, but only manual versions sold here. ➤

CORONA 1600S. 1965-68 (prod: see Corona 1500). Saloon, 4-seater coupé. F/R, 1587cc (S4 OHV). A bigger engine, a second carburettor, and a higher compression boost this one's output to 95bhp, and it's higher geared than the 1500 with a maximum 100mph claimed. Servo front disc brakes standard. Coupés only in Britain after '67. To judge from survivors we've met, these early Toyotas seem to last quite well.

CORONA 1900 MK II. 1969-72 (prod: see Corona 1500). Saloon, 4-seater coupé. F/R, 1858cc (S4 OC). Five main bearings and an upstairs camshaft for this one, while the hydraulically-actuated clutch is now of diaphragm type. Coupé not UK-available till late '70, but this one was tested to do the ton, did its 0-60mph in 13.5secs, and returned an overall 27mpg.

CROWN DE LUXE. 1969-71 (prod: 352,882 all types). Saloon, estate car. F/R, 2253cc (S6 OC). Well-equipped if undistinguished family saloon with seven-bearing 115bhp engine, a live axle and coils at the rear, and quad headlamps. Automatic and power front disc brakes standard for UK customers. UK available late 1968, and continued till restyle for '72 season. Later ones have even more inclusive equipment, ergo are better value.

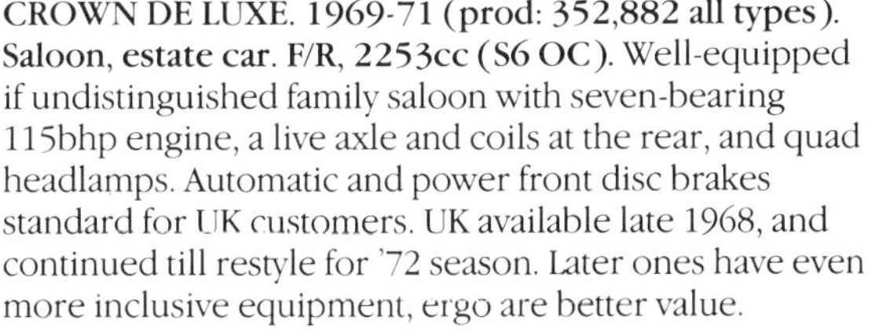

COROLLA 1100. 1967-70 (prod: 859,000 approx all types). 2-door saloon, 4-door saloon, estate car. F/R, 1077cc (S4 OHV). Unimpressive little tin sedan, though five mains a bonus in this class. Semi-elliptic rear suspension and drum brakes standard. Four-door, estate car, and automatic option not UK-available till '69. In 1971 came 1166cc engine and front discs.

TRABANT (GB)

The IFA was a post-World War II consortium of East German nationalised car firms, with the IFA vehicle based on a DKW. It was made from 1948 to 1956, renamed the Zwickau, and then the Trabant, from 1959. Still in production in the 1980s, it is essentially a pre-war DKW.

P600/601. 1963 to date (prod: 860,000 approx to 1973). 2-door saloon, estate car. F/F, 595cc (S2 TS). East German sub-utility DKW descendant with 26bhp air-cooled transverse twin engine and four-speed all-synchromesh 'box incorporating a free wheel. Separate chassis and rust-free glass-fibre bodywork, nominally available UK, 1965. Still made, but not exported to Western countries.

TRIDENT (GB)

The Trident was originally a TVR, a sleek Fiore-styled machine unveiled at the 1965 Geneva Show. However, TVR was in financial trouble, and Bill Last, a TVR dealer, bought the body moulds and set up his own manufacturing operation. The firm produced cars in Woodbridge and then Ipswich. It folded in 1974, but the car made a brief reappearance at Earls Court in 1976 before the firm folded finally in 1977.

◄ **CLIPPER. 1967-78 (prod: 225 approx all models). Coupé, convertible. F/R, 4727cc/4950cc/5562cc (V8 OHV).** Trevor Fiore's projected new TVR first seen at Geneva, 1964, later 'productionised' by W.J. Last using an Austin-Healey 3000 chassis with live rear axle. Servo front disc brakes, four-speed Ford 'box, power windows: convertibles very rare. Ford engines to '70, thereafter Chryslers available, but back to Ford for brief '76 revival.

VENTURER V6/TYCOON. 1969-78/1971-74 (prod: see Clipper). Coupé. F/R, 2994cc/2498cc (V6/S6 OHV). Styling as per Clipper, but use of lengthened Triumph TR6 frame spells irs not found on earlier cars. Kit-available. Venturers have Ford V6 engines, Tycoon with 150bhp fuel-injected Triumph unit and automatic. Revived 1976-78 Venturers are Ford-powered with live axle and coils at the rear: very few built. ►

TRIUMPH (GB)

Surprisingly, the name is no longer with us, having been dropped by Austin Rover in 1984: after the Leyland takeover of BMC, most felt that the dominant managers were those from Triumph, who had been under the Leyland wing since 1961. Triumph began making cars in 1923, although it was famous for its motorcycles before then. In 1936 the car and motorcycle sides of the business were divorced, with the car making firm going into receivership in 1939. In 1945, it emerged under the control of John Black's Standard. Triumph's heyday was in the 1960s, when it had a range of fine sports and middle-bracket saloon cars.

◄ **1800 SALOON 18T. 1946-48 (prod: 4000). Saloon. F/R, 1776cc (S4 OHV).** First Standard-made Triumph in full razor edge idiom with thin pillars. Steel-tube chassis, Standard-type transverse-leaf ifs, self adjusting hydraulic brakes, and right-handed four-on-the-column, 65bhp ohv engine as supplied to Jaguar for the 1½-litre. Very staid, but on the plus side all the Triumph clubs are very well organised.

1800 ROADSTER 18TR. 1946-48 (prod: 2501). 2/4-seater drophead coupé. F/R, 1776cc (S4 OHV). Mechanics as 1800 saloon, only shorter and lower. A splendid parody of Classicism with set-back radiator, exposed headlamps, triple wipers, and a dickey seat with a lid doubling as a second cowl. Correct colours are black or metallic grey. Gearchange not as bad as it sounds, but an expensive restoration project and not much of a performer.

2000 ROADSTER TRA. 1948-49 (prod: 2000). 2/4-seater drophead coupé. F/R, 2088cc (S4 OHV). 1800 Roadster with some extra cross bracing to the frame and a Vanguard power train – wet-liner engine, three-speed all-synchro 'box, hypoid rear axle, 9ins brakes – dropped in. A bit faster than the 1800, but you miss the extra ratio. Already worth heavy money.

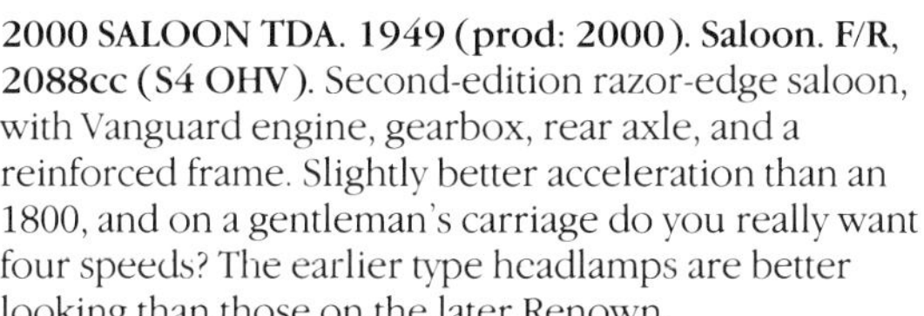

2000 SALOON TDA. 1949 (prod: 2000). Saloon. F/R, 2088cc (S4 OHV). Second-edition razor-edge saloon, with Vanguard engine, gearbox, rear axle, and a reinforced frame. Slightly better acceleration than an 1800, and on a gentleman's carriage do you really want four speeds? The earlier type headlamps are better looking than those on the later Renown.

RENOWN MK I TDB/MK II TDC. 1949-52/1952-54 (prod: 6501/2800). Saloon. F/R, 2088cc (S4 OHV). Fully Vanguardised razor-edge Triumph with box-section frame and coils at the front, still on 108ins wheelbase. Left-hand column shift and Vanguard-type instruments, though these latter set in polished wood. Overdrive option from June 1950. Mk II (1952) has an extra 3ins of wheelbase.

RENOWN LIMOUSINE. 1951-52 (prod: 190). Limousine. F/R, 2088cc (S4 OHV). Rare 111ins wheelbase version with sliding division (but no occasional seats), non adjustable front seat, and radio/heater installation. Overdrive available. They probably lengthened the saloon's wheelbase to use up leftover chassis, and the result was unloved when it appeared.

MAYFLOWER. 1950-53 (prod: 35,000). 2-door saloon, drophead coupé. F/R, 1247cc (S4 SV). Odd little unitary saloon using pre-war Standard 10 engine/gearbox (latter with bottom blanked off), coil ifs and hydraulic brakes. Flexible and frugal but razor-edge upper works don't blend well with slab sides and handling just isn't. Reasonable rust record and a lively following. Ten dropheads made 1950 but none survives.

TR-X. 1950 (prod: 3). 3-seater convertible. F/R, 2088cc (S4 OHV). Walter Belgrove's aerodynamic dream car with pop-out headlamps and also hydro-electric assistance for overdrive (standard), seats, windows, hood and radio aerial. Double-skinned light alloy body with the hydraulics between the skin. Chassis essentially Vanguard but twin carbs give 72bhp and a promised 90mph. The Korean War was a convenient excuse for not making any more. Two survive.

TR2. 1953-55 (prod: 8628). 2-seater sports. F/R, 1991cc (S4 OHV). Successful development of a strange lash-up seen at the '52 Show with twin carb 90bhp 2-litre Vanguard derived engine, coil front suspension, 9ins drum brakes and plain bomb crater grille. Overdrive and wire wheels available and also factory hardtops for '54. With overdrive does 108mph and 35mpg. Low hung doors awkward and handling lethal, but very reliable. Quite a few stayed home, but survivors expensive.

TR3. 1955-57 (prod: 13,377). 2-seater sports. F/R, 1991cc (S4 OHV). Improved TR2 with triple overdrive when specified (TR2 had it only on top), scuttle ventilator, egg crate grille and room for an occasional rear seat. Usual options available and TR3s had 95bhp with front disc brakes and roller bearing back axle from late '56. Home deliveries less than 10 per cent, so again both rare and expensive.

TR3A. 1957-61 (prod: 58,236). 2-seater sports. F/R, 1991cc/2138cc (S4 OHV). Not an official designation but applied to full '57 spec TR3s with 100bhp engine, full width grille, recessed headlamps, grille mounted sidelamps and exterior door handles. Options as for TR2/3. Better brakes and flat panel behind seats from late '59, while some '61s have the bigger engine. More made of these than any other four-cylinder TR but less than 2000 stayed home.

TR4. 1961-65 (prod: 40,253). 2-seater sports. F/R, 2138cc (S4 OHV). A complete redesign by Michelotti, resulting in a car a foot longer than the TR3 with a wider track, full-width pressed-steel body, power bulge for the carburettors (SU to late '62, Stromberg thereafter), bigger boot, all-synchro 'box and collapsible steering column. Servo brakes, wire wheels, and the Surrey top that anticipated Porsche's famed Targa are options: so, in theory, was a 1991cc engine.

DOVE GTR4. 1961-64 (prod: 55 approx). 2+2-seater coupé. F/R, 2138cc (S4 OHV). Alpine-style coupé conversion (by Harrington) for Doves of Wimbledon, almost a hatchback. Rear seat is for children only, but bigger 15 gallon tank a bonus. Carried a 500lbs weight increment, and acceleration suffers accordingly. Usual TR4 options, but reputedly no TR4As converted.

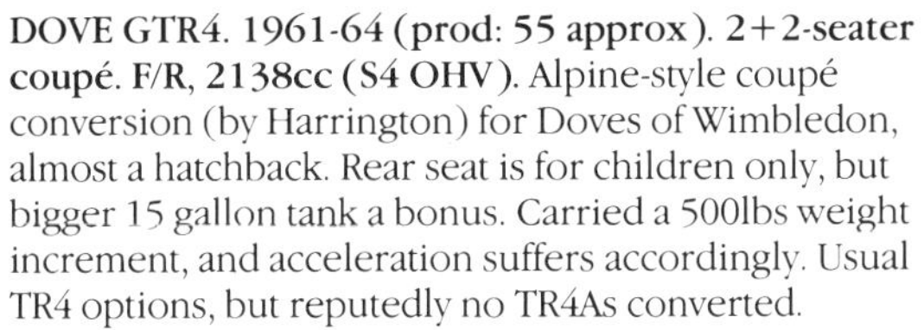

TR4A. 1964-67 (prod: 28,465). 2-seater sports. F/R, 2138cc (S4 OHV). Another 100lbs of avoirdupois, the price of coil and semi trailing arms irs – though a few US-market cars kept the live axle – a/c electrics optional, and diaphragm clutch. Recognition features are a new grille and sidelamps streamlined into the side flashes. Usual options. Will do around 110mph and 0-60 in 11.4secs, but these later fours are thirstier than the TR2s and TR3s.

TR5/TR250. 1967-68 (prod: 2947/8484). 2-seater sports. F/R, 2498cc (S6 OHV). First six-cylinder TR with 115mph on tap, servo brakes and radial ply tyres standard, and also Rostyle wheels, though there's a desirable wire option. Home-market TR5 with Lucas fuel injection (troublesome on early cars), TR250 with two Strombergs and a few less brake horses for the USA, this latter recognisable by the go-faster stripes on the nose.

TR6. 1969-76 (prod: 94,619). 2-seater sports. F/R, 2498cc (S6 OHV). 124bhp engine (150bhp pre '73), but other changes include wide rim wheels, full-width Karmann-styled nose, deletion of the bonnet bulge, a squared off tail, and a plain single-bar grille. One piece hard-top replaces Surrey type '73, when overdrive (standard from '74) limited to top two ratios. Again, twin Strombergs on USA versions.

HERALD/HERALD S. 1959-62/1961-63 (prod: 76,890). 2-door saloon. F/R, 948cc (S4 OHV). Cheap family saloon with separate chassis, all-independent suspension, rack and pinion steering and incredible 25-foot turning circle. Uprated 38bhp Standard Ten type engine gives 35-40mpg. Twin-carb coupé engine optional from September '59. S model (February '61) is a stripped version with less chromium and equipment. Front disc brakes available from October '61.

HERALD COUPE/CONVERTIBLE. 1959-61/1960-61 (prod: 15,153/8262). 2+2-seater coupé, 2+2-seater convertible. F/R, 948cc (S4 OHV). Pretty little cars with twin SUs, 45bhp, and 75mph, without a notable increase in thirst. Specifications otherwise as saloon, same swing-axle rear end. Convertibles UK-available October '60, front disc brakes on the last ones. Usual chassis-corrosion problems have reduced many to the role of kit-car donor, but Herald coupés generally are becoming collectable.

HERALD 1200. 1961-68 (prod: 201,142/5319/43,295/39,819). 2-door saloon, coupé, convertible, estate car. F/R, 1147cc (S4 OHV). Bigger engine and a higher axle ratio (4.11:1) now, also script on bootlid and bonnet, rubber bumpers, and a front disc brake option. Diaphragm clutches from early '66. Estates came out a month later than the rest of the range, coupés rare and discontinued '64. All should give 40mpg with reasonable driving.

HERALD 12/50. 1962-67 (prod: 53,267). 2-door saloon. F/R, 1147cc (S4 OHV). De Luxe Herald with near-Spitfire tune engine (8.5cr, high-lift camshaft), front disc brakes, luxury trim, fine-barred aluminium grille, padded dash, and folding sunroof, plus the usual chassis and forward-tilting bonnet that lets the dirt in as well as aiding maintenance. Popular in its day, but unless it's mpg you're after, go for the later 13/60.

HERALD 13/60. 1967/71 (prod: 82,650). 2-door saloon, convertible, estate car. F/R, 1296cc (S4 OHV). Bigger 61bhp engine with the 12/50's front disc brakes, though on saloons the sunroof's now an extra. Recognisable by its Vitesse-style single slant headlamps and horizontal barred grille. Apart from familiar corrosion problems, a splendid hack that'll hold 75 all day. Convertibles becoming expensive. Production statistics include ckd kits sent for export.

VITESSE 1600. 1962-66 (prod: 22,814/8447). 2-door saloon, convertible. F/R, 1596cc (S6 OHV). Back to pint-sized sixes on an elongated Herald with twin carbs, 70bhp, close-ratio 'box, front disc brakes, and those 'Chinese' quad headlamps. Overdrive optional and desirable: without it you're stuck with 22mpg. Reinforced chassis, but handling tricky. Sunroofs available on saloons March '63, rev counters standard from '64 models. Stromberg carbs on the last cars.

VITESSE 2-LITRE MK 1. 1966-68 (prod: 12,977/6944 incl Mk II). 2-door saloon, convertible. F/R, 1998cc (S6 OHV). 95bhp 2-litre engine from the 2000 saloon in its GT6 tune, twin Strombergs and synchro on bottom, with usual overdrive option. Also has wider rims, better brakes, and some assorted scriptitis. It'll do 95mph, but those swing axles can't really cope, and the tail hangs out a treat. Try Mk II instead. Convertibles now very desirable.

VITESSE 2-LITRE MK II. 1968-71 (prod: see 2-litre Vitesse Mk I). 2-door saloon, convertible. F/R, 1998cc (S6 OHV). Thank goodness, this one has the revised rear suspension with reversed lower wishbones. Dampers lever-arm rather than telescopic. Carburation and overdrive as for Mk I and cosmetic changes limited to Rostyle wheels. Fun, but don't expect more than 25mpg, and remember that there's no more room than in a Herald. A very few Vitesse estates were made, but never officially.

SPITFIRE I. 1962-65 (prod: 45,753). 2-seater sports. F/R, 1147cc (S4 OHV). A sports Herald with a 12/50-plus engine (9:1 cr, twin SUs, 63bhp) but the same old chassis and suspension, and the same bonnet opening layout. Front disc brakes always standard, and here you have 90mph plus all the Herald splendours and miseries: it's a good thing you can't watch yourself at 10 tenths cornering. From 1964 available with centre-lock wire wheels, overdrive, and factory hardtop.

SPITFIRE II. 1965-67 (prod: 37,409). 2-seater sports. F/R, 1147cc (S4 OHV). Main changes here are under-bonnet with a hotter camshaft and 67bhp, which boost speed and acceleration. Has the diaphragm clutch of contemporary Heralds. Finish generally superior with carpets and leathercloth covering odd bits of bare metal. Problems are chassis rust and tyre wear if one over-indulges the famous U-turn. Take a good look at halfshafts before buying any of this family.

SPITFIRE III. 1967-70 (prod: 65,320). 2-seater sports. F/R, 1296cc (S4 OHV). Introduced March '67 with the 1.3-litre, 75bhp engine plus bigger front brake calipers. Quick identification points are higher bumpers with flashers underneath the front ones, a wooden facia, and a smaller steering wheel. Top speed is now 95mph, and a second has been shaved off the 0-50mph time. Options as for earlier Spitfires.

SPITFIRE IV. 1970-74 (prod: 70,021). 2-seater sports. F/R, 1296cc (S4 OHV). This one gets revised styling and rear suspension, synchromesh on first and a higher (3.89) axle ratio, plus plastic underriders and yet another new facia. Not as fast as Mk III, smaller fuel tank from '73, which is last year of wire wheel option. Later 1500 engine on late American Mk IVs, but not in Britain until Mk V introduced in 1975.

2000 MK I. 1963-69/1965-69 (prod: 113,157/7488). Saloon, estate car. F/R, 1998cc (S6 OHV). Twin-carburettor Standard Vanguard 6 engine in new unitary Triumph with all-synchro 'box, servo disc/drum brakes, and all-independent suspension (coils and semi-trailing arms at the rear). A cheap alternative to the Rover 2000, with over 90mph and reasonable mpg. Overdrive and automatic options, estate cars from October '65, and full-flow ventilation from '67.

2000 MK II. 1969-77/1969-75 (prod: 92,053/7118). Saloon, estate car. F/R, 1998cc (S6 OHV). Lower bonnet line, longer nose and tail, bigger boot, full-width grille with inbuilt indicator/sidelamp clusters and turbo wheel trims identify this one from outside. Facia and trim are improved, too. Mechanical changes include a/c electrics and a bigger brake servo, with engine power increased during '75, when estate cars (always rare) were discontinued. ➤

◄ **2.5 PI MK I. 1968-69 (prod: 8658/371). Saloon, estate car. F/R, 2498cc (S6 OHV).** The press called this one a 'hot rod' and it was good for 105mph, thanks to the new 132bhp fuel injected 'six' also fitted to the TR5. Rostyle wheels standard, automatic and overdrive available. Estate cars special order items. These early fuel injection engines were troublesome, so go for your big Triumph in carburettor form.

2.5 PI MK II. 1969-75 (prod: 43,353/4102). Saloon, estate car. F/R, 2498cc (S6 OHV). Styling and cosmetics as for 2000 Mk II, plus a separate rev counter, a vacuum reservoir for the brakes, and a power steering option (you could also have this last on late 2000s). Carburettor versions available from mid '74, evolving into 1975's 2500S with 106bhp and overdrive as standard, a good buy. ➤

◄ **1300. 1965-70 (prod: 113,008). Saloon. F/F, 1296cc (S4 OHV).** Herald-type engine in a front-drive saloon with north-south engine and all-synchro four-speed 'box set underneath, which means a better linkage than on Minis. Trailing-link rear suspension, rack and pinion steering (it felt rather dead) and front disc brakes. Comfortable and well-appointed, but not terribly interesting.

1300TC. 1967-70 (prod: 35,342). Saloon. F/F, 1296cc (S4 OHV). Bringing a promising little saloon to life with the twin-carb, 75bhp Spitfire engine, a brake servo, a four-branch manifold, and the inevitable TC badging. Less exciting than a Vitesse, but it'll do 90mph as against the standard article's leisurely 75-80mph and it should manage 30mpg. ➤

1500. 1970-73 (prod: 66,353). Saloon. F/F, 1493cc (S4 OHV). This time they've married the fwd saloon specification to a single-carburettor 61bhp unit of the type that eventually found its way into the MG Midget. No twin-carb versions till 1973; servo brakes standard, and rear-end layout simpler, by a dead axle and coils. Over 85mph, but a little fussy, and fuel economy not its strongest point.

GT6 MK I. 1966-68 (prod: 15,818). Coupé. F/R, 1998cc (S6 OHV). Fastback Spitfire with E-type Jaguar-style rear hatch and the 2-litre Vitesse engine with its twin Strombergs. Options include wire wheels and overdrive. It touches 105mph, 0-60 takes 12secs, and offers a potential 25mpg, but this time the Herald back end is being tried beyond its endurance, and the result is hairy handling and a bumpy ride. Go for later Marks.

GT6 MK II. 1968-70 (prod: 12,066). Coupé. F/R, 1998cc (S6 OHV). Getting the GT6 right, or grafting on the Mk II Vitesse rear suspension, and a new cylinder head boosting output to 105bhp. Add a wooden facia, raised bumpers, padded steering wheel spokes, and proper ventilation, and it almost makes up for those Rostyles (there's still a wire option though). Overdrive gives almost too high a motorway top, but this one could be a useful sleeper in the investment market.

GT6 MK III. 1970-73 (prod: 13,042). Coupé. F/R, 1998cc (S6 OHV). Rear end treatment as on the Spitfire IV, chopped off tail, ventilated disc wheels, deeper screen, and overdrive switch in the gearshift knob, though for '73 they revert to an older-type rear suspension, Spitfire-style. On the credit side, these last ones have brake servos, stronger bumpers, and tinted glass, and those who know say that the 'retrograde' step hasn't had too adverse a result.

TOLEDO. 1970-76 (prod: 130,488 incl Dolomite 1300). 2-door saloon, 4-door saloon. F/R, 1296cc (S4 OHV). Marriage of the 1300 engine and hull (initially in two-door form only) to a conventionally located gearbox and driveline with a live axle and coils at the back. Four-door models from '72, servo front disc brakes (desirable) on '73 models, radial-ply tyres standard 1975. Not a very inspiring little car: the bigger-engined Dolomites are preferable.

STAG. 1970-77 (prod: 25,877). Coupé, convertible. F/R, 2997cc (V8 DOC). The car the Daimler SP250 might have been, with two extra seats thrown in. Lots of luxury, a 145bhp twin-carburettor engine, all-independent springing, power front disc brakes, and (too light) power steering. There's a built-in rollbar in the roof, headlights are quad type, and potential's 115mph and 22mpg. Overdrive available with manual transmission, but automatic Stags are in the majority. ➤

TURNER (GB)

Jack Turner began his company by producing, fairly unsuccessfully, pure racing cars. In 1954, he turned to making small, economical and practical sports cars which were immensely popular in the USA. The company went into voluntary liquidation in 1966, partially because Turner's health made the necessary restructuring impossible.

◄ **SPORTS. 1951-52 (prod: 7 approx). 2-seater sports. F/R, 1767cc (S4 OHV).** Bespoke special using twin-tube frame, all-independent transverse springing, Morris rack and pinion steering, and twin leading shoe hydraulic brakes. Engines to customer's choice: data for Lea-Francis unit, but Vauxhall (Wyvern, Velox) and MG (TD) also fitted. Stark, cycle-winged bodywork on most, though some had all enveloping bodies.

A30 SPORTS. 1955-57 (prod: 90). 2-seater sports. F/R, 803cc (S4 OHV). Austin A30 engine, gearbox, front suspension and hydromech brakes offered up to a classical Turner tubular frame with trailing arms and torsion bars at the back. Light and not unpleasing glass-fibre bodywork spells 10cwt, ergo 80mph and 45mpg. Like most Turners, kit-available. ➤

◄ **950 SPORTS. 1957-59 (prod: 170, incl Turner-Climax versions). 2-seater sports. F/R, 948cc (S4 OHV).** A30 Sports with A35 engine giving 34-43bhp according to tune and carburation, thus a 90mph potential. Full hydraulic brakes: a few with Coventry-Climax FWA engine (see *Turner-Climax*). Almost all exported, mainly to USA and South Africa.

MK I SPORTS. 1959-60 (prod: 160, incl Turner-Climax versions). 2-seater sports. F/R, 948cc (S4 OHV). Still the same chassis and suspension, common to all production Turners save the GT, but with new bodyshell restyled at both ends and minus the tail fins of earlier Austin-engined cars. Front disc brakes available, 95mph on tap with twin-carburettor motor to Sprite tune. ➤

MK II/MK III SPORTS. 1960-63/1963-66 (prod: 150/90 incl Turner-Climax versions). 2-seater sports. F/R, 997cc/1340cc/1498cc (S4 OHV). Specifications as for Mk I Sports, only with Triumph Herald front suspension and Ford engines (Anglia, Classic, Cortina). Also sold with Coventry-Climax unit. Mk III identifiable by large scoop in bonnet top and elliptical tail lights. Most powerful catalogued engine gave 80bhp. ➤

◄ **TURNER-CLIMAX. 1959-66 (prod: see 950/ Mks I/II/III). 2-seater sports. F/R, 1098cc/1216cc (S4 OC).** Turner two-seaters with 75bhp FWA or 90bhp FWE Coventry-Climax units, front disc brakes, and wire wheels. Mechanical and styling changes otherwise as for pushrod cars, though even with the smaller unit these are good for 100mph and 0-50 in well under 10secs. Alexander-Turner GT coupé was strictly a racer, and not made in series.

GT. 1961-65 (prod: 9). 2+2-seater coupé. F/R, 1498cc (S4 OHV). All-new square-tube frame with welded-up floorpan, Herald front end, and usual Turner rear suspension, plus wire wheels and front disc brakes. Styling (by Jack Turner) somewhat in the Reliant sports idiom. Five-bearing Cortina engine standard but 1340cc Classic and Coventry-Climax cited as options. ➤

TVR (GB)

Somehow, TVR has survived to this day, and is still making exciting sports cars. Yet its history has been full of ups and downs. TVR Engineering was set up in 1947 by Trevor Wilkinson with series production of its Sports Saloons starting in 1954. In 1962 the firm went under, with business carried on by a subsidiary company, Grantura Engineering. TVR was purchased by Martin and Arthur Lilley in 1965, but was sold again in the early 1980s. It has always made exciting sports cars, even if they have had a slight kit-car reputation, and the mid-1980s Rover V8-engines models are real road-burners.

◄ **GRANTURA I. 1958-60 (prod: approx 100). 2-seater coupé. F/R, 1172cc/997cc/1489cc/1098cc/1216cc (S4 SV/OHV/OC).** Backbone frame, VW-type torsion-bar-suspension at both ends, Austin-Healey 100 drum brakes, BMC final drive unit, Consul II windscreen, and the squat TVR coupé body. Wire wheels standard, but under the bonnet you get what you pay for, with matching 'box: flathead or 105E Ford, Coventry-Climax ohc, or BMC B-type in MGA tune. Rather a hotch-potch and later ones probably preferable.

GRANTURA II/IIA. 1960-61/1961-62 (prod: approx 400 both types). 2-seater coupé. F/R, 1588cc/1622cc (S4 OHV). Rack and pinion steering standard, with front disc brakes on Mk IIA. Engines and gearboxes usually MGA with 95-100mph available, though Coventry-Climax and 105E Ford in some, and possibly even some 1340cc Classics as well. ➤

◄ **GRANTURA III. 1962-64 (prod: approx 90). 2-seater coupé. F/R, 1622cc/1798cc (S4 OHV).** Redesigned multi-tubular frame common to all remaining TVRs of the period: coils and wishbones at front and rear, rack and pinion steering, front disc brakes, centre-lock wheels, and a slightly longer wheelbase. Overdrive available: back end still BMC, engines MGA to late '63, thereafter MGB.

GRANTURA IV/1800S. 1964-66/1966-67 (prod: approx 90/78). 2-seater coupé. F/R, 1798cc (S4 OHV). Wider track chassis, Manx-tailed body, and spare wheel under the floor instead of under the suspension. MGB's 95bhp engine standard. 1800S differs only in having bigger 15 gallon tank, but model made by a new, stable management, therefore detail workmanship probably a lot better. ➤

◄ **VIXEN S1/S2/S3. 1967-68/1968-70/1970-72 (prod: 117/438/168). 2-seater coupé. F/R, 1599cc (S4 OHV).** Settling down, with five-bearing Ford engines and all-synchro 'boxes across the board, plus 1800S's bigger fuel tank. Servo brakes and bolt-on bodywork (preferable) on S2, wheelbase lengthened during this series's run. S3 with cast-alloy bolt-on wheels and Cortina GT motor tune. No overdrive offered with Ford fours.

GRIFFITH 200/400. 1963-65 (prod: approx 310). 2-seater coupé. F/R, 4727cc (V8 OHV). Grantura III frame, servo brakes, wire wheels and the 289 American Ford engine with outputs of up to 271bhp. 200s retain BMC back end, 400s with big bonnet bulges, wide rims, Kenlowe fans. A hairy 150mph, but few stayed home, and rhd almost never seen. ➤

TUSCAN V8/V8 SE. 1967/1968-70 (prod: 28/45). 2-seater coupé. F/R, 4727cc/4950cc (V8 OHV). Again a crossbreed with American Ford V8 engine and all-synchro 'box. All on 90ins wheelbase, but most SEs have wide body and wider rims, and better appointments. Also standard on SEs, the full-house 271bhp engine, though some have the even more potent 5-litre engine. A real bomb.

◄ **TUSCAN V6. 1969-71 (prod: 101). 2-seater coupé. F/R, 2994cc (V6 OHV).** Tuscans with similar differential to V8 version, but Ford of Britain's 128bhp V6 wedded to the American four-speed 'box. Cast alloy wide rims, Vixen body, servo brakes, and a dual overdrive option. More manageable than a V8, but still good for 120mph.

UNIPOWER (GB)

Andrew Hedges and Tim Powell were responsible for this small and high quality GT coupé, built at Perivale, Middlesex from 1966 to 1968 by Universal Power Drives, makers of forestry tractors. Subsequently, a new company, Unipower Cars Ltd, took over production, but this eventually folded in 1970: AC Cars Ltd have resurrected the name in the mid-1980s.

GT. 1966-70 (prod: 75). 2-seater coupé. R/R, 998cc/1275cc (S4 OHV). Fascinating little car only 40ins high, with Mini power pack (locked steering) just in front of the rear 'axle', glass-fibre body bonded to a tubular space-frame, all-coil springing and dual-circuit disc/drum brakes. Hard to get in, but when you are, there's 100mph with the small Cooper engine, and 120mph with the big one. Frontal radiator, and right-hand, sill-mounted gearshift. ►

VANDEN PLAS (GB)

In 1923, Belgian coachbuilders Van Den Plas set up an English offshoot, which was bought by the Austin company after World War II. Initially, it supplied coachwork for Austins, but became a manufacturer in its own right in 1960 with the Princess range. The name now applies only to luxury versions of some current Austin-Rover models.

◄ **4-LITRE. 1959-68 (prod: approx 2100). Saloon, limousine, landaulette. F/R, 3995cc (S6 OHV).** The good old '52 long-chassis Austin A135 (1250 already made) rebadged with BMC's artificial label. Options list now include automatic and power steering, both desirable. Quite a few chassis made for the Black Line, saloons rare and landaulettes very rare indeed. Collectors beware: it's 215ins long and weighs well over 2 tons.

3-LITRE MKS. I/II. 1959-61/1961-64 (prod: 4719/7984). ➤ Saloon. F/R, 2912cc (S6 OHV). Luxury Austin Westminster with loads of wood, leather and sound damping and a VDP grille. Overdrive and automatic available: Mk I's an A99 offshoot, and Mk II's to A110 specification with high-lift camshaft, twin exhausts and floor change. Power steering available from August '62. Mild collector value not shared by its Austin and Wolseley cousins.

◄ 1100/1300. 1963-68/1967-74 (prod: 39,732 both types). Saloon. F/F, 1098cc/1275cc (S4 OHV). Four-door ADO 16 with all the fancy trim – VDP grille, veneer-and-leather, armrests, picnic tables, clock radio, sunroof option and sound damping so heavy that you only *feel* valve bounce. Mk. II (late '67) with cutback tail fins and ventilated wheels, some early ones with the twin-carburettor 1100 engine still, though all from April '68 with the 1300 and single SU.

PRINCESS 4-LITRE R. 1964-68 (prod: approx 7000). ➤ Saloon. F/R, 3909cc (S6 IOE). Rolls-Royce's twin-carburettor B60 engine with twin electric fuel pumps in an A110-type hull. Automatic, power steering, and power disc/drum brakes are part of the package, as are picnic tables and all the other VDP trimmings: you paid extra for electric dampers (desirable). Rounded-off rear wings and no tail fins. 100mph and 18mpg, but forget all about fun-driving. Good ones can come surprisingly expensive.

VAUXHALL (GB)

The Vauxhall Ironworks in London specialised in marine engineering before making cars, the first of which appeared in 1903. During the Edwardian era, the firm's staples were large touring cars, with the classic 30/98 and Prince Henry-type sports cars adding lustre to the image. In 1925, however, the firm's poor finances saw a takeover by America's General Motors, which still controls Vauxhall. The firm then changed direction, going down-market very successfully, although until the early 1980s it had always been in the shadow of Ford and Austin/Morris. It has struggled hard to regain market share, but none of its modern volume sellers are British designs.

◄ I TWELVE-FOUR. 1940-46 (prod: 6). Saloon. F/R, 1442cc (S4 OHV). Short-lived revival of pre-war unitary 12/4 with 102ins wheelbase and six-light bodyshell, identical to '39 model save for new 1940-type grille. Torsion-bar front suspension, hydraulic brakes, umbrella-handle handbrake, and three-on-the-floor. Tough engine, 65mph and 35mpg, but like all Vauxhalls, a rust trap. Genuine post-war examples exceedingly rare.

HIY TEN-FOUR/HIX TWELVE-FOUR. 1946-47/1946-48 (prod: 44,047). Saloon. F/R, 1203cc/1442cc (S4 OHV). Forties' four-light Ten hull with exposed rear spare wheel and new grille not used on any pre-war Ten, same 98ins wheelbase common to both types, and usual Vauxhall mechanics. Production began March '46, Ten dropped in the summer of '47. Rust and front suspension are problems, but there's a good club for GM Vauxhalls. ►

◄ **J FOURTEEN-SIX. 1939-48 (prod: 30,511 post-war). Saloon. F/R, 1781cc (S6 OHV).** Structure and suspension as for H- and I-types, though this bigger six-light type has a projecting boot and all-synchro 'box. Subtle bonnet-louvre and grille changes distinguish post-war cars, plus some rather nasty bits of plastic on the dash. Forget all about handling, and put up with those camshaft-driven wipers, a Vauxhall disease for nearly 20 years. If you can find a rust-free one, the performance will surprise you – nearly 75mph and 28mpg.

LIX WYVERN. 1948-51 (prod: 55,409). Saloon. F/R, 1442cc (S4 OHV). Really only the H-type with streamlined front end, projecting boot, concealed spare wheel, and alligator bonnet, plus disc wheels and column shift. Frugal and reliable, but on 35bhp you'll stagger up to 60 – just. For performance, choose a Velox. Later cars (1950 on) have worm and peg steering and (usually) leather upholstery. ►

◄ **LIP VELOX. 1948-51 (prod: 76,919). Saloon. F/R, 2275cc (S6 OHV).** From the outside, identical to a Wyvern apart from its bumper overriders and cream wheels. With a 55bhp 'six' pulling only 21cwt, it's fast and quite a handful on a twisty road. And you'll miss the 14's synchronised bottom gear...

WYVERN EIX. 1951-52/1952-57 (prod: 5313/105,275). Saloon. F/R, 1442cc/1508cc (S4 OHV). Longer, wider car based on '49 Chevy's styling, though unitary, of course. Pushbutton doors, coil front springing and hypoid rear axle. Short-stroke 1508cc engine (lots more urge) from April '52, recirculating ball steering '53, new bonnet and grille '55, slimmer pillars and wrap-round rear window '56. New grille again and (thank goodness) electric wipers on seldom-seen '57s. ►

VELOX EIP/EIPV. 1951-52/1952-57 (prod: 13,277/ 222,019 to end 1956). Saloon, Grosvenor estate car, Dormobile estate car. F/R, 2275cc/2262cc (S6 OHV). Companion to E-Wyvern, though coloured wheels now common to both species. Short-stroke engine April '52, other updates as for Wyvern, though from '55 rear wheels are spatted on sixes. Estate cars 1957 only: the Grosvenor is hearse-like and very rare. With later engine, you get 80mph and 30mpg.

CRESTA EPIC. 1955-57 (prod: 166,504). Saloon. F/R, 2262cc (S6 OHV). Vauxhall's answer to the Ford Zodiac, though it shares the Velox's 65bhp single-carburettor engine. Extra refinements when you choose Cresta include leather trim, two-toning inside and out, heater, clock, mascot and lockable filler cap. All with rear-wheel spats. Styling changes as for other E-types, though from '56 you could have a 'three-phase colour scheme'(!).

VICTOR F. 1957-59 (prod: 390,747 all Fs). Saloon, estate car. F/R, 1508cc (S4 OHV). Dreadful, gaudy '55 Chevrolet-shape on 13ins wheels with dog's leg screen, wrap-round rear window, and flutes banished to the bonnet sides. Bonuses are a hydraulically-actuated clutch and synchro on bottom once more. Early ones have exhausts exiting through the rear bumper, a new form of rust trap. Newton-drive two-pedal control and estate cars available from early '58, some less official overdrive conversions, too.

VICTOR F SERIES II. 1959-61 (prod: see Victor F). Saloon, estate car. F/R, 1508cc (S4 OHV). Much the same as before, only with the hooded headlamps of later Series Is, and all the horrible side-chrome deleted. Engine output up from 48 to 55bhp, full-width grille, single central bonnet rib instead of two, and wrap-round bumpers, '61s with five-barred grilles. Rust always a problem, though Vauxhall engines go on for ever.

VICTOR FB. 1961-63/1963-64 (prod: 328,640). Saloon, estate car. F/R, 1508cc/1595cc (S4 OHV). No flutes any more, but total restyle makes for a bearable and (in theory) less rustprone shape: the FB's also roomier with a bigger boot. Pressurised cooling, side chrome on De Luxe models, and an all-synchro four-on-the-floor option. Bigger engines and clutches and a new facia for '64, when servo front disc brakes also available.

VX4/90 FB. 1961-63/1963-64 (prod: n/a). Saloon. F/R, 1508cc/1595cc (S4 OHV). Sporty Victor with twin-carb 71bhp high-compression engine, individual front seats, servo front disc brakes, four-on-the-floor, a different grille, and colour side flashes. Higher axle ratio mentioned in initial announcements not fitted. It will do 90mph and 24mpg, but it's noisy and doesn't handle well. Bigger engine (85bhp) for '64 models.

VICTOR FC. 1964-67 (prod: 219,814). Saloon, estate car. F/R, 1595cc (S4 OHV). More room inside, curved side panels and thinner pillars, plus a steering column ignition lock (extra), duo-servo rear brakes and some more power, up to 70bhp. Powerglide automatic available June '66, new grille on '67s. Last of the pushrod Victors.

VX4/90 FC. 1964-67 (prod: 13,449). Saloon. F/R, 1595cc (S4 OHV). The VX's output is up to 85bhp, and it gets a new crosshatch grille, a better facia, and a radial-ply tyre option. Colour side flashes retained for external identification. Limited slip diffs on '66s and '67s, but no automatic option on this one.

VICTOR FD 2000. 1967-72 (prod: see Victor FD 1600). Saloon, estate car. F/R, 1975cc (S4 OC). As for FD 1600, but with a bigger version of the ohc engine giving 104bhp, a higher axle ratio. Alternator, servo front disc brakes, automatic (Borg-Warner to '69), and heated rear window are in options list. Other changes as for FD 1600, and 1970-72s badged as 2000 SLs.

VICTOR FD 1600. 1967-72 (prod: 198,085 all FDs and Ventora). Saloon, estate car. F/R, 1599cc (S4 OC). The Victor comes into line with the latest Viva, but more important is Vauxhall's new engine with hemi-head and cogged-belt ohc. Its 83bhp spells 90mph even in basic form, and steering is now by rack and pinion. Front disc brakes extra, so is four-on-the-floor with or without overdrive. Estate cars from May '68, GM Strasbourg automatic transmission available for '70, when cars renamed Victor Supers.

VX4/90 FD. 1969-72 (prod: 14,277). Saloon. F/R, 1975cc (S4 OC). Back after a lapse of two seasons, the VX4/90 now has twin Strombergs and overdrive as part of the package, as well as rear-wing stoneguards, Rostyle wheels, a body coachline, and a central grille bar. Usual comprehensive instrumentation, but (for the first time on a VX) automatic is available. Not quite good for 100mph.

PA VELOX/CRESTA. 1957-60 (prod: 81,841). Saloon, estate car. F/R, 2262cc (S6 OHV). Revised sixes with an extra 1½ins of wheelbase, hydraulic clutch, all-synchro 'box, and a '57 American shape with dog's leg screen and tailfins, though the awful three-piece rear window isn't used after '58. Cresta has usual luxury extra equipment. Estate cars from '59, new curved-top grille and a servo-brake option for 1960. Good performers if you can stand the looks.

PASX VELOX/PADX CRESTA. 1960-62 (prod: 91,923). Saloon, estate car. F/R, 2651cc (S6 OHV). New, square-dimensioned engine with wedge-shaped combustion chambers in basic '57 shape with bigger wheels and tailfins, lower-geared steering, and yet another grille pattern. Dual overdrive and Hydramatic available, also servo front disc brakes (or just the servo, if you prefer drums). Spot a Cresta by its anodised wheel trims.

VELOX/CRESTA PB. 1962-64/1964-65 (prod: 87,047). Saloon, estate car. F/R, 2651cc/3294cc (S6 OHV). Reskinned six on lines of FB Victor, but with more rounded tail. Three-on-the-column still, but with overdrive and Hydramatic options: servo front disc brakes now standard. Estate cars (by Dormobile) from '64. The '65 models have 3.3-litre engine, acrylic paintwork, and two-speed wipers but, alas! two-speed Powerglide as the self-shifting option.

CRESTA PC. 1965-72 (prod: 53,912). Saloon, estate car. F/R, 3294cc (S6 OHV). There's no Velox any more, only a Cresta De Luxe option with quad headlamps. Mechanics little changed, though bodies updated to match FC Victors. Output now 123bhp, and four-on-the-floor rounds out a wide range of transmission choices. No estates after 1968.

VISCOUNT. 1966-72 (prod: 7025). Saloon. F/R, 3294cc (S6 OHV). PC Cresta double-plus, that is, lots of sound damping, bigger wheels, wider rims, power steering and windows, heated rear window, vinyl top, reclining seats, radio, and walnut veneer facia. Powerglide standard, but four-on-the-floor listed at same price. Will just about pull the ton on a 3.46 rear axle. Last of the traditional big GM Vauxhalls.

VENTORA/VICTOR 3300. 1968-72 (prod: see Victor FD 1600). Saloon, estate car, F/R, 3294cc (S6 OHV). Crossbred FD Victor with the big six engine in 123bhp form, front disc brakes, and proper pull-up handbrake lever. Victor 3300 designation used on estate cars. Four-speed manual with or without overdrive: automatics are Powerglide to '69, with the preferable GM-Strasbourg thereafter. Vinyl roof option on saloons, and Ventora II designation applied to 1970-72 models.

VIVA HA. 1963-66 (prod: 309,538). 2-door saloon. F/R, 1057cc (S4 OHV). Angular British version of the German Opel Kadett, with 44bhp engine, wedge-shaped combustion chambers, all-synchro four-speed 'box, floor change, rack and pinion steering and semi-elliptics at the rear. Drum brakes standard, but discs at the front yours for only £12 extra. Higher-geared steering for '65, and '66 range includes SLs with polished aluminium grilles, colour side flashes, and better trim.

BEDFORD BEAGLE. 1964-73 (prod: n/a). Estate car. F/R, 1057cc/1159cc/1256cc (S4 OHV). Dormobile conversion of the HA Bedford van, no frills and even less sound-damping, though van-type doors give excellent loading height and will handle almost anything. Same 4.125 back axle as the cars: gets later uprated engines in 1967 (1159cc) and 1972 (1256cc). Always, however, drum brakes and not very good ones at that. Personal experience suggests 40mpg on light loads.

VIVA HA 90. 1965-66 (prod: 11,794). 2-door saloon. F/R, 1057cc (S4 OHV). Basically a 1966-specification HA de luxe with some extra performance – over 80mph and 0-50mph in 13secs – thanks to a 60bhp high-compression engine, a Stromberg carb, and revised manifolding. Propshaft reinforced, too. Servo front disc brakes standard, but HBs are generally better cars.

VIVA HB. 1966-70 (prod: 566,391). 2-door saloon, 4-door saloon, estate car. F/R, 1159cc (S4 OHV). More capacity and power, coils and a live axle at the rear, and a new, attractive shape, with more room as well as extra length. Automatic available on DL/SL versions from February '67, estate cars June '67. Collapsible steering columns and four-door saloon option for 1970.

VIVA HB 90. 1966-70 (prod: 78,296). 2-door saloon, 4-door saloon, estate car. F/R, 1159cc (S4 OHV). The HB in high performance form with 60bhp, 9:1 cr engine, Stromberg instead of Solex carburettor, insulated rubber mounts for engine, front suspension and steering, and a lower axle ratio to boost acceleration. Good for 85mph. Like other DLs and SLs, available with automatic, and other changes as for standard HB. Crayford made a handful of convertibles, too.

BRABHAM VIVA HB. 1967-68 (prod: n/a). 2-door saloon. F/R, 1159cc (S4 OHV). Turning the HB into a mini-GT with an extra 9bhp, straight-through exhaust, wide rim wheels and tenuous Jack Brabham connection. Front disc brakes are, of course, standard, but no automatic on this one, though predictably there's a go-faster flash round the top of the grille.

VIVA HB 1600. 1968-70 (prod: 13,517). 2-door saloon, 4-door saloon, estate car. F/R, 1599cc (S4 OC). Stiffer suspension and low-profile tyres on yet another Vauxhall cross-pollination, this time an HB hull with the 83bhp 1.6-litre cogged-belt ohc engine from the FD Victor. Front disc brakes standard, Borg-Warner automatic available, and four-door saloons from late '69 for '70.

VIVA GT. 1968-70 (prod: 4606). 2-door saloon. F/R, 1975cc (S4 OC). This time they've slipped the 2-litre FD engine into a Brabham replacement, and slanted it at 45 degrees. Twin Strombergs and 104bhp spell a genuine ton, and there's a close-ratio four-speed 'box. Brakes and final drive are Victor, too, and the suspension's been beefed up.

VERITAS (D)

This West German company was founded by former BMW employees who wanted to build sports cars based on the pre-war BMW 328: at that time (1948), BMW had not resumed manufacturing. The firm was forced to reorganise in 1950, being renamed Veritas Nürburgring, but closed in 1953 – immediate postwar Germany was no place to build sports cars . . .

◄ **METEOR. 1947-48 (prod: 78 all types). 2-seater sports. F/R, 1971cc (S6 OHV).** Early post-war special using BMW 328 chassis/mechanical parts, with new camshaft and head and roller-bearing crankshaft. Hurth gearbox, various tunes up to 128bhp, and slab-sided aerodynamic bodywork. Only marginally 'street', but fun as an historic racer.

SATURN/SCORPION/COMET. 1949-50 (prod: see Meteor). Sports coupé, sports cabriolet, 2-seater sports. F/R, 1988cc (S6 OC). Still BMW-type chassis, but now with seven-bearing hemi-head Heinkel unit giving 100/120bhp, five-speed synchromesh 'box, and de Dion back end. Dry-sump lubrication with twin oil pumps, coupés and convertibles (Saturn, Scorpion) on longer wheelbase. Some cars with BMW engine and four speeds. ►

VESPA (F)

This minicar was designed by the Piaggio aircraft firm, the creator of the successful Vespa scooter. Production, however, was undertaken in the A.C.M.A. factory in France rather than in Italy. The car actually had considerable *chic* appeal, and its high build quality was one reason for it lasting from 1958 to 1961.

◄ **400. 1958-61 (prod: 34,000 approx). 2-seater cabriolet. R/R, 393cc (S2 TS).** Pretty little French minicar with rolltop convertible body *à la* Fiat Topolino, all-independent springing (swing axles at the back), hydraulic brakes, and four-speed synchro 'box. Slide out tray for battery in nose, 50mph and 50mpg. Marketed in the Channel Islands, but no regular imports to the mainland.

VOLGA (USSR)

The Volga was the first postwar successor to the somewhat basic Pobieda car, both being products of the giant Gorky auto works: they were made at the works alongside each other for three years. Volga is one of the few Russian car manufacturers which makes products basically for home consumption.

M21/M22. 1955-72/1961-72 (prod: n/a). Saloon, estate car. F/R, 2445cc (S4 OHV). Tough Russian family saloon with five-bearing wet-liner engine, unitary construction, and lots of inclusive equipment – vast tool kit, driver-controlled radiator blind, radio, bed-seats, two-speed wipers and so on. Engineering conservative, handling lumpy and heavy, and performance uninspired. Always three speeds, but floor change offered with rare rhd. ►

M24. 1969 to date (prod: n/a). Saloon. F/R, 2445cc (S4 OHV). Much the same old mechanics with coil-spring ifs, live rear axle and drum brakes, albeit now with a servo. Restyled as early sixties American, dual-choke carburation, alternator, and four speeds with synchro on first, 90mph claimed. Seen at Earls Court in '70 and '71, but imports negligible.

VOLKSWAGEN (D)

A huge car manufacturing concern, born originally of Hitler's attempt to provide low cost motoring for the masses. Ferdinand Porsche designed the original car, although very few were actually made before 1939. After World War II, during which it had made military vehicles for the Wehrmacht, Volkswagen came under British control, from which it was released in 1949, producing the Beetle. This one-model reliance ultimately had serious effects and even after the takeover of Audi and NSU Volkswagen's losses grew ever larger, with only a new range for 1974 (including the Golf) reviving the firm's fortunes. VW is also a true multi-national company producing cars in several countries, including Brazil, Mexico and Yugoslavia.

1100 STANDARD. 1946-53 (prod: 527,508 all 1131cc saloons). 2-door saloon. R/R, 1131cc (HO4 OHV). The now familiar formula of rear-mounted air-cooled flat-four engine and all-torsion-bar springing; first Beetle into Britain though not many sold, and official imports don't begin till mid-'53. Minimal brightwork, no synchromesh and cable-operated mechanical brakes. All with divided rear windows. 16ins wheels to October '52, 15ins thereafter. Curiosity value.

1100 EXPORT/DE LUXE. 1949-53 (prod: see 1100 Standard). 2-door saloon, cabriolet. R/R, 1131cc (HO4 OHV). First fully-equipped model and first Beetle imported in quantity into Britain, from '53. Hydraulic brakes May '50: from October '52 with synchromesh and chromium plated hubcaps, bumpers, and headlamp rims. One-piece oval rear window (April '53) almost invariable on RHD cars. Some folding-top saloons, but early Karmann cabriolets (and the much prettier Hebmüller two-seater) not imported here.

1200 STANDARD. 1954-64 (prod: 7,267,899 all saloon models). 2-door saloon. R/R, 1192cc (HO4 OHV). Basic stripped Beetle with bigger 30bhp engine, vacuum ignition control and better cylinder-head cooling. Main styling/mechanical changes as for 1200 De Luxe below, but cable-operated brakes to April 1963 (!) and never synchromesh at all. Listed here to 1962, but hardly any imported.

1200 DE LUXE. 1954-64 (prod: see 1200 Standard). 2-door saloon. R/R, 1192cc (HO4 OHV). Up-engined de luxe, on 15ins wheels, of course. Twin exhausts and tubeless tyres 1956. Improvements in 1958 are a bigger screen and rear window, there's a front anti-roll bar from '60, and by '61 you've got a 34bhp engine, automatic choke, bigger brake master cylinder, synchro on bottom, and redesigned steering. Saxomat automatic clutch (rare in Britain) available on later cars. ➤

◄ **1200 KARMANN CABRIOLET. 1954-65 (prod: 262,686 all Beetle cabriolets to 1974). 4-seater cabriolet. R/R, 1192cc (HO4 OHV).** Fully openable four-seater first listed 1951, and a regular Beetle item (though not always with same mechanics) to the end of German production. Mechanical changes as on 1200 De Luxe, UK-available from 1955, but not many rhd cars around. Usual Beetle splendours and miseries, but relatively scarce and might become collectable.

KOMBI. 1951-74 (prod: 3,514,783 all light commercials). Estate car/minibus. R/R, 1131cc/1192cc/1493cc/1584cc (HO4 OHV). VW's light commercial with full forward control, cam and lever steering, and lower overall gearing. Mechanics otherwise stock. First of the modern mobile-home generation, and conversions are legion. Very dependable if tricky on the hands. The 1192cc engine arrived in '54, the 1.5-litre in '64, and the 1.6-litre in '68. In the latter year the model was also restyled. Front disc brakes from 1971. ➤

◄ **1200 KARMANN-GHIA COUPE. 1955-65 (prod: 364,401 all coupés to 1974). 2+2-seater coupé. R/R, 1192cc (HO4 OHV).** Ghia's pretty and curvaceous sporty model: mechanics as for stock 1200 with same year-by-year changes. Better aerodynamics make for more straightline speed (77mph as against 68), but it weighs more than a saloon and will be a bit slower off the mark. Handling's better too. Rear seat for children only. UK-available from '57, but rhd not very common.

1200 KARMANN-GHIA CABRIOLET. 1957-65 (prod: 80,899 all cabriolets to 1974). 2-seater cabriolet. R/R, 1192cc (HO4 OHV). Two-light ragtop development of the coupé with same mechanics and specification changes, plus the usual VW problems, notably funny handling in crosswinds. Rhd seldom seen, though listed in Britain from 1958. Too rare and collectable to use as a donor-car for kits. ➤

1300 BEETLE. 1965-70 (prod: 2,726,154). 2-door saloon, Karmann cabriolet, Karmann-Ghia coupé, Karmann-Ghia cabriolet. R/R, 1285cc (HO4 OHV). Bigger 40bhp engine with the all-synchro 'box of later 1200s, revised front end, greased-for-life steering joints, slotted wheels. From '68, two-speed wipers, 12-volt electrics, dual-circuit brakes with a front-disc option, collapsible steering column. Also available that year, a three-speed 'stick automatic' version (acceleration nil, avoid). Coupés and cabriolets in Britain 1966/67 only.

1500 BEETLE. 1966-70 (prod: 1,888,282). 2-door saloon, Karmann cabriolet, Karmann-Ghia coupé, Karmann-Ghia cabriolet. R/R, 1493cc (HO4 OHV). Last and most powerful of the pre-MacPherson-sprung Beetles, with the old torsion bars at either end. Its 44bhp gave 80mph, and dual-circuit disc/drum brakes are now standard. Also has bigger flywheel, wider rear track (should help handling) and softer rear springs with supplementary stabiliser. Improvements as for 1300, with 'stick automatic' available from '68. Post-'70 Karmann-Ghias had 1600cc engines as well as the revised chassis.

1200 BEETLE. 1967-70 (prod: 585,817). 2-door saloon. R/R, 1192cc (HO4 OHV). Styling marches on, but on this one you still have a 1954-size engine (34bhp), six-volt electrics, and drum brakes in our period, though they're of dual-circuit type from 1968. Nice, reliable hack which translates into a nice and easily insurable kit-car if you're content with maiden-aunt performance.

1500/1500 VARIANT. 1961-63 (prod: 738,010/203,046 incl 1600). 2-door saloon, estate car. R/R, 1493cc (HO4 OHV). A 'better Beetle', but is it? Main major differences under the skin amount to more room, the option of a proper, car-type wagon, and round-section torsion bars if you care to look underneath. Automatic choke and all-synchro 'box, but still six-volt electrics and drum brakes on these. Plus, it's faster than contemporary Beetles: minus, it uses more fuel.

1500S. 1963-65 (prod: see 1500). 2-door saloon, estate car. R/R, 1493cc (HO4 OHV). The 'S' suffix spells an extra carburettor, nine more brake horses (54 instead of 45), 85mph, and appreciably better acceleration in the upper ranges, though these engines don't like the sort of cheap petrol you can stuff into a Beetle's tank. All S-cars sold in Britain are to de luxe specification.

1500S/1600 KARMANN GHIA. 1963-65/1965-69 (prod: 42,563 both types). 2+2-seater coupé. R/R, 1493cc/ 1584cc (HO4 OHV). No cabriolets this time, and rather more angular styling, with the traditional Karmann motif confined to the bonnet. Full wrapround rear window and more room. Latter-day improvements on 1600 model (fuel injection, automatic) available though this up-engined type wasn't normally listed in Britain.

1600. 1966-73 (prod: 601,286 fastbacks; other styles see 1500). 2-door saloon, 2-door fastback saloon, estate car. R/R, 1584cc (HO4 OHV). New engine, front disc brakes, and optional fastback (not to everyone's taste). Originally offered with six-volt electrics and twin Solex carburettors: 12-volts 1967, plus electronic fuel injection and automatic options from '68 along with dual-circuit brakes as standard. MacPherson front suspension for '68 automatics and for all cars from '69 onwards. Revised front and rear end styling, 1970.

411. 1968-72 (prod: 266,521 incl 1972 412 models). 2-door saloon, 4-door saloon, estate car. R/R, 1679cc (HO4 OHV). Final extension of the Beetle theme with 98½ins wheelbase, and room for four doors. Brakes are stock '68 Volkswagen, with servos on some late cars. All had 12-volt electrics, four-speed manual or three-speed stick automatic, MacPherson front suspension with coils and trailing arms at the back. Fuel-injection engine (80bhp as against 68 with twin Solexes) from '70, when Variant estate car added to range.

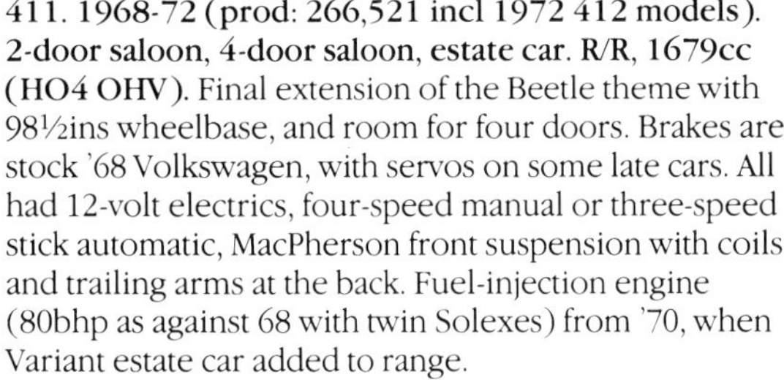

VOLKSWAGEN-PORSCHE (D)

Seemingly a curious marriage, but one which made sense at the time. Porsche wanted a way to break into the mass sports car market, but did not have the capacity to do so, while VW desired to move its image up-market. The problem was that the resultant car was just too expensive, lasting from 1969 to 1975. Still, they outsold Jaguar's E-type . . .

914/4. 1969-73 (prod: 65,351). Roadster. R/R, 1679cc (HO4 OHV). Poor man's Porsche with Targa-type body, using 80bhp fuel-injected VW 411 engine, five-speed all-synchromesh 'box, all-coil springing (MacPherson at front) and disc brakes all round. Inner pair of quad headlights retract. Porsche Sportomatic transmission available, 100+ mph and good handling, but lacking in bottom-end punch. Sold as a Porsche in America, but seldom seen in Britain.

914/6. 1969-72 (prod: 3333). Roadster. R/R, 1991cc (HO6 DOC). 914/4 chassis and body, but rather more Porsche as it uses the 911's flat-six in twin-carburettor 110bhp form. Radially finned brakes; identifiable by its twin headlamps only. 120mph, 0-50mph in 6.3secs, and 25mpg, but no right-hand drive and pretty rare anywhere. All later cars of this make were flat-fours. ➤

VOLVO (S)

Along with Saab and Abba, probably Sweden's best known export. The company was founded in 1927 under the management of Assar Gabrielson and with backing from the SKF ball-bearing firm. Before World War II the company built solid and uninspired middle range products, but the PV444 gave the company a reputation for cars with good roadholding and fine build quality which it keeps to this day. In 1975 the firm acquired Daf and founded Volvo Car BV, although the parent company has only a 30 per cent stake in the Dutch company.

◄ **PV544. 1959-61/1962-65 (prod: 246,995). 2-door saloon. F/R, 1583cc/1778cc (S4 OHV).** Famed fastback with 1942 Ford styling and a rally winner in its day, though never marketed in Britain, ergo lhd if you find one. Six-volt electrics, twin SU carburettors, four-speed all-synchro 'box (but there are some three-speeders, too), all-coil springing, and drum brakes. Will do 95mph in its hottest form (bigger engine from '61). Very collectable in some parts of Western Europe.

121/122. 1956-62/1962-67 (prod: 202,421 all models). 4-door saloon. F/R, 1583cc/1778cc (S4 OHV). Basic unitary four-door with '55 Chrysler styling, the familiar five-bearing engine in single-carburettor form, and suspension and gearbox as PV544, though all UK models (from '59) are four-speeders, apart from automatic options ('66 on). Front disc brakes '65, sealed chassis lubrication '66. Early engines only give 60bhp, but 1.8-litre versions have 85bhp and should go as well as twin-carb 1.6-litres. ➤

◄ **122S. 1957-62 (prod: see 121/122). 4-door saloon. F/R, 1583cc (S4 OHV).** The first Volvo to sell seriously in Britain. Specification as for 121/122 in essence, but with twin-SU engine giving 85bhp and 85-90mph. Drum brakes, six-volt electrics, and as indestructible as Volvos usually are, but the rust will have had a long innings, so better to go for later members of this family.

122S-B18. 1962-67 (prod: see 121/122). 4-door saloon. F/R, 1778cc (S4 OHV). The 122S with the bigger engine, plus 12-volt electrics, front disc brakes, and (on later cars) progressively better rust protection. Overdrive optional. 1965 and subsequent models recognisable by their horizontal grille bars: these give over 90mph and 24mpg on 95bhp.

131/132S. 1961-70 (prod: 359,118 all two-door models). 2-door saloon. F/R, 1584cc/1778cc (S4 OHV). Better-looking than four-door 120s, but only sold in Britain from 1965, which means 1.8-litre engines and front disc brakes, plus usual overdrive option. Automatic available from '67 when 100bhp twin-carburettor 132S with servo brakes also listed here. Last imported 1969.

221/222. 1962-69 (prod: 83,177). Estate car. F/R, 1778cc/1985cc (S4 OHV). Wagon version of 120 model, UK-available late 1962, usually with single Zenith carburettor and always officially with straight four-speed all-synchro 'box. Disc front brakes '65, and output increased in '67 when twin-carburettor 222 becomes available. Some late ones (from 1968) with 2-litre engine.

123GT. 1966-67 (prod: see 131). 2-door saloon. F/R, 1778cc (S4 OHV). Sporting two-door saloon with 115bhp engine, twin SUs, overdrive, and servo brakes: limited-slip differential available. Advertised to do 108mph, but only a handful imported, and not many made anyway. Might become collectable.

P1800/P1800S. 1961-63/1963-69 (prod: 29,993). 2-seater coupé. F/R, 1778cc/1985cc (S4 OHV). Attractive sports coupé originally made for Volvo by Jensen, and made famous in TV's *The Saint* series. Servo front disc brakes and twin-carburettor engine on all, overdrive standard for Britain. S models (108bhp to '66, 115bhp thereafter) take over in '63, sealed cooling '67, dual circuit braking, electric cooling fan and 2-litre engine 1969. Still a bit of a sleeper, but there's already some collector-interest.

P1800E. 1969-72 (prod: 11,414). 2-seater coupé. F/R, 1985cc (S4 OHV). Main change here (apart from the alternators already seen on late P1800S cars) are the Bosch electronic fuel injection and automatic option (latter from '71). Overdrive again standard for UK, and chassis engineering remains classic Volvo 120. The Reliant-style GT estate didn't happen until 1972. ➤

◄ **144. 1966-68/1968-75 (prod: 94,800/429,648). 4-door saloon. F/R, 1778cc/1985cc (S4 OHV).** Into the built-in safety era on a ponderous family saloon on a 102ins wheelbase hull, with the usual Volvo engine and suspension, all-disc servo brakes, and a speed in the low 90s with the original engine. Overdrive, automatic and limited slip differentials available. A/c electrics '68, 2-litre 118bhp engine standard on '69 models, and a fuel-injected 124bhp development from '71.

144S. 1967-68/1968-74 (prod: see 144). 4-door saloon. F/R, 1778cc/1985cc (S4 OHV). This one's a 122S replacement with twin horizontal SUs boosting power from 85 to 115bhp in 1.8 litre form – which means nearly 100mph, 70 in third and a 0-50mph time of 8.6 secs. Overdrive standard for Britain, but no automatic option. The 2-litre engine came in 1969. Other improvements as for 144. ➤

◄ **142/142S. 1967-68/1968-74 (prod: 6640/406,346). 2-door saloon. F/R, 1778cc/1985cc (S4 OHV).** Watch it, the production breakdown is for cylinder capacity, not the number of carburettors. All comments and changes as for 144 family, though it was introduced later: the old 131 was allowed to work itself out as a bargain-basement Volvo. Just as ugly as the four-door.

145/145S. 1967-68/1968-74 (prod: 9200/259,117). Estate car. F/R, 1778cc/1985cc (S4 OHV). Classical four-door Volvo wagon with the tough old five-bearing engine (2-litre from the '69 model year) and the usual choice of tune. In its day, recognised 'U' housewife wear in the commuter suburbs and still a good hack if the rust hasn't got in. Production breakdown and changes as for 144/145, plus the bonus of a built-in rear window wash/wipe from early 1970. ➤

164. 1968-73 (prod: 104,850). 4-door saloon. F/R, 2978cc (S6 OHV). Built like a tank and about as exciting, with a massive seven-bearing 145bhp pushrod six and the usual Volvo chassis engineering. Power disc brakes all round as on 140s, a live axle and coils at the back, and 110mph on tap. Lots of options – automatic, limited slip diff., overdrive, power steering, sun roof – though no wagons. Later engines come with electronic fuel injection and more power. ➤

WARTBURG (D)

The Wartburg grew out of the IFA firm, which was a union of all the major nationalised – East German – car factories, including DKW, Audi and Phanomen. From 1956, the Eisenach works – pre-war home of BMWs – started producing front-drive, two-stroke engined machines.

◄ **312. 1962-66 (prod: approx 150,000). 4-door saloon, estate car. F/F, 991cc (S3 TS).** East German variation on the three-cylinder DKW theme, with separate chassis, four-on-the-column plus a free wheel, rack and pinion steering, a beam-axle back end, and heavy-to-work brakes. A big car for 1-litre: 170ins long, and lots of room. UK available July '64 (wagons, 1965): these latter still being sold here well into 1967.

353 KNIGHT. 1966 to date (prod: 330,000 approx to end 1974). 4-door saloon, estate car. F/F, 991cc (S3 TS). More headroom with its new four-light body: also now with front-mounted 'box, floor change, sealed-for-life suspension and spare wheel stowed in the front wing. All-synchro 'box and estates late '67, disc front brakes '75, UK imports ceased '77. Plus: lots of inclusive equipment and panels detach for quick replacement. Minus: awful handling, ghastly brakes, and 25mpg. ➤

WARWICK (GB)

The designer of the Peerless, Bernard Rodger, started making the Warwick GT after the failure of his previous manufacturing venture. All he did, in effect, was to up-date the existing design, and the car was made from 1960 to 1962 at Colnbrook in Buckinghamshire until the money ran out.

◄ **2-LITRE. 1960-62 (prod: n/a). 2-door sports saloon. F/R, 1991cc (S4 OHV).** Revival of the Peerless GT, again with Triumph TR3 engine and 'box (triple overdrive standard), front suspension and final drive unit, plus the de Dion rear end and front disc brakes with optional servo. Centre-lock wire wheels available. It's 80lbs lighter than a Peerless, which should help, but contemporary reports were unkind about the fit and finish of the glass-fibre body.

3½-LITRE. 1961-62 (prod: n/a). 2-door sports saloon. F/R, 3528cc (V8 OHV). Interesting heart transplant – the familiar Buick (later Rover) aluminium V8 into the Peerless/Warwick glass-fibre-bodied structure. Standard tune was 185bhp; but 240bhp promised with some tweaking. Driveline was a four-speed ZF 'box with Laycock overdrive and a 3.7:1 ZF final drive unit. Intended to sell in the USA, but the money ran out first. Distant relative of Gordon-Keeble. ➤

WILLIAM (F)

Imported into this country by Crayford, this minicar was still listed by the French Lambretta importer, M. William, as a Lambretta model in 1981. It was also built in Italy as the Lawil S3 Varzina, which in 1985 was the slowest car listed in the world!

◄ **FARMER. 1969-74 (prod: n/a). Open 2-seater. F/R, 125cc (S1 TS).** Or plain 'Willam' when Crayford attempted to market it in Britain, 1972. French version of Italian Lawil design, and very basic, with Lambretta scooter engine, four-speed crash 'box, transverse-leaf ifs, and 10ins wheels with drum brakes. No doors, only chains hung over empty space, barely 80ins long, but the commuters gave it the bird.

WOLSELEY (GB)

This firm ended its days as yet another badge-engineering exercise on British Leyland cars, but was one of the British motoring pioneers under the managership of Herbert Austin. In 1901, the firm became a part of Vickers, and from 1904 to 1910 the cars were marketed as Wolseley-Siddeleys. However, in 1927, the firm was absorbed by Morris, and thereafter its cars were luxury versions of Morrises until the BMC merger in 1952, when there was a rationalisation of design. The last true Wolseley was the 1500 of 1958, but it still retained an up-market image compared to Austin and Morris products.

EIGHT. 1946-48 (prod: 5344). 4-door saloon. F/R, 918cc (S4 OHV). 'U' version of the Series-E Morris with 33bhp ohv conversion, Wolseley bonnet and grille, and headlamps out of doors, but still six-volt electrics. Planned as a new model for 1940, it was Lord Nuffield's favourite car in his old age. Examples have made astounding prices at auctions, but they're still available in good order for three figures. ➤

TEN. 1939-48 (prod: 2715 post-war). Saloon. F/R, 1140cc (S4 OHV). First seen in January '39 as the snob's Morris Ten – same engine but a proper chassis in place of the Morris's rustprone unitary affair. Usual Nuffield engineering – wide-ratio four-speed synchromesh 'box, hydraulic brakes, cart springs, and such Wolseley refinements as a telescopic steering column and built-in jacks. No dropheads post-war. ➤

◄ **12/48 SERIES III. 1938-48 (prod: 5602 post-war). Saloon. F/R, 1548cc (S4 OHV).** Last flowering of the good old 69.5 x 102mm engine with roots going back to the Morris-Cowley. To 1938 specification with cruciform-braced frame, electric pump feed, Jackall jacks, sliding roof, opening screen, reversing lamp and leather trim. Same body as the contemporary sixes, so not very much urge.

14/60 SERIES III. 1939-48 (prod: 5731 post-war). Saloon. F/R, 1818cc (S6 OHV). Four-bearing six on a 104¾ins wheelbase, sharing the 12/48's 1939 styling and appointments. Twin-carburettor 60bhp power unit should give you 70mph, and this package includes twin horns and the notorious Wolseley nightpass system – a dipped beam linked to the passlamps. (It's now illegal, and if the bumper bolts shear, you've no dip at all.) ➤

◄ **18/85 SERIES III. 1939-48 (prod: 8213 post-war). Saloon. F/R, 2322cc (S6 OHV).** The classic police Wolseley, sharing its twin-carburettor 85bhp engine with the pre-war 2-litre MG: gear ratios much the same, too, though this won't matter on a Wolseley. Twin windtone horns and a built in radio aerial complement the usual de luxe trimmings common to 12/48s and 14/60s, and longer bonnet helps looks. In production from the autumn of 1945.

25 SERIES III. 1947-48 (prod: 75 post-war). Limousine. F/R, 3485cc (S6 OHV). Revival of Wolseley's big 1938-40 formal carriage on an impressive 141ins wheelbase, sole survivor of a range which included saloons and a drophead pre-war. Twin SUs fed by twin electric pumps, hence 105bhp. Heaters standard in both compartments. Rarer, more interesting, and probably less thirsty than a Humber Pullman. ➤

4/50. 1948-53 (prod: 8955). Saloon. F/R, 1476cc (S4 OC). Into badge engineering with what amounts to a MO-series Morris Oxford with upstairs-camshaft engine and a proper Wolseley front end with the famous illuminated radiator emblem. Spotlamp and heater standard equipment on this one, which did 75mph and 26mpg, but they'll all have rusted by now, and whence engine spares, one wonders?

OXFORD HIRE CAR. 1950-55 (prod: approx 200). Limousine. F/R, 1802cc (S4 OHV). Oddball made by Wolseley to Morris-Commercial specification – engine has affinities (albeit distant ones) with the old 14/28 Morris-Oxford, there's an underslung worm back end, brakes are rod-operated mechanicals, and wheels are good old 1929 artillery pattern. Most were London taxicabs, but a few six-light limousines made. Surprisingly, there's synchromesh...

6/90 SERIES I. 1954-56 (prod: 5776). Saloon. F/R, 2639cc (S6 OHV). Styling is enlarged 4/44, and the underparts are essentially 6/80, the coil-spring rear end excepted, but now the BMC C-type unit has replaced the old ohc type. Four-on-the-column, twin SUs fed by electric pump and, of course, lots of wood and leather. The facia's plastic, though.

6/80. 1948-54 (prod: 24,886). Saloon. F/R, 2215cc (S6 OC). MS-series Morris Six with the Wolseley treatment, though differences mainly cosmetic, as Morrises had ohc, too. Twin spotlamps, electric choke, and telescopic steering wheel, plus wood and real leather. Another police favourite. Faults as for Morris version, like rust, awkward maintenance, and woolly steering.

4/44. 1952-56 (prod: 29,845). Saloon. F/R, 1250cc (S4 OHV). From the BMC era, but 100 per cent Nuffield, with a unitary hull shape used only on bigger Wolseleys (and Rileys), a detuned single-carburettor T-type MG engine, and rack-and-pinion steering. Coils, however, instead of torsion bars at the front. One-piece curved screen looks better than the 4/50's vee, but the radiator cap's a dummy. Usual nasty four-on-the-column.

6/90 SERIES II/III. 1956-57/1957-59 (prod: 1024/5052). ➤ Saloon. F/R, 2639cc (S6 OHV). Looks like Series I, but Series II has semi-elliptics, thank goodness, at the back, a proper polished walnut facia once more, right-hand floor shift for manuals, and overdrive/automatic options. Series III (July '57) with bigger rear window, servo brakes, and lower-geared steering. Why bother with a Riley 2.6 – this is the same package, and easier to find.

◄ 15/50. 1956-58 (prod: 12,353). Saloon. F/R, 1489cc (S4 OHV). You've guessed – it's a 4/44 with single-carburettor BMC B-series engine (50bhp) offering 75mph. Usual mechanics plus illuminated radiator badge (of course), foglamps, and floor instead of column shift. Manumatic two-pedal drive (avoid) an option on this model, though no automatic.

1500. 1957-65 (prod: 100,832). Saloon. F/R, 1489cc (S4 ➤ OHV). Extended Morris Minor theme with the same excellent suspension and steering, the good old B-series engine, and a closer-ratio 'box which wasn't quite as good as it sounded on paper. Internal bonnet and boot lid hinges on Series II (1959): tell a Series III (Oct '61) by its A40-type rear lamp clusters, revised radiator side-grilles, and longer side chromium flashes. The 1200cc version (old-type A40 engine) is very rare and exclusively for the Irish Republic. The slow driver's Riley 1.5.

◄ 15-60/16-60. 1959-61/1961-71 (prod: 24,759/63,082). Saloon. F/R, 1489cc/1622cc (S4 OHV). Wolseley's contribution to the Farina round-game with all the luxury trimmings, single-carburettor engine, and floor change. Later 16/60 (Sept '61) has the 1.6-litre engine and an automatic option, but as always, no disc brakes. Everything lasts for ever save the unitary hull, but it's just about the dullest car imaginable.

6-99. 1959-61 (prod: 13,108). Saloon. F/R, 2912cc (S6 ➤ OHV). With Morris out of the six-cylinder league, the choice is now between unitary Farina shapes by Austin, Vanden Plas and Wolseley. This latter specification adds up to 102bhp with twin SUs and twin electric pumps, servo front disc brakes, and synchromesh on all three forward ratios, with triple overdrive. Automatic optional but the fog lamps are inclusive.

6-110 SERIES I/II. 1961-64/1964-68 (prod: 10,800/ 13,301). Saloon. F/R, 2912cc (S6 OHV). Output up to 120bhp on Series I, with a Panhard rod locating the rear axle. Power steering and air conditioning available from July '62. Series II (March '64) has four speeds instead of three and overdrive is therefore optional. Smaller wheels, too, though picnic tables and reclining seats are now part of the package. ➤

◀ **HORNET I. 1961-62 (prod: 28,455 all Hornets). 2-door saloon. F/F, 848cc (S4 OHV).** Mini with a Wolseley grille (and matching side grilles) plus the Riley Elf's ungainly rear-end bustle. Mechanical specification strictly stock, but there are some bonuses: wrap-round rear bumper, heater, screenwash, and one windtone horn. Nobody's favourite Mini.

HORNET II/III. 1963-64/1964-69 (prod: see Hornet I). 2-door saloon. F/F, 998cc (S4 OHV). Bigger, 38bhp engine and twin leading-shoe front brakes on Series II – predictably Series III (Sept '64) gets Hydrolastic springing, a diaphragm clutch, and key starting. AP automatic transmission available on '66 models. An oddball variant exclusive to Wolseley is the Viking Sport (1964) a top chop by W.J. Last of Trident fame. ➤

◀ **1100/1300. 1965-68/1967-73 (prod: 17,497/27,470). 4-door saloon. F/F, 1098cc/1275cc (S4 OHV).** Halfway house between Riley and MG members of the family: 1100s have twin-carburettor units in Riley tune, walnut veneer trim, and two-tone colour options, but fewer instruments than Rileys. 1300 engine available June '67, and Mk II cars (Oct '67) feature the usual cutback fins, the bigger single-carburettor motor, and an automatic option. Of minimal interest, but it's surprising there were so many.

18/85. 1967-72 (prod: 35,597). Saloon. F/F, 1798cc (S4 OHV). The name recalls the proud Flying Squad days, but it's just an Austin 1800 with walnut facia, leather trim, individual front seats, and power steering inclusive. Automatic versions have facia-mounted gear selectors. Mk II (August '69) with restyled interior and reclining seats, though there's a high-performance twin-carburettor S version with bigger brakes as well. ➤

ZAPOROZHETS (USSR)

Still made in 1985 under the ZAZ name, the Zaporozhets went into production in 1960. The car's layout was clearly Fiat 600 inspired, and from 1968 the export version, the Yalta, was available with a 1-litre Renault engine. Sold in LUAZ 4x4 form behind the Iron Curtain.

◄ **ZAZ-965. 1960-65 (prod: n/a). 2-door saloon. R/R, 748cc (V4 OHV).** Russian baby car of somewhat NSU shape with aircooled V4 engine at the back of a unitary hull incorporating all-independent suspension, rack and pinion steering, and four-speed synchromesh 'box. Centrifugal clutch is an optional extra. Still listed 1983, but capacity up to 887cc in 1965, later enlarged further to 1196cc. Shown at Earls Court, 1961, but no serious English sales.

Photographic Acknowledgements

The publishers are grateful to the following for supplying the photographs used in this book:

Manufacturers
Alfa Romeo Auto S.p.A.
Austin Rover Group Ltd.
BMW AG.
Citroen Cars Ltd.
Daimler-Benz AG.
Fiat Auto (UK) Ltd.
Ford Motor Co. Ltd.
Jaguar Cars Ltd.
Maranello Sales Ltd.
Morgan Motor Co. Ltd.
Porsche Cars Great Britain Ltd.
Renault UK Ltd.
Rolls-Royce Motors Ltd.
Vauxhall Motors Ltd.
Volvo Concessionaires Ltd.

One-Make and Marque Clubs and Registers
AC Owners' Club
Alvis Owner Club
Austin Ten Drivers' Club
BMW Car Club (Great Britain)
Bond Owners Club
Bristol Owners Club
Fairthorpe Sports Car Club
Post Vintage Humber Car Club
Jowett Car Club
Lancia Motor Club
Lea Francis Owners' Club
Maserati Club
Morgan Sports Car Club
Les Amis du Panhard et Levassor GB
Porsche Club Great Britain
Reliant Owners' Club
Singer Owners' Club
Skoda Owners' Club
Standard Motor Club
Tornado Register
Turner Register
F Victor Owners' Club

Libraries and Collections
A.F.N. Archives
Haymarket Publishing Ltd
David Hodges
National Motor Museum Photographic Library
Cyril Posthumus
Quadrant Picture Library

Special thanks are also due to the following for their help:

George Adams
Edward Album
Lorna Arnold
Kim Badland
Peter Burford
David Burgess-Wise
Miriam Carroll
Isabelle Chapuis
A.D. Clausager
Stan Cornock
Richard Crump
Dave Davies
K.W. Daws
Tom Dine
David Freeth
Graham Gauld
Trevor Gillard
Ken Hill
Barry Iles
Denis Jenkinson
Mark Konig
Stephen Lewis
Brian Long
Dave Malins
Ian McDavid
Adrian and Denize Polley
Jon Pressnell
David Preston
Ian Priestley
Ron Ruggins
D.G. Scott
Ernest Shenton
Jack Turner
Bryan Walls
Peter Woodend
Peter Zollner

Jacket pictures by Neill Bruce